Globalization and Transnational Collective Labour Relations

BULLETIN FOR COMPARATIVE LABOUR RELATIONS – 90

Globalization and Transnational Collective Labour Relations

International and European Framework Agreements at Company Level

General Editor

Roger Blanpain

Author

Stefania Marassi

Wolters Kluwer

Law & Business

Published by:
Kluwer Law International
PO Box 316
2400 AH Alphen aan den Rijn
The Netherlands
Website: www.kluwerlaw.com

Sold and distributed in North, Central and South America by:
Aspen Publishers, Inc.
7201 McKinney Circle
Frederick, MD 21704
United States of America
Email: customer.service@aspenpublishers.com

Sold and distributed in all other countries by:
Turpin Distribution Services Ltd
Stratton Business Park
Pegasus Drive, Biggleswade
Bedfordshire SG18 8TQ
United Kingdom
Email: kluwerlaw@turpin-distribution.com

ISBN 978-90-411-4748-6

Table of Contents

Global companies face pressure on their operations from a variety of social actors and from markets themselves. Their reactions vary markedly, but TCAs have emerged as a means by which companies can consider the governance of their global operations in partnership with global, European and national trade unions and workers' representatives.

(International Training Centre of the International Labour Organization, 'Key issues for management to consider with regard to Transnational Company Agreements (TCAs)', December 2010)

List of Abbreviations

BWI	Building and Wood Workers' International
CEC	European Confederation of Executives and Managerial Staff
CSR	Corporate Social Responsibility
EC	European Commission
ESSD	European Sectoral Social Dialogue Committee
EFA	European Framework Agreement
EFBWW	European Federation of Building and Woodworkers
EI	Education International
EIF	European Industry Federation
EMCEF	European Mine, Chemical and Energy Workers' Federation
EMF	European Metalworkers' Federation
EPSU	European Federation of Public Service Unions
EWC	European Works Council
ETF	European Transport Federation
ETUC	European Trade Union Confederation
FECCIA	European Federation of Managerial staff in the Chemical and Allied Industries
FECER	European Federation of Executives in the Sectors of Energy and Research
GATT	General Agreement on Tariffs and Trade
GME	General Motors Europe
GSP	Generalized System of Preferences
GUF	Global Union Federation
HRC	Human Rights Council
IAEI	International Arts and Entertainment Alliance

ICEM	International Federation of Chemical, Energy, Mine and General Workers' Union
ICFTU	International Confederation of Free Trade Unions
IFA	International Framework Agreement
IFBWW	International Federation of Building and Wood Workers
IFC	International Finance Corporation
IFJ	International Federation of Journalists
IFME	International Federation of Mining and Energy
ILO	International Labour Organisation
ILO Tripartite Declaration	ILO Tripartite Declaration of Principles concerning Multinational Enterprises and Social Policy
ILO Declaration 1998	ILO Declaration on Fundamental Principles and Rights at Work
IMF	International Metalworkers' Federation
ISO	International Organization for Standardization
ITC-ILO	International Training Centre of the International Labour Organization
ITF	International Transport Workers' Federation
ITGLWF	International Textiles Garment and Leather Workers' Federation
ITS	International Trade Secretariat
IUF	International Union of Food, Agricultural, Hotel, Restaurant, Catering, Tobacco and Allied Workers' Association
MNE	Multinational Enterprise
NCP	National Contact Point
OECD	Organisation for Economic Co-operation and Development
OECD Guidelines	OECD Guidelines for Multinational Enterprises
PSI	Public Services International
SAI	Social Accountability International
SE	Societas Europaea
TCA	Transnational Company Agreement
TFEU	Treaty on the Functioning of the European Union
UNI	United Global Union (previously known as Union Network International)

Acknowledgements

I would like to thank Professor Roger Blanpain who encouraged and supported me since I started writing my Master thesis at Tilburg University. His lectures on 'Comparative Labour Law' and 'International Labour Law' in 2010 have been a unique source of inspiration. His experience and in depth knowledge on labour law and related topics have shaped my way of understanding and thinking the complexity of labour relations. He guided me in writing this book with his valuable comments and support.

Moreover, I would like to express my deep appreciation to Professor Frank Hendrickx, thanks to whom I discovered the topic of this book. Since he was the first supervisor of my Master thesis, we had interesting conversations and sharing of opinions that have honed my idea about the development of transnational company agreements.

A special thank goes to my colleague Abiola Makinwa, who regularly inquired about the progress of the book and encouraged me to write and continue doing research.

Furthermore, I would like to thank my dearest friend Valentina, who is always very close to me even though the distance that divides us. She taught me to look on the bright side of life and to continue pursuing my dreams.

Last but not least, I would like to thank my mother Maria Grazia, my father Maurizio and my partner Piet. My deepest gratitude goes to them.

My parents gave me the possibility to study abroad and to nurture the dream to study international and European Labour Law at Tilburg University. They have been and they will always be my reference point in life. My mother taught me to never give up and to always believe in myself; my father taught me to put things in perspective.

Piet shared this journey with me with his constant support. He engaged in conversations that helped me to look at the topic of the book from other perspectives. He took care of me during the long days and evenings of writing by making sure that in the house there were always snacks to keep my energy level and concentration up. He believed in me all throughout the process of writing this book and for this reason I am deeply grateful.

Introduction

The process of globalization has brought about numerous challenges for multinational enterprises (hereinafter: MNEs) as well as for trade unions and workers' representatives. In particular, the emergence of a global market-driven economy has fundamentally altered the context these actors operate in.

The elimination of tariff barriers and the consequent expansion of world trade flows, together with the increased competition in the labour market, have had deep consequences on the business strategies of MNEs. In the words of Thomas Friedman, "[T]he more you let market forces rule (...) the more efficient and flourishing your economy will be (...). [G]lobalization (...) has its own set of economic rules (...) that revolve around opening, deregulating and privatizing your economy."[1]

Against this background and in order to remain competitive in the global market, MNEs decided to outsource and delocalize their production to low-wages countries. This in turn has raised general concerns as to the potential negative externalities in the countries where the companies – or even their business partners – operate. At the same time, the bargaining power of trade unions remained mainly limited to the national level, while the conduct of MNEs' operations surpassed national borders and became truly globalized.[2] The increasing gap in action radius that follows from this forced trade unions to look out for ways to coordinate their activities globally and respond to the internationalization of MNEs' activities.

In response to these evolutions several initiatives were undertaken both by public and private actors to ensure the accountability of MNEs for their conduct in the absence of an international framework that directly regulate their behaviour. Some of these initiatives go back to the 1970s and include the OECD Guidelines for Multinational Enterprises (hereinafter: OECD Guidelines), the ILO Tripartite Declaration of principles

1. Thomas Friedman, *The Lexus and The Olive Tree* (Anchor Books 2000) 8-9.
2. Konstantinos Papadakis, 'Introduction' in Konstantinos Papadakis (ed), *Cross-Border Social Dialogue and Agreements: An Emerging Global Industrial Relations Framework?* (International Institute for Labour Studies 2008) 1.

concerning multinational enterprises and social policy (hereinafter: ILO Tripartite Declaration) as well as the development of unilateral corporate codes of conduct.[3]

Since the end of the 1980s, one can also witness the emergence of transnational company agreements (hereinafter: TCAs) to face the same challenges. These agreements are concluded between MNEs and trade unions (and workers' representatives) and are applicable across all MNEs' operations.[4]

This book focuses on TCAs, a category that encompasses both international framework agreements (hereinafter: IFAs) and European framework agreements at company level (hereinafter: EFAs). In particular, the book intends to identify the similarities and differences between IFAs and EFAs and, more specifically, shed light on how the distinction between these two categories of TCAs is perceived in practice by the signatory parties. The ultimate goal of the research documented in this book is to evaluate if the distinction between IFAs and EFAs can still be drawn.

This book is a revised and updated version of the Master Thesis that the author defended in June 2011 as a conclusion of the LL.M. 'International and European Labour Law' at Tilburg University.[5]

The research is constructed around a comparative analysis of a selected number of IFAs and EFAs. For reasons of both practical feasibility and qualitative selection, the study will be limited to agreements concluded by MNEs with more than 80,000 employees in 2013.

[I] CONTENT OF THE BOOK

[A] Chapter 1

Chapter 1 is divided into three sections. The first section is devoted to outline the phenomenon of globalization and the initiatives that have been undertaken by public and private actors to regulate the conduct of MNEs. Amongst other topics, it examines the concept of corporate social responsibility (hereinafter: CSR), corporate codes of conduct, transnational collective bargaining (hereinafter: TCB) and TCAs. In addition, it investigates the reasons that lead MNEs and trade unions to conclude TCAs.

The second section introduces the origin, development and current practice of concluding IFAs. The pace that has characterized the conclusion of IFAs since the late 1980s (the first IFAs was concluded in 1988) is analysed as well as the possibility to regard IFAs as an emerging form of global social dialogue.

---

3. *Ibid.*, 5. See also Isabelle Schömann, 'Transnational Company Agreements: Towards an Internationalisation of Industrial Relations' in Isabelle Schömann et al., *Transnational Collective Bargaining at Company Level – A New Component of European Industrial Relations?* (ETUI aisbl 2012) 198. Romuald Jagodzinski, 'Transnational collective bargaining: a literature overview' in Isabelle Schömann et al., *Transnational Collective Bargaining at Company Level – A New Component of European Industrial Relations?* (ETUI aisbl 2012) 21-22.
4. Arturo Bronstein, *International and Comparative Labour Law: Current Challenges* (Palgrave Macmillan 2009) 115.
5. Stefania Marassi, A legal Assessment on International Framework Agreements and European Framework Agreements (Tilburg 2011).

The third section studies the origin, evolution and current practice of concluding EFAs. It also takes a closer look at three key issues related to these agreements. First, it examines the initiatives undertaken by the European Commission to formalize this emerging mode of governance. Second, it analyses the role of European Works Councils (hereinafter: EWCs) in initiating, negotiating and concluding EFAs as well as their respective relationship with trade unions. Third, it outlines the possibility to include these agreements within the current legal framework of European social dialogue.

[B] Chapter 2

Chapter 2 is devoted to a detailed comparative analysis of the texts of IFAs and EFAs concluded by MNEs with more than 80,000 employees in 2013. In order to identify which are – if there are – the similarities and differences between IFAs and EFAs, the analysis therefore takes the following characteristic aspects of these agreements into consideration: titles, signatory parties, sectors involved, content, addressees, duration, revision, renewal, termination and follow-up procedures.

[C] Chapter 3

Chapter 3 analyses three legal issues concerning IFAs and EFAs: first, the legal status of these agreements; second, their legal effects; third and last, the relationship between these texts and other norms. A comparative analysis will be carried on the texts of IFAs and EFAs that meet the requirements set in Chapter 2.

This chapter pays particular attention to the possibility to qualify IFAs and EFAs as national collective agreements. Moreover, it is questioned whether these agreements fall within the concept of soft law or hard law and, therefore, if they have legally binding effects. In addition, this chapter sheds light on the relationship between the agreements at issue and other norms, especially national laws, local laws and collective agreements.

CHAPTER 1

Transnational Collective Labour Relations

§1.01 THE IMPACT OF GLOBALIZATION ON TRANSNATIONAL COLLECTIVE LABOUR RELATIONS

[A] Introduction

Chapter 1, §1.01 of the present book will examine the main features of globalization and its potential adverse impact on the living and working conditions of workers in MNEs and throughout the global supply chain. Moreover, it will analyse the different endeavours undertaken by public and private actors to ensure that MNEs are accountable for their conduct and respect internationally recognized labour rights in their business operations.

[B] Globalization

The World Commission on the Social Dimension of Globalization has described the phenomenon of globalization by saying that "[g]lobalization has set in motion a process of far-reaching change that is affecting everyone. New technology, supported by more open policies, has created a world more interconnected than ever before. This spans not only growing interdependence in economic relations – trade, investment, finance and the organization of production globally – but also social and political interaction among organizations and individuals across the world".[6]

The elimination of tariff barriers has led MNEs to increase their activities beyond national borders. This trend has then fuelled a rapid expansion of international commerce around the globe. The World Trade Report 2013 indicates that a rapid

6. World Commission on the Social Dimension of Globalization, 'A Fair Globalization: Creating Opportunities for All' (2004) X <www.ilo.org/public/english/wcsdg/docs/report.pdf> accessed 20 February 2014.

growth in international trade flows has characterized the last 30 years, more specifically '[s]ince 1980, world trade has grown on average nearly twice as fast as world production.'[7]

At the same time, one has witnessed a swift expansion of foreign direct investments outflows, which, after a decline in 2012, is expected to increase even further to reach 'levels of $1.6 trillion in 2014 and $1.8 trillion in 2015'.[8]

Moreover, the rapid technological development has been one of the main driving forces in this process of sweeping changes, coupled with the increase of easier and faster ways of communication and transmission of knowledge and information. An information society is what characterizes the present world; in other words, a society in which new technologies are able to secure that information can travel worldwide in intense pace.[9] We live in what Al Gore has defined as a 'Global Mind' in his recent book 'The Future –Six Drivers of Global Change'. According to the US former Vice President, "the simultaneous deployment of the Internet and ubiquitous computing power have created a planet-wide extension of the human nervous system that transmits information, thoughts, and feeling to and from billions of people at the speed of light".[10]

By the same token, the emergence of a global economy has had a deep bearing on the system of production. This is no longer limited at national level but now involves MNEs as key actors, namely businesses that operates across national borders[11] and whose number has sharply increased over the past three decades[12] reaching around 82,000 in 2008, with approximately 810,000 subsidiaries and about 77 million workers.[13] MNEs operate "with intricate spiderwebs of supply chains connecting to hundreds of other enterprises in dozens of countries."[14] In other words, MNEs conduct their activities with a network of subsidiaries, suppliers, contractors and subcontractors.[15] Hayter describes this situation as follows:

> Today, the production of many manufactured goods and services often takes place on a production line which stretches from a multinational company across borders, weaving through many different sizes of firms in the formal and informal

7. WTO, 'World Trade Report 2013: Factors Shaping the Future of World Trade' (2013) <www.wto.org/english/res_e/booksp_e/world_trade_report13_e.pdf> accessed 20 September 2013.
8. UNCTAD, 'World Investment Report 2013' (2013) UNCTAD/WIR/2013, IX.
9. Roger Blanpain and Michele Colucci, *The Globalization of Labour Standards: The Soft Law Track*, vol. 52 Bulletin of Comparative Labour Relations (Kluwer Law International 2004) 1-2.
10. Al Gore, *The Future – Six Drivers of Global Change* (Random House 2013) 44.
11. Karen Jones, 'Corporate Codes, IFAs and Multi-National Corporate Social Responsibility 10 Years after the UN Global Compact' in Roger Blanpain (ed.), *Labour Markets, Industrial Relations and Human Resources Management: From Recession to Recovery*, vol. 80 Bulletin of Comparative Labour Relations (Kluwer Law International 2012) 138. (Jones defines a multinational corporation as a "business that has a physical presence and resides in more than one country").
12. Kees J. Vos, 'New Modes of Governance in Industrial Relations' in Roger Blanpain (ed.), *Labour Markets, Industrial Relations and Human Resources Management: From Recession to Recovery*, vol. 80 Bulletin of Comparative Labour Relations (Kluwer Law International 2012) 51.
13. UNCTAD, 'World Investment Report 2009' (2009) UNCTAD/WIR/2009, 8.
14. Gore (n. 10) 4.
15. Susan Hayter, 'The Social Dimension of Globalization: Striking the Balance' in Roger Blanpain (ed.), *Confronting Globalization – The Quest for a Social Agenda*, vol. 55 Bulletin of Comparative Labour Relations (Kluwer Law International 2005) 2-3.

> economy and involving workers in different countries in a unitary global production system.[16]

As an example, Miller points out that Nike, a world famous American multinational, has more than 700 suppliers.[17]

Over the years, MNEs have more and more outsourced (part of) their activities and/or relocated their businesses across the globe. This allows them to remain competitive on the global market (or at least to tread water) and potentially increase their revenues by capitalizing on the lower labour standards existing in the host countries and in the countries where their business partners operate. By entrusting some tasks to these companies, MNEs can have the final product more efficiently and at a lower price.

This change in the system of production has a number of advantages and disadvantages. The (developing) low-wages host countries have gained benefits from the global economy. The delocalization of MNEs' operations on their territories indeed has boosted the local economy and facilitated the creation of more jobs for the population. The investment inflows in the developing countries has several (economic) advantages as indicated in the 1992 Preamble of the World Bank Guidelines on the Treatment of Foreign Direct Investment. According to this document:

> a greater flow of foreign direct investment brings substantial benefits to bear on the world economy and on the economies of developing countries in particular, in terms of improving the long term efficiency of the host country through greater competition, transfer of capital, technology and managerial skills and enhancement of market access and in terms of the expansion of the international trade.[18]

However, if many are the advantages connected to the emergence of globalization, one may not overlook that a global economy entails some disadvantages too. In fact, as already said, MNEs now more than ever are called to face the increased competition from other businesses. In order to cut the costs of production and respond to the consumers' needs to have cheaper products, MNEs' management sometimes takes the decision to relocate the production processes to countries with poorer and unhealthier working conditions. In other words, MNEs are on the lookout of investment-friendly countries, which are prone to lower labour conditions and disregard human rights and environmental standards in order to have a comparative advantage over other countries and, consequently, attract more foreign investments.[19] Inflows of capital, investment and trade to developing countries have the advantage of creating jobs, improving the country economy and, accordingly, the living standard of the population. However, this practice may also lead to a 'race to the bottom' in terms of labour, human rights

16. *Ibid.*, 3.
17. Doug Miller, 'The ITGLWF's Policy on Cross-Border Dialogue in the Textiles, Clothing and Footwear Sector: Emerging Strategies in a Sector Ruled by Codes of Conduct and Resistant Companies' in Konstantinos Papadakis (ed.), *Cross-Border Social Dialogue and Agreements: An Emerging Global Industrial Relations Framework?* (International Institute for Labour Studies 2008) 168-169.
18. World Bank Group, 'Legal Framework for the Treatment of Foreign Investment' Volume 2: Guidelines' (1992) Report No. 11415, 35.
19. Bronstein (n. 4) 86 ff.

and environmental standards as these countries have tried forcefully to attract more and more foreign investors and commerce, at times to the detriment of the living and working conditions of their national population and workforce.

The fear of MNEs to lose competitiveness on the global market and consequently their search for cheaper production options go hand in hand with the endeavour of (developing) countries to attract investment, capital and trade inflows, sometimes by lowering labour standards in order to have a cheaper workforce.[20]

The consequences of MNEs' conduct in the global market has been, and still is, a core issue on the international stage. Corporate social responsibility has represented a response to the internationalization MNE's activities. More specifically, the idea behind this concept is that actions of MNEs are "part of the economy, society, and the environment in which they operate"[21] and, for this reason, these businesses should behave ethically, respecting core labour standards as well as human rights and environmental standards recognized by the international community. This leading concept, a "politically correct buzz word" as called by Jones,[22] will be examined in-depth in the next section.

[C] Corporate Social Responsibility

CSR practices have become a common feature in the emerging market economy and, more particularly, a new mode of corporate governance aimed at enhancing the standards of living for people within and outside the company, while at the same time maintaining the productivity of the enterprise.[23] The European Commission has defined CSR as a "concept whereby companies integrate social and environmental

20. Rober Howse and Brian A. Langille and Julien Burda, 'The World Trade Organization and Labour Rights: Man Bites Dog' in Virginia A. Leary and Daniel Warner (eds), *Social Issues, Globalisation and International Institutions: Labour Rights and the EU, ILO, OECD and WTO* (Martinus Nijhoff Publishers 2006) 159. ("On this view labour standards have often been characterized as producing 'rigidities' in markets and frustrating development. Labour rights are thus a cost and a tax upon development – one which international investment will seek to avoid and which rational governments should refrain from imposing. Labour rights are a set of luxury goods to be purchased with the wealth generated by growth and after the event."). For a different view see Hoe Lim, 'The Social Clause: Issues and Challenges' (International Labour Organizations – Bureau for Workers' Activities 2001) <http://www.actrav.itcilo.org/actrav-english/telearn/global/ilo/guide/hoelim.htm> accessed 24 August 2014. (Even though developing countries embrace the neo-liberal idea that higher labour standards creates rigidities in the labour market and as a result hinder the economic development, according to *Lim* it is not proven that higher labour standards hamper the inflows of investment. In fact, "while labour costs may be an important factor to TNCs, this does not mean that countries which enforce core labour standards will necessarily risk negative repercussions on FDI flows. This is because it is not proven that there is a causal link between core labour standards and labour costs.").
21. Attila Kun and József Hajdú, 'Conceptualization of Corporate Social Responsibility in the Context of Labor Law' in Roger Blanpain (ed.), *Rethinking Corporate Governance: From Shareholder Value to Stakeholder Value*, vol. 77 Bulletin of Comparative Labour Relations (Kluwer Law International 2011) 176.
22. Jones (n. 11) 135.
23. On the concept of CSR see: Michael Hopkins, 'Corporate Social Responsibility: an issues paper' (2004) International Labour Office Working Paper No. 27, 1 <www.ilo.org/legacy/english/integration/download/publicat/4_3_285_wcsdg-wp-27.pdf> accessed 12 February 2014.

concerns in their business operations and in their interaction with their stakeholders on a voluntary basis".[24] The ILO has further specified that CSR is a "voluntary, enterprise-driven initiative and refers to activities that are considered to exceed compliance with the law".[25]

Two interconnected factors lie behind the emergence of CSR practices: first, the emergence of a globalized market; second, the lack of international instruments that are directly applicable to MNEs and ensure their compliance with international labour standards (but also human rights and environmental standards).[26]

As to the first factor, the emergence of a market-driven economy has displayed that MNEs can more easily take advantage of their economic position to the detriment of the working conditions of workers in the global supply chain. Cheaper salaries and lower working conditions may lead to increasing competitiveness in the international landscape, a factor that the management of MNEs may take into consideration when developing the business strategy. However, at the same time, by infringing internationally recognized labour standards MNEs can lose their reputation before the different stakeholders.

The fear to endanger the public image has been the catalyst behind CSR practices. Upon pressure by civil society, among which trade unions, MNEs have started assuming their social responsibility as business organizations.[27] They have often welcomed this call positively and have undertaken spontaneous and voluntary regulatory initiatives to outline their business behaviour and improve workers' conditions sometimes beyond the minimum legal requirements.[28]

Concerning the second factor, to date, 189 legally binding ILO Conventions have been adopted by the International Labour Conference. States are the addresses of these

24. Commission (EC), 'Promoting a European Framework for Corporate Social Responsibility' (Green Paper), COM (2001) 366 final, 18 July 2001, 6.
25. ILO, 'InFocus Initiative on Corporate Social Responsibility (CSR)' (2006) Governing Body, 295th session, GB.295/MNE/2/1, 1 <http://www.ilo.int/public/english/standards/relm/gb/docs/gb295/pdf/mne-2-1.pdf> accessed 12 February 2014.
26. Konstantinos Papadakis, 'Introduction and Overview' in Konstantinos Papadakis (ed.), *Shaping Global Industrial Relations – The Impact of International Framework Agreements* (Palgrave Macmillan 2012) 1.
27. Paul Tony Edwards et al., 'Corporate Social Responsibility in Multinational Companies: Management Initiatives or Negotiated Agreements?' (2007) Discussion Paper No. 185, International Institute for Labour Studies, 2, <www.ilo.org/public/english/bureau/inst/publications/discussion/dp18507.pdf> accessed 1 April 2014. See also Colin Crough, 'Modelling the Firm in its Market and Organizational Environment: Methodologies for Studying Corporate Social Responsibility' (2006) 27(10) Organization Studies 1533, 1536 ("CSR is essentially 'corporate externalities recognition', in other words, the behaviour by firms that voluntarily take account of the externalities produced by their market behavior"); Kun and Hajdú (n. 21) 177 ("CSR is a construct of four aspects: 1. Economic responsibility mainly towards shareholders; 2. Legal responsibility as no corporation can be regarded as socially responsible without being in full compliance with legal requirements; 3. Ethical responsibility, namely to do what is rights, just and fair, even when there is no obligatory legal framework to do so; 4. Philanthropic responsibility, i.e. charitable donations, recreations facilities for employees and their familiars, among other things").
28. Élodie Béthoux and Claude Didry and Arnaud Mias, 'What Codes of Conduct Tell Us: Corporate Social Responsibility and the Nature of the Multinational Corporation' (2007) 15(1) Corporate Governance: An International Review 77, 78. Moreover, two additional reasons are behind CSR practices. The International Organization of Employers has envisaged in philanthropy and

Conventions though, not MNEs. Upon ratification, ILO Conventions bind States, which are then obliged to implement them into national law. Only then, MNEs have to abide by the ILO standards as applied in the national jurisdiction.

The absence of an international legal framework directly addressing the infringement of fundamental labour rights by MNEs in host countries is a drawback that civil society is attempting to face by calling for voluntary (self-) regulatory initiatives by these corporations. A consensus for 'political regulation', namely "the establishment of legally binding social norms and standards by national governments and/or international institutions",[29] has not been reached yet.[30] However, voluntary (self-) regulatory CSR initiatives have emerged as a response to the shortcomings stemming from the absence of an applicable international legal framework.

Different types of voluntary (self-) regulatory instruments fall within the category of corporate social responsibility:[31]

(a) codes of conduct and documents containing a set of guiding corporate principles that are established by international organizations, such as the United Nations (UN), the International Labour Organizations (ILO) and the Organization for the Economic and Co-operation Development (OECD);
(b) corporate codes of conduct;
(c) negotiated agreements between MNEs, on the one side, and trade unions and/or workers' representatives, on the other side (also called TCAs);
(d) initiatives promoted by non-governmental organizations, such as certification initiatives (e.g. Fair Trade and Social Labelling) and social accountability standards (e.g. SA 8000,[32] a framework developed by Social Accountability

competitiveness the driving evolution of some documents containing MNEs' unilateral commitment to internationally recognized labor standards. See International Organizations of Employers, 'Corporate Social Responsibility: An IOE Approach' (2003) <http://www.ioe-emp.org/fileadmin/ioe_documents/publications/Policy%20Areas/csr/EN/%282003-03-21%29%20Corporate%20Social%20Responsibility.pdf> accessed 1 April 2014.

29. Volker Telljohann et al., 'European and International Framework Agreements: Practical Experiences and Strategic Approaches' (Eurofound, Office for Official Publications of the European Communities 2009) 7, available at <http://www.eurofound.europa.eu/pubdocs/2008/102/en/2/EF08102EN.pdf> accessed 14 March 2014.
30. An attempt was made in 2003, when the UN Sub-commission on Promotion and Protection of Human Rights adopted the draft "Norms on the responsibilities of transnational corporations and other business enterprises with regard to human rights". See UNCHR (Sub-Commission), 'Norms on the responsibilities of transnational corporations and other business enterprises with regard to human rights' (2003) UN Document E/CN.4/Sub.2/2003/38/Rev.2.
31. This list is based on the categories used by Bronstein (n. 4) 113-114 and Konstantinos Papadakis, 'Introduction and Overview' (n. 26) 1-2.
32. Others standards developed within the framework of corporate social responsibility are those created by the International Organization for Standardization (ISO). In November 2010, the ISO released 'ISO 26000', an international voluntary standard that "provides guidance on the underlying principles of social responsibility, recognizing social responsibility and engaging stakeholders, the core subjects and issues pertaining to social responsibility (...) and on ways to integrate socially responsible behaviour into the organization (...). This International Standard emphasizes the importance of results and improvements in performance on social responsibility". See ISO, 'ISO 26000' available at <www.iso.org/obp/ui/#iso:std:iso:26000:ed-1:v1:en> accessed 20 January 2014.

International (SAI) and adhered to by many businesses for the improvement of working conditions at the workplace).[33] ILO Conventions and UN Conventions are the reference points for this document.[34]

This book will analyse only the first three categories of (self-) regulatory instruments encompassed in the concept of CSR. However, the main focus will be on the third form of corporate governance embedded in the CSR's strategy of an enterprise, namely TCAs. Different scholars argue that these agreements represent a CSR's strategy used to harmonize and enhance labour standards across the worldwide operations of a MNE.[35] However, another view on the topic considers these labour-management negotiated agreements as the starting point of the internationalization and/or Europeanization of industrial relations at company level and the origin of TCB.[36] This book does not intend to take a position between these two views. The aim pursued is to outline the framework in which this new form of social dialogue has emerged and carry out a comparative analysis of the two categories of TCAs, IFAs and EFAs.

[D] The Development of Public and Private Initiatives to Regulate MNEs' Conduct[37]

Sections §1.01[E] and §1.01[F] will provide an overview of the public and private initiatives undertaken to regulate MNEs' conduct and secure the compliance of internationally recognized labour rights, among others.

[E] Publicly-Driven Initiatives: Codes of Conduct and Other Documents

The first attempt to regulate corporate behaviour dates back to the 1960s-1970s. As of then this topic has drawn much attention not only of scholars but also – and especially – of international organizations such as the ILO, OECD, UN and in the North American Free Trade Agreement (hereinafter: NAFTA), more particularly in the North American Agreement of Labour Cooperation (hereinafter: NAALC). Specifically, these actors started thinking about how to face the negative social consequences stemming from MNEs' operations in host countries. To this end, they adopted different codes of

33. Website of SAI, <http://www.sa-intl.org/index.cfm?fuseaction=Page.ViewPage&pageId=490> accessed 20 January 2014. On this topic see also Jean-Michel Servais, 'International Labour Standards and Corporate Social Responsibility' in Roger Blanpain (ed.), *Confronting Globalization – The Quest for a Social Agenda*, vol. 55 Bulletin of Comparative Labour Relations (Kluwer Law International 2005) 23.
34. These instruments will not be addressed in this book.
35. Papadakis, 'Introduction and Overview' (n. 26) 1-2; Bronstein (n. 4) 113.
36. Telljohann et al., 'European and International Framework Agreements: Practical Experiences and Strategic Approaches' (n. 29) 41; See also IOE, 'Fact Sheet for Business: International Framework Agreements (IFAs)' (2013) <http://www.ioe-emp.org/fileadmin/ioe_documents/publications/Policy%20Areas/international_industrial_relations/EN/_2013-11-21__Fact_Sheet_for_Business_-_IFAs__final_.pdf> accessed 14 March 2014.
37. This terminology is used in Papadakis, 'Introduction' (n. 2) 5.

conduct and other documents containing a set of principles to guide MNEs' conduct. Next subsections will examine some of these documents in chronological order.

[1] Draft UN Code of Conduct on Transnational Corporations

The 1976 Draft UN Code of Conduct on Transnational Corporations has been the first attempt to introduce an instrument aiming at regulating transnational corporations' conduct. This draft code of conduct was never adopted though.[38] This failure, however, has not discouraged other international organizations to get involved in the search of a way to address the spill-over effects of multinational corporations' activities. Hence, in the same period, before the OECD and the year after the ILO adopted codes of conduct to guide corporate operations.

[2] OECD Guidelines for Multinational Corporations and ILO Tripartite Declaration of Principles concerning Multinational Enterprises and Social Policy

Turning now to the initiatives developed by the ILO and the OECD to advocate good practices for companies, it is beyond doubt that the behaviour of MNEs has been on the agenda of these organizations for many years. Above all, the overriding concern behind the initiatives undertaken by these organizations has been how to ensure that the benefits that MNEs operations bring to the development of host countries does not work to the detriment of workers' labour standards. The emergence of MNEs and the expansion of their activities in the 1960s have then led before the OECD and just after the ILO to commence dealing with the potential costs that MNEs' operations may have on the social progress in the host countries.[39]

As the political environment was not inclined to adopt legally binding rules that MNEs had to comply with, both the OECD and the ILO adopted soft law instruments, the 1976 OECD Guidelines for Multinational Corporations (hereinafter: OECD Guidelines) and one year after the ILO Tripartite Declaration of Principles concerning Multinational Enterprises and Social Policy (hereinafter: ILO Tripartite Declaration). These codes of conduct represent public initiatives aimed at seeking to advance responsible businesses, which respect internationally agreed labour standards. In addition to that, they are a tool in the hands of these companies, which can further their positive public image before different stakeholders by stating that they adhere to core labour standards.

Even though these codes of conduct have not the status of legally binding instruments, Blanpain and Colucci argue that "(t)hey are, however, morally binding as constituting rules society at large accepts and promotes". The two scholars go on by saying that "(t)hese principles can become part of the 'hard' law in as far as they

38. The last draft was made in 1990. For the text see Proposed Text of the Draft Code of Conduct on Transnational Corporations, U.N. E.C.O.S.O.C., 2d Sess., Annex, U.N. Doc. E/1990/94 (1990).
39. Blanpain and Colucci (n. 9) 21.

constitute general principles of law, which many legal systems, including that of the EU recognizes as source of law."[40]

Before examining in detail the OECD Guidelines and the ILO Tripartite Declaration, it is worth mentioning that private initiatives aimed at regulating MNEs' conduct now exist next to these publicly-driven codes of conduct. In particular, the most recent development of codes of conduct has taken place at company level with an increasing number of MNEs adopting corporate codes of conduct, namely voluntary self-regulatory instruments of corporate social regulation. Corporate codes of conduct represent the third and last phase of the development of this type of instruments, which, according to a Eurofound report, has followed a threefold path.[41] The first code of conduct was concluded at the beginning of the twentieth century. Only as from the 1970s one has assisted at the involvement of the ILO and OECD in outlining what the behaviour of MNEs should look like. Finally, only in the last decade of the twentieth century, MNEs have addressed the shortcomings of their activities and have adopted voluntary corporate codes for various reasons, chiefly to channel a positive image of their business operations to different stakeholders (e.g., consumers, NGOs). Section §1.01 [F] [1] will be devoted to this last important stage especially in light of the connection existing between these unilateral instruments with multi-stakeholder instruments, namely TCAs.

Looking now in detail before at the OECD and after at the ILO initiative, in 1976, the OECD adopted the OECD Guidelines as part of the OECD Declaration and Decisions on International Investment and Multinational Enterprises.

This document was revised in 2011 and it represents an example of 'collective code of conduct'.[42] In particular, it contains a set of recommendations addressed to MNEs by 44 adhering governments and is not limited at promoting the respect of labour standards by MNEs but it has a larger scope of application (also, for instance, human rights and environmental standards).

Through the OECD Guidelines the adhering countries encourage MNEs to adopt a responsible business behaviour that respect human rights, environmental and labour standards, consumer interests, among others.[43] More specifically, the aim of the OECD Guidelines is as follows:

> ensure that the operations of these enterprises are in harmony with government policies, to strengthen the basis of mutual confidence between enterprises and the societies in which they operate, to help improve the foreign investment climate and to enhance the contribution to sustainable development made by multinational enterprises.[44]

---

40. *Ibid.*, 122.
41. Schömann et al., 'Codes of Conduct and International Framework Agreements: New Forms of Governance at Company Level' (Eurofound, Office for Official Publications of the European Communities 2008) V <www.eurofound.europa.eu/pubdocs/2007/92/en/1/ef0792en.pdf> accessed 14 November 2013.
42. Vos (n. 12) 56.
43. OECD, OECD Guidelines for Multinational Enterprises (2011), OECD Publishing, <http://www.oecd-ilibrary.org/governance/oecd-guidelines-for-multinational-enterprises_9789264115415-en> accessed 14 September 2014.
44. *Ibid.*

Chapter V of the Guidelines deals with 'Employment and Industrial Relations' and reaffirms the importance of several labour standards, among which the core labour rights contained in eight ILO fundamental Conventions. In particular, it recalls the observance of these standards by MNEs and clarifies that the OECD Guidelines and the ILO Tripartite Declaration go hand in hand with seeking to advance responsible business behaviour.[45]

As a means of implementation of the Guidelines, the 44 adhering governments need to set up National Contact Points (hereinafter: NCP),[46] whose role is to "further the effectiveness of the Guidelines by undertaking promotional activities, handling enquiries, and contributing to the resolution of issues that arise from the alleged non-observance of the guidelines in specific instances."[47] To date (14 April 2014), Chapter V of the Guidelines has received particular attention by NCPs, with more than half of the requests submitted (62 %) dealing with employment and industrial relations. More specifically, out of the approximately 300 specific instances filed to NCPs, 164 concern alleged breaches of freedom of association, collective bargaining and child labour. The American NCP is ahead, followed by the Dutch and the English NCPs. Furthermore, the majority of requests regards companies active in the manufacturing industry, followed by mining and quarrying and agriculture, and forest and fishing.

At the time of writing (14 April 2014), the most recent instance dates back to the beginning of 2014, when trade unions notified the Austrian NCP about the activities of a company involved in the manufacturing sector that allegedly violated Chapter V of the OECD Guidelines. Ultimately, the Austrian NCP did not handle the issue because the company reached an agreement with the employee's representatives.[48]

Moreover, the request submitted in October 2013 by an individual to the German NCP (then transferred to the Brazilian one) merits further attention in order to gain a better understanding of the type of issues dealt with by NCPs and what potential these bodies may have. Even though it does not directly deal with Chapter V of the OECD Guidelines, this case is very important. In fact, three German MNEs were allegedly considered responsible for the fire in the Tazreen factory in Bangladesh. These companies allegedly breached the General Policies and Human Rights Chapter in the Guidelines. At the time of writing, the case is still under analysis by the rapporteur.[49]

One year after the OECD Guidelines, the endeavour to address MNEs' conduct gathered momentum within the ILO. As a result, in 1977 the ILO Governing Body adopted the ILO Tripartite Declaration.[50] This document, which was revised in 2006, is a universal, non-binding instrument that sets guiding principles not only to MNEs but

45. *Ibid.*
46. For detailed information about the National Contact Points, see Blanpain and Colucci (n. 9) 60 ff.
47. Available at <http://mneguidelines.oecd.org/ncps/> accessed 1 May 2014.
48. OECD, 'Database of specific instances – Employment issues in Austria' <http://mneguidelines.oecd.org/database/instances/at0004.htm> accessed 1 May 2014.
49. OECD, 'Database of specific instances – Alleged violation of employee rights in Bangladesh' <http://mneguidelines.oecd.org/database/instances/br0021.htm> accessed 10 January 2014.
50. Governing Body (204th Session) Tripartite Declaration of Principles concerning Multinational Enterprises and Social Policy (Geneva, November 1977 as amended at its 279th (November 2000) and 295th Session (March 2006).

also to governments, employers' and workers' organizations in four main areas: employment, training, conditions of work and life and industrial relations.[51] The aim of the ILO Tripartite Declaration is to:

> encourage the positive contribution which multinational enterprises can make to economic and social progress and to minimize and resolve the difficulties to which their various operations may give rise, taking into account the United Nations resolutions advocating the establishment of a New International Economic Order, as well as subsequent developments within the United Nations, for example, the Global Compact and the Millennium Development Goals.[52]

A follow-up mechanism to the ILO Tripartite Declaration was established since the adoption of this code of conduct: a survey is periodically sent to all ILO Member States and the most representatives employers and workers' organizations. These actors need to give an answer as to how MNEs operating in their countries have respected the principles contained in the ILO Tripartite Declaration. The responses to the questionnaire are then analysed by the ILO Governing Body, which can adopt recommendations.[53]

The Eighth Survey, which covers the period 2000-2003, is the most recent and public available document containing an analysis of the data retrieved by sending the questionnaire to the mentioned actors. The low rate of responses to this survey has been one of the main reasons behind the choice to reassess different means of implementation of the ILO Tripartite Declaration.[54] As a result, the monitoring mechanism through periodic surveys has been halted for several years. However, a decision has been taken to resume the survey mechanism and conduct the Ninth Survey, which covers the period 2009-2012. To date, this survey is still in process and the International Labour Office will provide the analysis of the responses to the Governing Body by the 323rd session in March 2015.[55]

[3] ILO Declaration on Fundamental Principles and Rights at Work

Even though it does not introduce a set of principles addressed to MNEs, the ILO Declaration on Fundamental Principles and Rights at Work (hereinafter: ILO Declaration 1998) and its follow-up merit further analysis.[56]

51. Information available at: ILO, 'Tripartite declaration of principles concerning multinational enterprises and social policy (MNE Declaration) – 4th Edition' <www.ilo.org/empent/Publications/WCMS_094386/lang--en/index.htm> accessed 14 November 2013.
52. ILO Tripartite Declaration (n. 50).
53. Information available at: ILO, 'Follow-up Surveys' <www.ilo.org/empent/Informationresources/WCMS_101251/lang--en/index.htm> accessed 12 January 2014.
54. Governing Body (301th Session) Proposal for evaluating the effect given to the Tripartite Declaration of Principles concerning Multinational Enterprises and Social Policy (Geneva, March 2008).
55. Governing Body (317th Session) Tripartite Declaration of Principles concerning Multinational Enterprises and Social Policy (MNE Declaration): Operational plan for promotional activities and proposal for the new survey (Geneva, 6–28 March 2013) 1.
56. International Labour Conference (86th Session) Declaration on Fundamental Principles and Rights at Work and its Follow-up (Geneva 18 June 1998).

The principles contained in the ILO Tripartite Declaration were reaffirmed in the ILO Declaration 1988, which is a non-binding instrument adopted in response to the ongoing debate on the social dimension of globalization and, more specifically, on the interplay between, on the one hand, increasing international trade and, on the other hand, internationally recognized labour standards. This relationship, according to Lim, is "about ensuring that countries with lower labour standards do not gain an 'unfair advantage' in trade at the expense of countries with higher labour standards".[57] More particularly, Servais notes that "if a country allows its companies to employ their workers in deplorable working conditions and for miserable wages (...) it will be able to export its products at a lower price and thus obtain an unfair advantage over its competitors".[58]

An attempt to provide a solution to the potential negative externalities global trade may have on labour standards was made by the World Trade Organization (hereinafter: WTO). A proposal for the introduction of a social clause was already considered in the Havana Charter (1948) and it was tabled during several negotiations rounds:[59] from the Tokyo Round (1973-1979) to the Uruguay Round (1986-1994) and ultimately before the WTO Singapore Conference in 1996.

A unanimous consensus was not reached though. This was the result of the opposition of developing, low-wages States, which feared that the introduction of such a clause would have hindered the flows of trade and therefore the possibility to enhance their economy and the living conditions of their population. This strong resistance led the international community to look for another *forum* where to find a solution to the difficult interplay between international trade and labour rights. Despite recognizing the importance that labour rights have in the context of the WTO, the 1996 Ministerial Declaration of the WTO explicitly stated that the ILO is the competent body to deal with labour standards, not the WTO.[60]

57. Lim (n. 20).
58. Jena-Michel Servais, *International Labour Law* (2nd rev. ed., Kluwer Law International 2009) 34. Moreover, Servais notes that the concern about the linkage between trade and labor standards dates back at least to 1788 "when Jacque Necker, a minister of State and banker, wrote (...) that a country that did away with the weekly day of rest would undoubtedly obtain an advantage, but only if it was the only one to do so: the situation would revert to the *status quo ante* if other countries followed suit".
59. Bronstein (n. 4) 95 ff. ("a social clause was envisaged in the draft Chapter of the International Trade Organization (Havana Charter, 1948) but this never came into force. Only certain elements of the Havana Charter were later incorporated into the GATT agreement, which did not contain any specific provision concerning labour apart from the rule which allowed for the prohibition of imported goods produced by prison labour. However, even in the 1970s, the United States brought the issue of labour standards before the Tokyo Round, though with no success. (...) The social clause again came to the forefront during the Uruguay Round negotiations (1986-94) (...). It was again rejected in the WTO Singapore Conference in 1996, which adopted a Declaration which emphatically stated that while the WTO was competent on trade issues it was also committed to respect for internationally recognized core labour standards (...). However, it added that labour issues fall within the competence of the ILO, not of the WTO, and that labour standards should not be used for protectionist purposes").
60. WTO, Singapore Ministerial Declaration (13 December 1996) WT/MIN(96)/DEC. Even though a social clause was not introduced at the WTO, some States use unilateral social clauses in their trade relations. For instance, in 1976 the US introduced a trade scheme, the Generalized System of Preferences (GSP), according to which approximately 5000 products imported from one of the

Only two years after, the ILC Declaration 1998 was adopted at the 86th session of the International Labour Conference. This non-binding document highlights the efforts of the ILO to promote the respect of the core labour rights that are set forth in the fundamental eight ILO fundamental Conventions. Out of the 189 ILO Conventions adopted since 1919,[61] eight ILO Conventions have been considered as encompassing the fundamental labour rights that should be respected regardless of the ratification by the Member State in which workers conduct their activities. The eight ILO fundamental Conventions are the following: ILO Conventions Nos. 87 and 98 on freedom of association and collective bargaining, ILO Conventions Nos. 138 and 182 on minimum wage and the elimination of the abolition of the worst forms of child labour, ILO Conventions No. 110 and 111 on elimination of discrimination and ILO Conventions Nos. 29 and 105 on the abolition of forced labour.

In particular, the ILO Declaration 1998:

> Declares that all Members, even if they have not ratified the Conventions in question, have an obligation arising from the very fact of membership in the Organization, to respect, to promote and to realize, in good faith and in accordance with the Constitution, the principles concerning the fundamental rights which are the subject of those Conventions, namely:

(a) Freedom of association and the effective recognition of the right to collective bargaining;
(b) The elimination of all forms of forced or compulsory labour;
(c) The effective abolition of child labour;
(d) The elimination of discrimination in respect of employment and occupation.[62]

If the environment was still not fertile for the introduction of a social clause neither at WTO level nor at the ILO, a consensus could still be reached on a non-binding document aimed at enhancing the observance of core labour standards worldwide and, more specifically, at achieving universal ratifications of the eight ILO fundamental Conventions.

---

123 (developing) States are subject from trade benefits such as a duty-free entry. In order to benefit this preferential treatment, the beneficiary States need to respect internationally recognized labor rights. This system was introduced also in the European Union, which has a revised GSP in force since 1 January 2014. For more information on the US GSP, see the Official website of the Office of the United States Trade Representative on the U.S. GSP: < www.ustr.gov/trade-topics/trade-development/preference-programs/generalized-system-preference-gsp > accessed 15 November 2014. As to the EU GSP, see theOfficial website of the European Commission on the EU GSP: <http://ec.europa.eu/trade/policy/countries-and-regions/development/generalised-scheme-of-preferences/index_en.htm > accessed 15 November 2013. See also Bronstein (n. 4) 108-110.

61. ILO, NORMLEX (Information System on International Labour Standards' available at <http://www.ilo.org/dyn/normlex/en/f?p=NORMLEXPUB:1:0::NO::: > accessed 2 May 2014.
62. ILO Declaration 1998 (n. 56) para. 2.

Table 1.1 Number of Ratifications Eight ILO Fundamental Conventions[63]

ILO Convention	*Number of Ratifications*
ILO Convention No. 87	152
ILO Convention No. 98	163
ILO Convention No. 29	177
ILO Convention No. 105	174
ILO Convention No. 100	171
ILO Convention No. 111	172
ILO Convention No. 138	166
ILO Convention No. 182	178

Source: Data available on the website of the ILO <www.ilo.org/dyn/normlex/en/f?p = 1000: 10001:0::NO> accessed 14 April 2014.

[4] UN Global Compact and Initiatives of the Special Representative for Human Rights and Transnational Corporations and Other Business Enterprises

Notwithstanding the failed attempt to introduce a Draft Code of Conduct on Transnational Corporations, the UN did not renounce to draw its attention to, and raise awareness on, the potential infringements of human rights, labour rights and environmental standards by MNEs. As a result, at the beginning of the 21st century, it launched the UN Global Compact, a "strategic policy initiative for businesses that are committed to aligning their operations and strategies with ten universally accepted principles in the areas of human rights, labour, environment and anti-corruption."[64]

The UN Global Compact falls within the corporate social responsibility framework and aims at ensuring that corporate conduct is aligned with what are considered the ten core principles every business operation should uphold. Four of the ten principles (from principle 3 to principle 6) are devoted to labour standards and, in particular, to the fundamental labour rights enshrined in ILO Declaration 1998.[65]

This initiative is particularly significant and has drawn the attention of the public at large because it seeks to set the boundaries to companies' conduct and to attain a sustainable development. The UN Global Compact has been embraced by several

63. To date (14 April 2014), 185 States are members of the ILO. Only three countries (Marshall Islands, Palau and Tuvalu) have ratified none of the ILO Fundamental Conventions. Moreover, China has not ratified 4 of the 8 ILO Fundamental Conventions (Nos. 29, 105, 87 and 98), the United States of America have not ratified 6 of these ILO Conventions (Nos. 29, 87, 98, 110, 111, 138) and India 4 of them (Nos. 87, 98, 138 and 182).
64. Official website of the UN Global Compact <www.unglobalcompact.org/AboutTheGC/index.html> accessed 23 February 2014.
65. Principle 3 is devoted to the protection of freedom of association and collective bargaining; Principle 4 deals with the elimination of all forms of forced and compulsory labor; Principle 5 examines the effective abolition of child labour; and finally Principle 6 concerns the elimination of discrimination in respect of employment and occupation.

companies, whose number has sharply increased reaching 12,000 over 145 countries and leading to what is now considered the "the largest voluntary corporate responsibility initiative in the world".[66] Even though the number of MNEs adhering to the UN Global Compact is still rather limited if one considers the total amount of MNEs currently active on the international arena, this initiative does not lose of importance as some of the largest companies have decided to embrace the principles contained in this document.[67]

In addition to the UN Global Compact, a Special Representative of the Secretary-General for human rights and transnational corporations and other business enterprises was appointed in 2005.[68] Within the context of the 'Protect, Respect and Remedy' Framework, in 2011 the Special Representative prepared the report 'Guiding Principles on Business and Human Rights for implementing the UN "Protect, Respect and Remedy" Framework'.[69] This document was unanimously endorsed by the Human Rights Council in Resolution 17/4 of 16 June 2011.[70] The Guiding Principles represent an important step to address the potential adverse impact of businesses' behaviour on human rights via the establishment of international standards. In particular, these "Guiding Principles are grounded in recognition of:

(a) States' existing obligations to respect, protect and fulfil human rights and fundamental freedoms;
(b) The role of business enterprises as specialized organs of society performing specialized functions, required to comply with all applicable laws and to respect human rights;
(c) The need for rights and obligations to be matched to appropriate and effective remedies when breached."[71]

[5] North American Agreement of Labour Cooperation

The NAALC, a labour protocol annexed to the NAFTA in 1993, is another instrument introduced with the aim of ensuring - even if indirectly -[72] that MNEs are socially responsible for their activities.

66. Official website of the UN Global Compact (n. 64).
67. Blanpain and Colucci, (n. 9) 126.
68. The mandate of the Special Representative for human rights and transnational corporations and other business enterprises are specified in UNCHR Res 2005/69 (2005) UN Doc E/CN.4/RES/2005/69.
69. UNCHR, 'Report of the Special Representative of the Secretary-General on the issue of human rights and transnational corporations and other business enterprises, John Ruggie' (2011) UN Doc A/HRC/17/31.
70. HRC, 'Human rights and transnational corporations and other business enterprises' (2011) UN Doc A/HRC/RES/17/4.
71. UNCHR, 'Report of the Special Representative of the Secretary-General on the issue of human rights and transnational corporations and other business enterprises, John Ruggie' (n. 69).
72. Blanpain and Colucci, (n. 9) 7 and 41 ("The NAALC imposes legal obligations on the three member countries, Canada, Mexico and the United States, not on multinational enterprises, although there is, due to possible (indirect) involvement of companies in NAALC procedures,

NAFTA is an agreement concluded by the United States of America, Canada and Mexico for the promotion and encouragement of trade flows among these countries by creating a free trade area with no tariff barriers. The NAALC was added to the NAFTA to establish a linkage between trade and labour in response to the pressure wielded by American trade unions, who feared a relocation of American and Canadian companies to the lower-wage Mexico.[73] As a result, even if the NAALC does not refer to the ILO labour standards, this document ensures that no deregulation takes place in the three State Parties, which "shall ensure that [their] labor laws and regulations provide for high labor standards, consistent with high quality and productivity workplaces, and shall continue to strive to improve those standards in that light."[74]

[F] Privately Driven Initiatives

Next to the mentioned publicly driven initiatives, MNEs have adopted voluntary, (self-) regulatory documents containing their commitment to abide by internationally recognized labour standards in all countries where they conduct their activities. One has then witnessed the development of new modes of corporate governance, a category that encompasses different tools such unilateral codes of conduct[75] and TCAs. Both these instruments will be examined in the following sections.

[1] Corporate Codes of Conduct

Over the last decades, MNEs have expanded their operations worldwide. This trend has raised the concern as to whether MNEs' behaviour is aligned with the principles of sustainable development. According to these principles, "enterprises should make decisions based not only on financial factors such as profits or dividends, but also on the immediate and long-term social and environmental consequences of their activities".[76]

As a response to this concern and the related pressure exercised by different actors (e.g., consumers, non-governmental organizations, trade unions and workers) MNEs have voluntarily taken an action. Several MNEs (for the most part based in the US)[77] have started regulating their business behaviour via unilateral corporate codes of conduct.[78]

---

when complaints of non compliance are made, undoubtedly public relations pressure on enterprise to see that their policies and actions comply with the 11 labour principles of the NAALC").

73. Bronstein (n. 4) 103.
74. The North American Agreement on Labor Cooperation (adopted 14 September 1993, entered into force 1 January 1994) 32 I.L.M 1499 (NAALC), Article 2. For more information on the NAACL, see Bronstein (n. 4) 103-106.
75. Edwards et al. (n. 27) 3. In this paper, the authors argue that sometimes codes of conduct are concluded through negotiations with (international) trade union federations.
76. Bronstein (n. 4) 113.
77. *Ibid.*, 115.
78. According to Papadakis, several thousands of codes of conduct have been adopted so far. Papadakis, 'Introduction and Overview' (n. 26) 5.

Corporate code of conducts can be defined as "unilateral recommendations through which the main decision-making bodies of companies set up rules of behaviour for managers and employees (sometimes also for suppliers and subcontractors) that reflect the principles and values of corporate social responsibility."[79] Despite their emergence dates back to the 1970s,[80] only from the 1990s these instruments have attracted increasing attention by MNEs, which have started establishing rules of corporate behaviour on different issues, such as human rights, environmental and labour standards as well as bribery and corruption.

By adopting these texts, MNEs intend to counter the allegations of violations of labour rights in the countries where the corporations and/or their subsidiaries, suppliers, contractors and/or subcontractors operate. This is because over the past several scandals have shed light on the allegedly adverse working conditions of workers of MNEs' suppliers.[81]

By adopting corporate codes of conduct, MNEs attempt to gain a marketing boost and recuperate credibility and a good reputation in the eyes of employees, consumers, NGOs and other stakeholders. The emergence of a globalized world in fact has contributed to raise the diffidence and the discontent of the vast majority of these actors towards the economic policies undertaken by MNEs.

Furthermore, there are other reasons behind the adoption of these codes. By way of example, Bronstein argues that MNEs conclude corporate codes of conduct for avoiding the potential interferences of host countries.[82] Furthermore, Gallin notes that MNEs adopt corporate codes of conduct for circumventing the involvement of trade unions and/or workers' representatives, which instead is present in bilateral instruments like TCAs. According to this scholar, "in some cases, companies adopted codes as part of a union-avoidance strategy by pre-emption, preferring to unilaterally offer a paternalistic package than have a recognized negotiating body to deal with".[83]

One can argue that these unilateral tools are very important because some of them address not only the MNEs' behaviour but all the economic activities in global supply chain. In other words, they set rules of behaviour also for MNEs' suppliers, contractors and subcontractors, whose workers are not employees of MNEs. In particular, some corporate codes of conduct state that if suppliers and (sub-) contractors do not respect the basic human rights, environmental and labour standards set in these texts, the MNE will interrupt the business relationships with these legal entities. A different behaviour would hinder MNEs' credibility before their stakeholders and could potentially lead to a decrease in production and profit. In these cases, the

79. Schömann et al., 'Codes of Conduct and International Framework Agreements: New Forms of Governance at Company Level' (n. 41) 1.
80. Vos (n. 12) 55.
81. Niklas Egels-Zandén, 'Clean Clothes Campaign' in Thomas Hale and David Held (eds), *The Handbook of Transnational Governance: Institutions and Innovations* (Polity Pr 2011) 261. (The author argues that the codes of conduct concluded in 1997 by four Swedish garment retailers are the outcome of several scandals around H&M, Lindex, KappAhl and Indiska).
82. Bronstein (n. 4) 105.
83. Dan Gallin, 'International Framework Agreements: A Reassessment' in Konstantinos Papadakis (ed.), *Cross-Border Social Dialogue and Agreements: An Emerging Global Industrial Relations Framework?* (International Institute for Labour Studies 2008) 34.

bargaining power vested in MNEs' stakeholders is so high that these corporations prefer to interrupt the relationships with their business partners rather than risking to lose their reputation and the related economic consequences.

Several positive aspects follow from the adoption of these unilateral voluntary instruments. As identified by Richard Locke, Thomas Kochan, Monica Romis and Fei Qin, the effectiveness of codes of conduct in improving the working and living conditions of workers in the MNEs' global supply chain is still a matter under discussion.[84] However, their study conducted on 800 Nike's suppliers (about 600,000 workers) in 51 countries (2004) has displayed the potential positive impact corporate codes of conduct may have on the labour standards in factories in developing countries. In addition to that, these instruments may have an impact in the development of a positive and constructive system of industrial relations within a company.[85]

Next to positive aspects, there are a number of shortcomings connected to the adoption of corporate codes of conduct, especially due to their nature of voluntary and unilateral instruments. One of these aspects is the lack of involvement of workers, workers' representatives and trade unions in the decision-making process that leads to the adoption of corporate codes of conduct. This feature sets apart these instruments from TCAs; in the latter workers' representatives and/or trade union play an active role in the negotiation and conclusion of the text. Furthermore, the monitoring procedures of corporate codes of conduct do not entail any involvement of social partners and are left to the discretion of MNEs' management.[86] Moreover, this form of social regulation has been harshly criticized because it mainly addresses propaganda and marketing purposes and it is limited to respond to the negative publicity made by the media about the inconsistency of certain corporate policies with international labour standards.[87]

[2] Transnational Collective Bargaining

In response to the increasing internationalization of economy and the consequent delocalization of MNE's activities, the need to develop new tools of corporate governance emerged. TCB represents one of the answers to the quest for a tool that overcomes the difficulties brought about by globalization.

84. Richard Locke et al., Beyond corporate codes of conduct: Work organization and labour standards at Nike's suppliers, (2007) (1-2) International Labour Review 21, 21-22.
85. Schömann et al., 'Codes of Conduct and International Framework Agreements: New Forms of Governance at Company Level' (n. 41) 73 ff.
86. André Sobczak, 'Legal Dimensions of International Framework Agreements in the Field of Corporate Social Responsibility' in Konstantinos Papadakis (ed.), *Cross-Border Social Dialogue and Agreements: An Emerging Global Industrial Relations Framework?* (International Institute for Labour Studies 2008) 116 (the author affirms that "as these codes do not always pay enough attention to their implementation they are thus often considered as 'window-dressing' and seen as part of the companies' public relations strategies"); see also Schömann et al., 'Codes of Conduct and International Framework Agreements: New Forms of Governance at Company Level' (n. 41) 74. (Concerning the implementation, monitoring and enforcement of codes of conduct, only sometimes external auditors support the MNEs' management).
87. IFBWWW, 'IFBWWW Experiences with Global Company Agreement' (2004) 2 <http://www.newunionism.net/library/organizing/IFBWW%20-%20Experiences%20with%20Global%20Company%20Agreements%20-%202004.pdf> accessed 3 February2014.

Even though the use of the term 'transnational collective bargaining' is still debatable, scholars have given different definitions to it.[88] By way of example, Costa and Rehfeldt define TCB as "collective bargaining practices between employer and employee representatives aiming to reach transnational agreements (global, European or other regional) whose content can be symbolic or far-reaching".[89]

Over the last years, TCB has started playing an important role in the multi-faceted system of industrial relations. When dealing with this topic, the first question that needs a clarification is a question of terminology:[90] what does 'transnational' mean and what differentiates it from 'national', 'supranational' and 'international'?

To answer this question, Senatori relies on the definition of TCAs given by the European Commission in 2008.[91] According to him, "the enfranchisement from any formal linkage to the territory, and hence from institutional framework, is the ingredient that differentiates transnational bargaining (as well as transnational law in broader terms) form other forms of regulation that go beyond national boundaries, such as the 'international' and the 'supranational'".[92]

The transnational legal order is fundamentally different from a supranational legal order, which is a key feature of the European Union. In the latter, one assists at the "establishment by an international authority of labor standards that would be directly binding on each State, with no need for ratification".[93] In other words, supranational labour law consists of EU primary and secondary legislation. In addition to that, European framework agreements concluded between European social partners and transposed into European Directives according to Article 155(2) Treaty on the Functioning of the European Union (hereinafter: TFEU) also form part of supranational labour law.

Furthermore, the transnational legal order diverges from the international order, which consists of international labour standards created as from 1919 in a trilateral forum, the ILO, and set forth in ILO Conventions and Recommendations. In a different way, the transnational legal order is characterized by the private, rather than public, initiative of different actors, such as MNEs and trade unions or workers' representatives. In addition, it does not aim at setting norms addressed to national governments.[94]

88. Romuald Jagodzinski, 'Transnational Collective Bargaining: A Literature Review', in I. Schömann et al., *Transnational Collective Bargaining at Company Level – A New Component of European Industrial Relations?* (ETUI aisbl, 2012) 24.
89. Isabel da Costa and Udo Rehfeldt, 'Transnational Restructuring Agreements: General Overview and Specific Evidence from the European Automobile Sector' in Konstantinos Papadakis (ed.), *Shaping Global Industrial Relations – The Impact of International Framework Agreements* (Palgrave Macmillan 2011) 146. See also Jagodzinski, 'Transnational Collective Bargaining: A Literature Review' (n. 88) 24 ("TCB, understood as negotiations and consultations within sectoral social dialogue").
90. This issue has been taken into consideration by several authors. See for instance Jones (n. 11) 138.
91. For this definition, see page §1.01 [F] [3].
92. Iacopo Senatori, 'Transnational Company Bargaining and the Discourse of the European Commission: A Critical Overview' (2013) Working Paper, 2, available at <http://www.labourlawresearch.net/sites/default/files/papers/SENATORI.pdf> accessed 10 March 2014.
93. Bronstein (n. 4) 92.
94. Edoardo Ales and Giorgio Verrecchia, 'Transnational: The Emerging Multifaced Dimension of Industrial Relations' in Salvo Leonardi et al., *European Action on Transnational Company*

Similarly to Senatori, also Ales describes the linkage between transnational labour law, in particular TCB, and the three other existing dimensions of industrial relations. This scholar points out that "(t)he transnational dimension of collective relations is consequently to be understood as that multinational one created by workers' and enterprises' representatives (or by an individual representative) when they agree (or accept to agree) rules that are applicable beyond the national context (a 'positive' point of differentiation from the national dimension), without belonging to the supranational or international dimension by virtue of such fact (a 'negative' point of differentiation from the supranational or international dimension)."[95]

The clarification on the terminology used leads us to examine the different levels TCB can have. First of all, TCB can take place at company level[96] on a global scale, leading to the conclusion of IFAs, namely agreements concluded between MNEs and mostly global union federations and applicable in all worldwide operations of the MNE.[97] At European level, TCB has a threefold dimension. This concept indeed has been used within the context of cross-industry, sectoral and company level negotiations.[98]

Before outlining these three levels, it is worth explaining that the first attempt to recognize the importance of transnational industrial relations at European level dates back to 2004 when the European Commission adopted the Communication 'Partnership for change in an enlarged Europe' (in the section 'Preparing further developments'). The significance of this new European approach towards industrial relations was reiterated in the 2005 Social Agenda. Chapter 1, §1.03 of this book will examine in detail this issue.

If now one examines the first dimension of TCB at European level, the cross-industry level, only three agreements concluded within the framework of Articles 154-155 TFEU resulted in the adoption of a Council Directive and can be included in the supranational system of industrial relations outlined above. Other Community-wide

---

Agreements: A Stepping Stone towards a Real Internationalisation of Industrial Relations? (IRES 2012) 35 <https://www.ires.it/files/rapporti/02_2012_EUROACTA-1.pdf> accessed 14 February 2014.

95. *Ibid.*
96. On a different view see Jagodzinski, 'Transnational Collective Bargaining: A Literature Review' (n. 88) 49 ("The view that transnational collective agreements signed at the level of multinational companies represent a form of TCB is not universally shared among the research community", citing Josez Harmen Even, Transnational collective bargaining in Europe. A proposal for a European regulation on transnational collective bargaining (Boom Juridische Uitgevers 2008)).
97. Da Costa and Rehfeldt, 'Transnational Restructuring Agreements: General Overview and Specific Evidence from the European Automobile Sector' (n. 89) 145. Jagodzinski, 'Transnational Collective Bargaining: A Literature Review' (n. 88) 50.
98. Da Costa and Rehfeldt, 'Transnational Restructuring Agreements: General Overview and Specific Evidence from the European Automobile Sector' (n. 89) 145-146. See also André Sobczak, 'Ensuring the effective implementation of transnational company agreements' (2012) 18(2) European Journal of Industrial Relations 139, 139. Romuald Jagodzinki, 'European Works Councils and Transnational Company Agreements - Balancing on the Thin Line between Effective Consultation and Overstepping Competences' in Isabelle Schömann et al., *Transnational Collective Bargaining at Company Level - A New Component of European Industrial Relations?* (ETUI aisbl, 2012) 164.

agreements concluded between European social partners at this level of negotiations did not follow the EU decision-making process leading to a Council Directive and their implementation was left to "procedures and practices specific to management and labour and the Member States" (Article 155(2) TFEU).[99] The number of these voluntary agreements (also called autonomous agreements) is more than the framework agreements implemented via a Council Directive. Arguably, these autonomous agreements belong to the transnational dimension of collective industrial relations at EU level.[100]

In addition to the cross-industry level, TCB at European level can take place also at sectoral level through numerous European Sectoral Social Dialogue Committee (hereinafter: ESSD). Just as for the cross-industry level, autonomous agreements that have not been implemented via a Council Directive are considered as falling within the transnational dimension of collective relations.[101]

The last dimension of TCB at European level is the one taking place at company level.[102] This collective bargaining practice has resulted in the conclusion of TCAs, a category that comprises both IFAs and EFAs. More specifically, while IFAs are the outcome of TCB that takes place at company level on a global scale, EFAs are the outcome of TCB taking place at European level.

The focus of this book is on TCAs. These agreements have been considered as the 'stepping stone towards the development of a global IR [industrial relations] framework'[103] and they intend to give a response to the adverse effects on working conditions stemming from the market economy led by MNEs.[104] However, next to TCAs, Chapter 1, §1.03 will provide an overview of the emergence and development of EU transnational collective bargaining at cross-industry and sectoral level.

[3] Transnational Company Agreements

TCAs are voluntary, negotiated instruments concluded between the management of MNEs and trade unions and/or workers' representatives. Due to their nature of negotiated texts, these agreements represent a step forward towards the recognition and promotion of internationally recognized labour standards. The European Commission defines TCAs as follows:

> agreements comprising reciprocal commitments the scope of which extends to the territory of several States and which has been concluded by one or more representatives of a company or a group of companies on the one hand, and one or more workers' organisations on the other hand, and which covers working and

99. Bronstein (n. 4) 203. ("These agreements are to be implemented in each EU Member State through national collective bargaining or by other means that rely on social dialogue").
100. Ales and Verrecchia (n 94) 36.
101. *Ibid.*, 37.
102. Fernando Rocha and Pere J. Beneyto, 'Trade Unions and Europeanisation of Industrial Relations: Challenges and Perspectives' in Salvo Leonardi et al., *European Action on Transnational Company Agreements: A Stepping Stone towards a Real Internationalisation of Industrial Relations?* (IRES 2012) 133-134.
103. Vos (n. 12) 52.
104. Papadakis, 'Introduction' (n. 2) 4-5.

employment conditions and/or relations between employers and workers or their representatives.[105]

This definition clearly identifies the aspect of 'transnationality' that was described in the previous section of the book. The trans-border dimension characterizes the scope of application of these agreements, which are not focused on companies whose activities are limited at the national territory. Rather these agreements are concluded by companies that operate across national borders on the territory of several States. In addition, the element of 'privatization of industrial relations' is displayed in the definition since TCAs are concluded between the management of a company and trade unions and/or workers' representatives. National States do not play an active role in the negotiation, conclusion as well as implementation of these agreements.

A number of scholars and organizations (e.g., European Commission) have expressed their views as to what TCAs stand for. According to Herrnstadt, TCAs represent an emerging mode of governance at company level and a means for determining the commitment of MNEs to CSR.[106] Other scholars, and *in primis* the European Commission, focus on the fact that most TCAs are concluded by companies headquartered in Europe and thus consider these agreements as a European phenomenon. Accordingly, TCAs are considered an important new form of social dialogue embedded within the framework of European industrial relations.[107] Furthermore, Stevis argues that TCAs, and more specifically those agreements concluded by MNEs beyond Europe, may represent an emerging form of global social dialogue.[108] Similarly, Vos notes that TCAs "are supposed to support the emergence of global social dialogue and global IR framework".[109]

As to the origin of these agreements, Gallin, Da Costa and Rehfeld point out that this new form of industrial relations dates back to the 1960s.[110] In these years, the challenges posed by the new corporate structure of MNEs called upon trade unions to attempt to coordinate their activities beyond national borders. As a result, three

105. Commission, 'The role of transnational company agreements in the contexts of increasing transnational integrations' (Staff Working Document), SEC (2008) 2155, 6.
106. Owen E. Herrnstadt, 'Are International Framework Agreements a Path to Corporate Social Responsibility?' (2007) 10(1) The Journal of Business and Employment Law 187, 188.
107. Commission, 'Transnational company agreements: realising the potential of social dialogue' (Staff Working Document), SWD (2012) 264 final, 2 ff. See also Reingard Zimmer, 'Establish a Legal Frame for Transnational Collective Agreements in Europe: A Difficult Task' in Salvo Leonardi et al., *European Action on Transnational Company Agreements: A Stepping Stone towards a Real Internationalisation of Industrial Relations?* (IRES 2012) 32.
108. Dimitris Stevis, 'International framework agreements and global social dialogue: Parameters and prospects' (2010) Employment Working Paper No. 47 <www.oit.org/wcmsp5/groups/public/@ed_emp/documents/publication/wcms_122176.pdf> accessed 14 April 2014.
109. Vos (n. 12) 58.
110. Gallin, 'International Framework Agreements: A Reassessment' (n. 83) 15-16. Isabel da Costa and Udo Rehfeldt, 'Transnational collective bargaining at company level: Historical Developments' in Konstantinos Papadakis (ed.), *Cross-Border Social Dialogue and Agreements: An Emerging Global Industrial Relations Framework?* (International Institute for Labour Studies 2008) 45.

international trade secretariats (hereinafter: ITSs)[111] worked towards the creation of a system of industrial relations which could respond to the increasing internationalization of MNEs' activities.[112] The ITSs intended to create world works councils, which could guarantee employees' participation in the decision-making process of MNEs operating worldwide. Their initiatives were not directed at the conclusion of what we now know as IFAs. However, their successful attempt to coordinate trades unions' activities worldwide is noteworthy.[113]

Following this endeavour, the first TCA was concluded in 1988 between the International Food Federation, Agricultural, Hotel, Restaurant, Catering, Tobacco and Allied Workers' Association (hereinafter: IUF) and the French company Danone (then called BSN). Since then and especially since 2000, many MNEs have become familiar with this new form of social regulation at company level and the pace at which TCAs spread has rapidly increased.[114] Currently, more than 160 companies have signed more than 250 TCAs covering a small, but still significant part of the global workforce (more than 10 million workers worldwide).[115]

To give some examples of TCAs, one can look at the 'European framework agreement for professional integration of young people', which was concluded by the French MNE Safran and IndustriALL Global Union on 28 March 2013. This agreement focuses on the enhancement of vocational training of young people, for instances via traineeships or apprenticeship.[116]

Another example is the 'Global Framework Agreement' concluded by Banco do Brasil S.A. and United Network International for the Americas on 30 May 2011 and

111. The International Federation of Chemical and General Workers' Unions, the International Metalworkers' Federation and the International Union of Food and Allied Workers' Association. See also Élodie Béthoux, 'Transnational agreements and texts negotiated or adopted at company level: European Development and Perspectives' (Background document) (2008) 5-6 <http://ec.europa.eu/social/BlobServlet?docId=4968&langId=en> accessed 10 April 2014.

112. International trade secretariats were organizations established in 1889 to represent the interests of a specific trade or occupation, for instance printers, tobacco workers and typographers. In 2002, their denomination was changed in global union federations. See John P. Windmuller, Stephen K. Pursey and Jim Baker, 'The International Trade Union Movement' in Roger Blanpain (ed.), *Comparative Labour Law and Industrial Relations in Industrialized Market Economies* (Kluwer Law International 2014) 75-100. For more information on the international trade union movement see Rebecca Gumbrell-McCormick, 'The International Labour Movement: Structures and Dynamics' in Peter Fairbrother, Marc-Antonin Hennebert and Christian Lévesque (eds), *Transnational Trade Unionism: Building Union Power* (Routledge 2013) 183-202.

113. Da Costa and Rehfeldt, 'Transnational collective bargaining at company level: Historical Developments' (n. 110) 45 ff. For more information about World Works Councils see S. Rüb, 'World works councils and other forms of global employee representation in transnational undertakings' Arbeitspapier No. 55 <http://www.boeckler.de/pdf/p_arbp_055.pdf> accessed 14 July 2014.

114. Commission, 'Mapping of transnational texts negotiated at corporate level', EMPL F2 EP/bp 2008 (D) 14511 4.

115. Commission, 'Transnational company agreements: realising the potential of social dialogue' (n. 107) 2.

116. Text available at <http://ec.europa.eu/employment_social/empl_portal/transnational_agreements/Safran_young_EN.pdf> accessed 5 March 2014.

renewed on 19 June 2013.[117] This agreement deals with different issues, such as fundamental labour rights, CSR and health and safety. Moreover, Article 1 gives a clear indication as to the parties' intention in concluding such an agreement, namely encouraging social dialogue as a significant to minimize conflict.

As one can understand from these two examples, the driving reasons behind the diffusion of these agreements are different and vary on the different interests of the signatory parties. Some TCAs are perceived as a vehicle to deepen the relationship between management and trade unions and consequently as a way to enhance social dialogue within the firm. In addition, some TCAs stem from the attempt of the enterprise's management to 'buy stability and peace' in situation of conflict with the workers' representatives.[118] Section §1.01[F][3][b][i] and §1.06[F][3][b][ii] of this chapter will provide an in-depth analysis of the reasons that drive trade unions and MNEs to conclude these agreements.

Within the broad category of TCAs, a classification has been made according to two different but intertwined criteria: the scope of application and the signatory parties.[119] If one considers the first criterion, two categories can be identified: first, TCAs whose scope of application is limited to Europe (EFAs); second, TCAs that have a global scope of application (IFAs).

If one takes into account the second criterion, different actors are involved in the conclusion of TCAs, such as global union federations (hereinafter: GUFs), European industry federations (hereinafter: EIFs), EWCs, national trade unions and other forms of workers' representation at company level. Hence, TCAs concluded by GUFs are called International Framework Agreements or 'global framework agreements' (hereinafter: GFAs)[120] and they usually have global scope of application, with some exceptions.[121] In particular, IFAs have been defined as:

> agreements concluded between a transnational company and an international union federation with the purpose of ensuring fundamental rights, typically by recognising the ILO core labour standards in all of the company's locations and establishing a formal ongoing relationship between the corporation and the union organisation. They are usually concluded in the context of Corporate Social Responsibility (CSR) initiatives as an alternative or in complement to unilateral codes of conduct.[122]

117. Text available at <http://ec.europa.eu/employment_social/empl_portal/transnational_agreements/BANCO%20DO%20BRASIL_EN.pdf> accessed 5 March 2014.
118. ITC-ILO, 'Key Issues for Management to Consider with regard to Transnational Company Agreements (TCAs)' (2010) 10 <http://lempnet.itcilo.org/en/tcas/admin/final-pub> accessed 5 March 2014.
119. Volker Telljohann et al., 'European and International Framework Agreements: New Tools of Transnational Industrial Relations' (2009) 3-4 Transfer 505, 508.
120. Papadakis, 'Introduction and Overview' (n. 26) 2.
121. Telljohann et al., 'European and International Framework Agreements: New Tools of Transnational Industrial Relations' (n. 119) 508 and 511 (the IFAs concluded by Chiquita, an American MNE, only applies to Latin America).
122. Commission, 'Mapping of transnational texts negotiated at corporate level' (n. 114) 5. See also Papadakis, 'Introduction and Overview' (n. 26) 2; Schömann et al., 'Codes of Conduct and International Framework Agreements: New Forms of Governance at Company Level' (n. 41) 1.

TCAs concluded by EIFs and/or EWCs are called European Framework Agreements and they usually have European scope of application.[123] National trade unions are involved in the conclusion of both IFAs and EFAs.

To complete this first overview of what TCAs are, one more issue will be dealt with: the country of origin of MNEs. All the data are retrieved from the database of the European Commission on TCAs.

Most of the companies that have concluded TCAs are headquartered in the European Union or in the European Economic Area (mainly in France and Germany). Among the countries outside Europe, enterprises headquartered in Switzerland (18) are the forerunner, followed by companies headquartered in the United States of America (13), Norway (7), Brazil (6), South Africa (3), Indonesia (2), Japan (2), Australia (1), Canada (1), Malaysia (1), New Zealand (1) and Russia (1).

Figure 1.1 Headquarter of MNEs

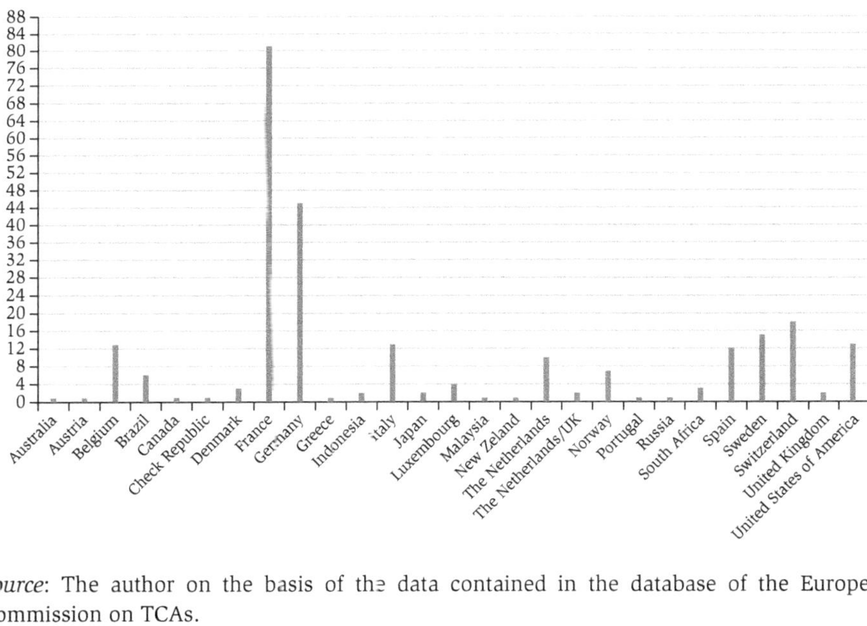

Source: The author on the basis of the data contained in the database of the European Commission on TCAs.

Even if the development of TCAs gathered momentum during the last two decades, one may not disregard the number of open questions that this evolving process of internationalization and Europeanization of industrial relations still pose. More specifically, the discussion revolves around chiefly three main areas: the actors entitled to

123. Telljohann et al., 'European and International Framework Agreements: New Tools of Transnational Industrial Relations' (n. 119) 508.

conclude TCAs; the legal status; and the legal effects of these agreements. These issues will be dealt with in-depth in the following chapters of the book.

To conclude, this section has shown that TCAs have the potential to be an important instrument for regulating the relationship between MNEs and trade unions and workers' representatives at transnational level. Due to the emerging internationalization of the economy, these actors need a tool capable of bridging the gap between MNEs' activities around the globe and the still territorial action of trade unions and/or workers' representative. TCAs may fill this gap and contribute to a process that will lead to the approximation of working conditions throughout the MNEs' business operations.

[a] Transnational Company Agreements versus Corporate Codes of Conduct

TCAs and corporate codes of conduct are a product of globalization with dissimilar impact on the labour market. In particular, while TCAs seem to 'represent a more pro-active approach to shaping company-wide social dialogue in a global context', corporate codes of conduct 'play a role in reinforcing a specific corporate culture'.[124]

TCAs and corporate codes of conduct differ in many aspects, starting from their nature: while the first are the outcome of the negotiations between management and trade unions and/or workers' representatives, the second are unilateral declarations drawn up by the management of companies. This difference has repercussions on the legitimacy of these instruments, which, as Sobczak points out, is higher in the case of TCAs due to their nature of negotiated tools.[125]

Moreover, in terms of content, the issues covered in corporate codes of conduct are usually not the same as those included in TCAs. In fact, while TCAs mainly cover labour standards, codes of conduct have a broader material scope of application since they focus on CSR and business ethics issues as well.

In addition to that, another significant difference between these two instruments concerns the compliance monitoring procedures. Corporate codes of conduct have been often criticized because monitoring mechanisms are usually dependent on the unilateral management's decision or are absent.[126] On the contrary, TCAs represent a significant step forward compared to corporate codes of conduct. In fact, for the most part, TCAs provide for dialogue-based monitoring systems, which guarantee the involvement of workers' representatives and/or trade unions in securing the compliance of these agreements by MNEs.

From the above-mentioned dissimilarities, one can argue that these two modes of governance at company level respond to different needs of MNEs and trade unions and/or workers' representatives, even though they are both voluntary instruments. Whereas TCAs can be regarded as a new form of social dialogue at company level with

124. Schömann et al., 'Codes of Conduct and International Framework Agreements: New Forms of Governance at Company Level' (n. 41) 1.
125. Sobczak, 'Legal Dimensions of International Framework Agreements in the Field on Corporate Social Responsibility' (n. 86) 115-116.
126. Jones (n. 11) 143. Gallin, 'International Framework Agreements: A Reassessment' (n. 83) 34.

the aim of enhancing, *inter alia*, the cohesion within the company and the collaboration with the social partners, corporate codes of conduct are considered as guidelines for the behaviour of the management.

[b] *The Position of Different Actors towards the Conclusion of Transnational Company Agreements*

The analysis of the motives behind the conclusion of TCAs is not new in the academic literature. Several scholars have written about the driving reasons and objectives that lead trade unions, workers' representatives and MNEs to initiate the negotiations and conclude these agreements.[127]

The following subsections will examine the motives behind the conclusion of TCAs on both the employees and management's side.[128]

[i] Trade Unions

GUFs and EIFs consider TCAs a very significant tool for pursuing numerous objectives. Literature has focussed its attention on the reasons that drive GUFs to conclude IFAs. However, most of the motives behind the conclusions of IFAs can be used for the EFAs too.[129]

Telljohann and Drouin identifies four main objectives pursued by GUFs in the negotiation and conclusion of IFAs.[130] These will be explained in the following paragraphs accompanied by examples.

As to the first objective, GUFs aim at fostering workers' rights and contributing to the process of approximation of the working conditions of the entire MNE's workforce

127. Jagodzinski, 'Transnational Collective Bargaining: A Literature Review' (n. 88) 51-52; Telljohann et al., 'European and International Framework Agreements: Practical Experiences and Strategic Approaches' (n. 29) 41 ff.; Telljohann et al., 'European and International Framework Agreements: New Tools of Transnational Industrial Relations' (n. 119) 513-519; Schömann, 'Transnational Company Agreements: Towards an Internationalisation of Industrial Relations' (n. 3) 210-212.
128. This book will not address the motives that lead EWCs and other forms of workers' representation to engage into transnational negotiations and concluded TCAs. For an in-depth analysis of the topic see: Schömann et al., 'Codes of Conduct and International Framework Agreements: New Forms of Governance at Company Level' (n. 41) 44-45; Reingard Zimmer, 'European Works Councils as Participants in Euro-Wide Collective Agreements: Analysis from a German Perspective' (2013) 4(4) ELLJ 313, 319-320; Jagodzinski, 'European Works Councils and Transnational Company Agreements – Balancing on the Thin Line between Effective Consultation and Overstepping Competences' (n. 98) 158-160.
129. In relation to EFAs, it is however important to note that many of these agreements have been concluded in order to address issues such as restructuring, anticipation and management of changes. For the motives that lead trade unions and EWCs to enter into negotiations with MNEs and sign these agreements see Telljohann et al., 'European and International Framework Agreements: Practical Experiences and Strategic Approaches' (n. 29) 56-58.
130. Renée-Claude Drouin, 'Promoting Fundamental Labor Rights Through International Framework Agreements: Practical Outcomes and Present Challenges' (2010) 31 Comparative Labor Law and Policy Journal 591, 599 ff. Telljohann et al., 'European and International Framework Agreements: New Tools of Transnational Industrial Relations' (n. 119) 513 ff.

(sometimes including the whole supply chain) by setting up rules that are applicable in all company's operations.[131] In other words, the signatory parties intend to introduce a global 'social floor', namely rights and entitlements accessible to all workers in the global economy.[132] In order to do so, the majority of the texts refer to the core labour standards contained in the eight ILO fundamental Conventions as well as in ILO Declaration 1998. As a result, by signing IFAs, MNEs voluntarily commit themselves to comply with the core labour standards set forth in the ILO Conventions and Recommendations mentioned in the text as well as with other values and principles mutually recognized by the MNEs? trade unions and and workers' representatives (e.g., ethics and environmental principles).

This motive is shared amongst GUFs. By way of example, according to the International Metalworkers' Federation (hereinafter: IMF), now part of IndustriALL Global Union, IFAs are "a global instrument with the purpose of ensuring workers' rights in all of the target company's locations."[133] In addition to that, the same GUF describes the reason behind the conclusion of these agreements by saying that "[t]hrough IFAs, the ILO's Core Labour Standards can be guaranteed in all facilities of a transnational company, which is especially helpful in transition and developing countries, where legislation is sometimes insufficient, poorly enforced or anti-worker."[134]

Concerning the second objective, IFAs are a significant tool to buttress social dialogue within a MNE.[135] The conclusion of these agreements can contribute and strengthen the development of social dialogue channels within corporations. More particularly, often the signatories of IFAs establish or use existing social dialogue channels within a MNE in order to ensure the implementation and monitoring of the agreement as well as the peaceful resolutions of the disputes arisen. These channels may encompass the involvement of trade unions as well as existing workers' representation bodies that are in charge of worker's information and consultation at company level (e.g., world work councils).[136]

In addition to that, in some circumstances the conclusion of IFAs can enhance and reinforce the dialogue between local trade unions and local management. In a number of IFAs, local and national trade unions play an important role, be it as they co-sign these agreements or they are the actors in charge of the implementation and/or monitoring procedures. By way of example, in the 'International Framework Agreement between SAAB AB and employee representatives Organisations in Saab AB and IF Metall and Industri All Global Union', Swedish trade unions not only co-signed the IFA but they currently have an active role in the implementation and monitoring of the

131. Mark Carley, 'Transnational Company Agreements. Dialogue, Rights, Anticipating Corporate Restructuring, Actors: A New Perspective' (Report of the French EU Presidency Conference, Lyon, 13-14 November 2008) 6, <www.travail-emploi-sante.gouv.fr/IMG/pdf/ATNEactes.pdf> accessed 29 March 2014.
132. Papadakis, 'Introduction' (n. 2) 2.
133. IMF, 'The Power of Framework Agreements' (2003) 3, <http://library.fes.de/pdf-files/gurn/00257.pdf> accessed 10 April 2014.
134. *Ibid.*, 4.
135. *Ibid.*, 4-5; Herrnstadt (n. 106) 190.
136. Drouin (n. 130) 601-603.

agreement. Under the heading 'monitoring and compliance', the agreements reads that "[i]mplementation and compliance with these provisions will be reported on and discussed once per year with the employee union representatives of maximum 4 person, 2 IF Metall, 1 Unionen and 1 Sveriges Ingenjorer at a Saab executive management meeting. The parties are always entitled to initiate discussions and reports on incidents occurred."[137]

To sum up, by strengthening social dialogue within a company, IFAs represent a valuable tool to build a 'conflict-free' environment and the establishment of a stable and long-lasting management-labour relationship.[138]

As to the third objective, international solidarity is an important aim pursued by GUFs with the conclusion of IFAs. A case study about the IKEA best describes this aim as follows:

> [w]ith the development of a global framework agreement, the BWI is becoming more relevant not only to developing countries but also to developed countries. International solidarity, for vast numbers of unions in developed countries, is seen primarily as political or moral support to unions in developing countries. Globalisation has changed the landscape of industrial relations, with more and more workers being employed directly or indirectly by MNCs. The BWI is evolving not only as an organisation for delivering solidarity but also as one that is directly involved in industrial relations at the global level.[139]

Regarding the fourth and final objective, both Telljohann and Drouin considers trade unions' cooperation and organization as one of the four chief objectives pursued by GUFs. More specifically, IFAs can be understood as organizing tools[140] in three different way: first, via the conclusion of IFAs, GUFs often come in contact with national and local trade unions. This enables them to strengthen their network and, in the long run, to better represent and defend the interests of all workers in MNEs' operations. Second, as outlined above, the conclusion of IFAs aims at enhancing social dialogue and accordingly contributing to solve the conflicts that may rise with the management. Due to the positive impact a 'conflict-free' working environment may have on MNEs' productivity, these companies may be more inclined to secure that their workers can enjoy the right of freedom of association and collective bargaining. IFAs may then be considered as a tool to support the creation of workers' organization.[141] Third, when concluding these agreements, GUFs may pursue the aim of increasing

137. Text available at <http://ec.europa.eu/employment_social/empl_portal/transnational_agreements/saab-gfa-en.pdf> accessed 10 June 2014.
138. Drouin (n. 130) 601-605. Telljohann et al., 'European and International Framework Agreements: New Tools of Transnational Industrial Relations' (n. 119) 519.
139. Peter Wilke, André Sobczak and Isabelle Schömann, 'Codes of Conduct and International Framework Agreements: New Forms of Governance at Company Level, Case Study: IKEA' (Eurofound, Office for Official Publications of the European Communities 2008) 8. See also Schömann et al., 'Codes of Conduct and International Framework Agreements: New Forms of Governance at Company Level' (n. 41) 41.
140. Gallin, 'International Framework Agreements: A Reassessment' (n. 83) 35 (the scholar stresses that the main difference between IFAs and corporate codes of conduct lies in the fact that IFAs are considered as organizing tools in addition to instruments addressing corporate behaviour).
141. Drouin (n. 130) 604.

their membership. In this respect, the report of the International Training Center of the ILO (hereinafter: ITC-ILO) explains that "[i]n one particular case, the signing of an IFA implied an automatic additional 20,000 new members for a particular GUF, upon signature".[142] In addition, according to UNI, "[i]f a company agrees to leave open the door to union organisation, then it's up to the unions to build on this. Increasingly UNI trade union alliances have been able to obtain agreements to allow trade union access to employers with success e.g. one UNI affiliate in Brazil can claim to have more than doubled its membership in this way."[143]

To sum up, this section has shown that trade unions' interests in promoting the conclusion of TCAs are diverse. However, all of them have a common feature: trade unions strive for enhancing the cooperation with the management of MNEs and for creating corporate policies that are mutually recognized.

[ii] Multinational Enterprises

The question as to what reasons drive MNEs to engage in transnational negotiations with trade unions and workers' representatives has drawn the attention of many scholars and institutions.[144] The answer rests upon the diverse business strategies undertaken by MNEs, whose interests in the conclusion of TCAs may differ according to several factors, such as the sectors in which they operate and the existence, if any, of working relationship with trade unions. All these factors may have an influence in the inclination of MNEs to conclude TCAs.[145]

Concerning these factors, Telljohann notes that MNEs will be more inclined to conclude IFAs (as well as corporate codes of conduct) if the brand of the company (especially in the textile sector) is well known. This is because a bad reputation before the public at large may hinder the MNE's position in the market. Similarly, the signature of TCAs will be more likely in companies active in a sector with a long history of strong and steady management-labour relation as well as dynamic (global) trade unions.[146]

The type of interaction between a MNE and trade unions and workers' representatives is connected largely to the type of business the company is involved. In fact, the economic sector and the management-labour working relationship are strictly interlinked. Referring to Gereffi, Hammer and Papadakis distinguish between producer-driven and buyer-driven value chains and specify that TCAs, IFAs in the case taken into consideration by the scholars, have a more suitable environment in the first type of global chain for a series of factors. First of all, in a producer-driven chain (such as in the

142. ITC-ILO (n. 118) 12.
143. UNI, 'Global agreements' <http://mail.uniglobalunion.org/Apps/iportal.nsf/pages/20090226_ml9xEn> accessed 9 April 2014.
144. Jagodzinski, 'Transnational collective bargaining: a literature overview' (n. 3) 46-47. Commission, 'Transnational company agreements: realising the potential of social dialogue' (n. 107) 5.
145. Schömann et al., 'Codes of Conduct and International Framework Agreements: New Forms of Governance at Company Level' (n. 41) 33-36.
146. Schömann et al., 'Codes of Conduct and International Framework Agreements: New Forms of Governance at Company Level' (n. 41) 35-36.

automobile sector) MNEs make use of suppliers and sub (contractors) but the production remain predominantly in control of the MNE. Moreover, traditionally, trade unions and workers' representatives played a stronger role and more influence companies characterized by this production system. These features are significant factors when examining the leaning of a specific industry sector in the development of negotiated instruments such as TCAs.[147]

Different is the case of MNEs active in a buyer-driven chain (such as in the textile industry), which rely upon different companies operating in low-wages countries by outsourcing segments of their production. In these MNEs, the influence and leeway of activities of trade unions and workers' representatives used to be very limited, if not totally absent.[148]

Now that the factors contributing to the creation of a suitable environment for transnational negotiations are outlined, this section will focus on the question initially posed: why do MNEs decide in the first instance to conclude TCAs? The literature on the topic identifies several reasons behind this choice and most of them are confirmed by the International Organizations of Employers (hereinafter: IOE). Papadakis examines the issue in detail by distinguishing three main categories: first, external factors that coerce MNEs to conclude TCAs; second, factors linked to the need to anticipate certain potential social risks; and third, factors linked to the pressure exerted by civil society.[149] The following paragraphs will outline all the three factors.

According to Papadakis, the Council Directive on European Works Councils plays a significant role in the first category.[150] This EU legislative act establishes the creation of transnational workers' representatives bodies in enterprises that meet a numerical threshold and are active in at least two different Member States. The establishment of European Works Councils is considered an important step for improving management-labour relationships since these bodies need to be consulted and informed when the issue at stake do not concern only one undertaking but has a 'transnational' character.

In addition, the same author notes that also cultural expectations and the role of actors such as the International Finance Corporation (hereinafter: IFC) work as coercive factors. In particular, concerning the first one, MNEs are inclined to conclude TCAs especially in countries where trade unions and workers' representatives have played an important role in the definition of working and employment conditions (as

147. Papadakis, 'Introduction and Overview' (n. 26) 6; Konstantinos Papadakis, 'Adapting International Framework Agreements in the Russian Federation, South Africa and Japan: Management and Motivations' in Konstantinos Papadakis (ed.), *Shaping Global Industrial Relations – The Impact of International Framework Agreements* (Palgrave Macmillan 2012) 64-65; Nikolaus Hammer, 'International Framework Agreements in the Context of Global Production' in Konstantinos Papadakis (ed.), *Cross-Border Social Dialogue and Agreements: An Emerging Global Industrial Relations Framework?* (International Institute for Labour Studies 2008) 93-95.
148. Papadakis, 'Introduction and Overview' (n. 26) 6; Papadakis, 'Adapting International Framework Agreements in the Russian Federation, South Africa and Japan: Management and Motivations' (n. 147) 64-65; Hammer, 'International Framework Agreements in the Context of Global Production' (n. 147) 93-95.
149. Papadakis, 'Adapting International Framework Agreements in the Russian Federation, South Africa and Japan: Management and Motivations' (n. 147) 62-68.
150. *Ibid.*, 63.

an example, Nordic countries).[151] As to the International Finance Corporation, this organization is member of the World Bank Group and sets environmental and social sustainability requirements that MNEs must meet in order to receive a loan.[152]

The second category identified by Papadakis, the anticipatory factors, relates to the importance of creating stable labour-management relations and a positive corporate image, especially when certain difficult managerial decisions have to be taken (e.g., restructuring).[153] Linked to this, Telljohann speaks about 'risk management' in particular when suppliers and (sub-) contractors are the subject of public campaigns against the poor and unhealthy living and working conditions of their workers.[154]

Finally, concerning the third category, civil society pressure is an important factor that drive MNEs to conclude TCAs. Trade unions usually wield pressure on MNEs, even though one may not exclude that also other groups, for example environmental groups, may start campaigns to encourage the conclusion of TCAs.

Next to the reasons that lead MNEs to conclude TCAs, there are several grounds behind the choice not to opt for this emerging mode of governance at company level. For instance, several issues concerning the legal status and the legal effects at national level of these agreements are still unsolved.[155] These factors contribute to deter enterprises from signing TCAs. MNEs indeed prefer to choose similar voluntary initiatives, for example corporate codes of conduct, which have a minor impact on the labour relations within the enterprise and its business partners.

§1.02 INTERNATIONAL FRAMEWORK AGREEMENTS

[A] Introduction

Chapter 1, §1.02 analyses the origin, development, status and main features of IFAs. A list of the IFAs concluded until May 2014 is included as Annex to this book (Table 1).

[B] A General Overview

As examined in Chapter 1, §1.01, the 1960s and 1970s witnessed the first attempt made by ITSs to mobilize, organize and coordinate trade unions' strategies at transnational

151. Schömann et al., 'Codes of Conduct and International Framework Agreements: New Forms of Governance at Company Level' (n. 41) 45-46 (IKEA IFA: *IKEA*: Basic motives on the part of IKEA management stemmed from pressures from environmental groups, reaction from customers and internal culture and values (to create a better everyday life).
152. See also Telljohann et al., 'European and International Framework Agreements: Practical Experiences and Strategic Approaches' (n. 29) 45; IOE, 'International Framework Agreements - An Employers' Guide' (2007) 8 <http://apirnet.ilo.org/resources/ifas-an-employers-guide> accessed 24 May 2014.
153. Papadakis, 'Adapting International Framework Agreements in the Russian Federation, South Africa and Japan: Management and Motivations' (n. 147) 65-67.
154. Telljohann et al., 'European and International Framework Agreements: Practical Experiences and Strategic Approaches' (n. 29) 45.
155. ITC-ILO (n. 118) 11.

level as a response to MNEs' activities.[156] In this period, corporations started running their business beyond national borders by, for instance, decentralizing their production. Outsourcing part of the production to subsidiaries, suppliers and (sub) contractors became, and still is, a major business strategy to reduce the costs of production.

In response to the (potential) negative externalities of these operations on workers' labour conditions, the international trade secretariats of the metalworking, chemical and food sectors buttressed a better workplace democracy through the establishment of world works councils in MNEs. These bodies could then ensure that workers or their representatives at company level were informed and consulted on issues that could destabilize their protection, e.g., in case of restructuring or transfer of undertakings. This step represented the origin of what nowadays many scholars define as transnational collective bargaining.[157]

This first endeavour to tackle the increasing globalization of the economy was followed by the ILO and OECD's initiatives to regulate MNEs' activities and the emergence of corporate codes of conduct. Only as from the late 1980s and especially since 2000, one has assisted at the development of TCAs. In particular, the process of transnational union coordination that started in the 1960s and 1970s gained momentum with the 'Common Viewpoint IUF/BSN', which is considered the first IFA. This agreement was concluded in 1988 between the French-based food multinational BSN-Danone and the International Union of Food, Agricultural, Hotel, Restaurant, Catering, Tobacco and Allied Workers' Association (hereinafter: IUF) and represents the outcome of the negotiations started in 1984 between the IUF's delegation and the management of BSN. The intention of the signatories was to extend the scope of application of the agreement to all the operations of the company worldwide.

As Gallin notes, the conclusion of the first IFA by BSN-Danone is result of the particular climate existing in the company, and more specifically it mirrors the ideas of its founder and CEO until 1996, Antoine Riboud. His political background, connected to the French Social Party and his ideas as a progressive Catholic, were at the basis of his recognition of trade unions as important figures within a corporation.[158] In particular, Mr Riboud stated during a meeting that "he wanted strong unions in his company because he could not imagine leading his company against its employees and without respecting their rights."[159]

The conclusion of this first IFA and the following TCAs represents a remarkable step in the MNEs' acknowledgement of GUFs as bargaining partners.[160] As Da Costa

156. Isabel da Costa and Udo Rehfeldt, 'Transnational Restructuring Agreements: General Overview and Specific Evidence from the Automobile Sector' in Konstantinos Papadakis (ed.), *Shaping Global Industrial Relations – The Impact of International Framework Agreements* (Palgrave Macmillan 2011) 147. See also Papadakis, 'Introduction' (n. 2) 5; Da Costa and Rehfedlt, 'Transnational collective bargaining at company level: Historical Developments' (n. 110) 43 ff.

157. Isabel da Costa and Udo Rehfeldt, 'Transnational Restructuring Agreements: General Overview and Specific Evidence from the Automobile Sector' (n. 156) 145-150. For a different interpretation see Jagodzinki, 'Transnational collective bargaining: A Literature Overview' (n. 3) 24 ff.

158. Gallin, 'International Framework Agreements: A Reassessment' (n. 83) 29.

159. *Ibid.*

160. Drouin (n. 130) 601. Schömann, 'Transnational Company Agreements: Towards an Internationalisation of Industrial Relations' (n. 3) 211.

and Rehfeldt point out, neither world work councils nor ITSs were recognized as such before.[161]

These agreements represent a valuable instrument to face the increasing internationalization of MNE's activities for they allow trade unions to represent and protect the interests of workers employed in the different operations of a MNE, irrespective of the countries where the company is active. Moreover, the signatories of some IFAs extend the scope of application of the agreements to the entire global value chain, thus including also suppliers and (sub-) contractors.

The following two sections will provide an overview of the existing GUFs and the model IFAs that these organizations have developed.

[1] Global Union Federations

GUFs are the key actors in the negotiation and conclusion of IFAs on the employees' side. In particular, they are organizations of national trade unions of a specific sector of industry or occupation[162] with the purpose of representing and furthering the interests of their members.[163]

Even though GUFs are the main signatories of IFAs, many agreements have been (co-) signed also by national trade unions and EWCs. The latter are bodies set up at company level, a feature that may allow a better interaction with the management of the company; on the contrary GUFs represent workers in an industrial sector or occupation, not in a specific company.[164] Despite the positive aspect connected to the involvement of EWCs, the conclusion of IFAs by these transnational bodies has raised questions as to their competence to sign the transnational agreements. In fact, neither the original Directive on European Works Council (Directive 94/45/EC) nor the 2009 Recast Directive confer to EWCs an explicit mandate to negotiate and conclude agreements. According to these EU legislative acts EWCs are bodies set up to be consulted and informed in case of management's decision that may have an impact on workers in different establishments of the company.[165] This issue will be examined in-depth in the section of this book devoted to EFAs.

Compared to the number of ITSs, which in 1914 reached 28, the number of GUFs is rather limited and has sharply declined over the years. Nowadays, only nine global federations are present in the international scenario: IndustriALL, Education International (hereinafter: EI), Public Service International (hereinafter: PSI), UNI Global Union (hereinafter: UNI), Building and Wood Workers International (hereinafter:

161. Da Costa and Rehfeldt, 'Transnational Restructuring Agreements: General Overview and Specific Evidence from the Automobile Sector' (n. 156) 147.
162. Windmuller and Pursey and Baker, 'The International Trade Union Movement' (n. 112) 91.
163. For more information about the IFAs' policy developed by IMF, ICEM, BWI and UNI see Michael Fichter, Markus Helfen and Katharina Schiederig, 'Transnational Solidarity around Global Production Networks? Reflections on the Strategy of International Framework Agreements' in Peter Fairbrother, Marc-Antonin Hennebert and Christian Lévesque (eds.), *Transnational Trade Unionism: Building Union Power* (Routledge 2013) 212-217.
164. Sobczak, 'Legal Dimensions of International Framework Agreements in the Field of Corporate Social Responsibility' (n. 86) 119-120.
165. *Ibid.*, 120.

BWI), International Transport Workers' Federation (hereinafter: ITF), IUF, International Federation of Journalists (hereinafter: IFJ) and International Arts and Entertainment Alliance (hereinafter: IAEI). The following paragraphs will outline the main features of these GUFs and will describe their involvement in IFAs.

IndustriALL is the most recent GUF resulting from the merger of three former GUFs, namely IMF, the International Federation of Chemical, Energy, Mine and General Workers' Unions (hereinafter: ICEM) and the International Textiles Garment and Leather Workers' Federation (hereinafter: ITGLWF). It represents workers in different sectors of industry that can be clustered in three main areas: mining, energy and manufacturing. In particular it advances the interests of 140 million workers operating in these sectors in 140 different countries.[166]

EI is a GUF representing 30 million employees involved in education in 170 countries. Two of the goals pursued by EI are the following: enhancing the economic interests of teachers and all other employees who work in educational organizations and fostering access to education to students around the globe.[167]

PSI is a global federation representing public workers active in a wide range of sectors, such as 'social services, health care, municipal and community services, central government, and public utilities such as water and electricity'. More specifically, 669 national trade unions are affiliated to this federation, which protects the economic interests of 20 million workers in 154 countries.[168]

UNI (before known as United Network International) (UNI) is a global federation representing the interests of more than 20 million workers involved in the service industry in 150 countries. For instances, workers represented by UNI perform their work in the cleaning and security industries as well as in the commerce, finance and sport sectors, just to mention a few.[169]

BWI is a global union federation striving to protect and enhance the interests of 12 million workers involved in the building (materials), wood and forestry sectors. In particular, 326 national trade unions are affiliated to this international federation, which covers workers in 130 countries worldwide.[170]

ITF is a GUF that advances the interests of over 4.5 million workers conducting their activities in the transport industry in around 150 countries. The promotion of trade unions around the globe and the assistance of approximately 700 affiliates are amongst the aims pursued by this federation.[171]

166. Official website of IndustriALL < www.industriall-union.org/about-us > accessed on 14 May 2014 < http://www.industriall-union.org/about-us > accessed on 14 May 2014.
167. Official website of EI < http://www.ei-ie.org/en/websections/content_detail/3247 > accessed on 14 May 2014.
168. Official website of PSI < http://www.world-psi.org/en/who-we-are > accessed on 14 May 2014.
169. Official website of UNI Global Union < www.uniglobalunion.org/about-us > accessed on 14 May 2014 at < http://www.uniglobalunion.org/about-us > accessed on 14 May 2014.
170. Official website of BWI < www bwint.org/default.asp?Language = EN > accessed 14 May 2014 < http://www.bwint.org/default.asp?Language = EN > accessed 14 May 2014.
171. Official website of ITF < www.itfglobal.org/about-us/moreabout.cfm > accessed 14 May 2014 < http://www.itfglobal.org/about-us/moreabout.cfm > accessed 14 May 2014.

IUF is a global union federation founded in 1920 to protect the interests of workers active in the following sectors of industry: 'agriculture and plantation, preparation and manufacture of food and beverage, hotels, restaurants and catering services and all stages of tobacco processing'. At international level 326 national trade unions are grouped in this federation, and over 126 million of workers in 126 countries are covered by its activities.[172]

IFJ is a GUF that protects the interests of a specific category of workers: journalists. Defending press freedom and political and cultural expression is one of the aims identified in the mission statement of this union federation. IFJ represents approximately 600,000 journalists in 134 countries.[173]

The International Arts and Entertainment Alliance (IAEA) is a GUF composed of three global union federations: the International Federation of Actors (FIA), the International Federation of Musicians (FIM) and the Media, Entertainment and Arts division of UNI (UNI-MEI).[174]

At the time of writing, GUFs have (co-) signed the majority of IFAs (more than 120 IFAs out of 145). The most active GUF is currently IndustriALL,[175] followed by UNI Global Union (and its regional organizations), IUF and BWI. The IFJ has concluded only one IFA and no agreement has been concluded by EI, IAEA and ITF. Furthermore, national trade unions have co-signed some of the IFAs and in one agreement concluded by Chiquita and IUF, the ILO Director is among the signatory parties.[176]

[2] Model International Framework Agreements

Given that there are no specific provisions conferring GUFs the mandate to negotiate and conclude IFAs, some GUFs have developed model agreements and guidelines to tackle the legitimacy issue.[177] The following paragraphs will examine two examples of a model IFA adopted by BWI and IMF.

On 16 November 2007 and on 3 December 2010[178] the BWI World Council approved a 'Model IFA'. The text refers to the main existing international instruments on human and labour rights (the Universal Declaration on Human Rights, the ILO

172. Official website of IUF <www.iuf.org/w/?q = node/149> accessed 14 May 2014 <http://www.iuf.org/w/?q = node/149> accessed 14 May 2014.
173. Official website of IFJ <www.ifj.org/about-ifj/mission-statement/> accessed 14 May 2014.
174. Official website of IAEA <http://www.iaea-globalunion.org/> accessed 14 May 2014.
175. The number of agreements concluded by IMF, ICEM and ITGLWF is counted in the number of agreements (co)signed by IndustriALL.
176. Another IFA in which the ILO Director-General played a role is the 'Global Agreement on Corporate Social Responsibility and International Industrial Relations', which was concluded in September 2005 and amended in May 2013. The ILO Director-General was present when the agreement was concluded. Information available at: BWI, 'BWI, IndustriALL and Lafarge sign a new global framework agreement in presence of ILO Director-General' (Press Release 2013) <www.bwint.org/default.asp?Index = 4937&Language = EN> accessed 14 May 2014.
177. Da Costa and Rehfeldt, 'Transnational collective bargaining at company level: Historical Developments' (n. 110) 61.
178. BWI, 'New BWI Model Framework Agreement' (Approved by BWI World Council on 3 December 2010) <http://www.bwint.org/default.asp?Index = 47&Language = EN> accessed 23 May 2014.

Declaration 1998, ILO Conventions and OECD Guidelines). Health and safety at work, decent work and welfare of workers are also addressed.

Next to the 'Model IFA', the World Council adopted a set of guidelines concerning how to initiate the procedures to conclude such an agreement, its content and the implementation and enforcement process.[179] In particular, the guidelines indicate that national affiliates (in particular those of the State where the corporation is headquartered) can be involved in the initiation of the negotiations leading to the conclusion of IFAs. Their role is particularly important when it comes to the implementation of the agreement. Concerning the content of the 'Model IFA', a reference is made to the core labour standards in the eight ILO fundamental Conventions and to issues such as health and safety at work, working hours, living wage and welfare of workers. In addition to that, some implementation mechanisms are laid down, for instance dissemination of the agreement among the workforce, suppliers and (sub-) contractors, local monitoring and the procedures to follow in case one of the parties infringes the agreement. Finally, a specific section is devoted to the duration of the agreement.

In addition to this model agreement, also IMF has adopted a 'Model IFA'. More specifically, in 1998, the IMF's Executive Committee adopted a Model Code of Conduct based on the ICTFU/ITSs Code of Labour Practice.[180] Despite the name given to this document was 'Model Code of Conduct', the aim pursued from the outset by the IMF's Executive Committee was to create negotiated codes between the GUF and MNEs. This is eventually what occurred since then. This 'Model Code of Conduct' may hence be considered as a 'Model IFA', whose core provisions concern the respect for ILO standards not only by the MNEs but also throughout the global venue chain and the establishment of implementation and monitoring procedures with the involvement of trade unions.[181]

[C] Features

This section is devoted to provide an overview of the main features of IFAs. More specifically, it explores two main facets of these agreements: the substantive aspect (the content) and the procedural aspect (implementation, monitoring and settle of disputes). Chapter 2 will provide a detailed analysis of the features of a selected number of IFAs and EFAs and it will draw a comparison between these agreements.

In terms of content, the texts of IFAs address different working and labour standards depending on several factors, such as the needs and interests of signatories,

179. BWI, 'BWI Guidance on International Framework Agreements (IFAs)' (2007) <http://www.bwint.org/pdfs/FinalnoteIFAWCNov07.pdf> accessed 23 May 2014.
180. The ICTFU/ITSs Code of Labour Practice is a document jointly developed in 1996 by the International Confederation of Free Trade Unions (ICFTU) and International Trade Secretariats. More information on the Code of Labour Practices are available atILO (ACTRAV), 'Labour and Business in the Global Market' available at <http://actrav.itcilo.org/actrav-english/telearn/global/ilo/guide/icftuart.htm> accessed 17 May 2014.
181. IMF, 'Background to International Framework Agreements in the IMF' (Background paper prepared for the IFA World Conference Frankfurt am Main, Germany, 26-27 September 2006) 2-4, <http://library.fes.de/pdf-files/gurn/00251.pdf> accessed 23 May 2014.

the history and the status of management-labour relations existing in the company, the type of company and the sector in which it operates.[182]

However, despite some differences in terms of content, studies on IFAs (and the differences with the European counterpart, EFAs) have identified a common pattern in the working and labour standards addressed in these agreements.[183] IFAs focus chiefly on the concept of corporate social responsibility and fundamental labour rights.[184] The text of these agreements frequently refers to the ILO Declaration 1998 and adheres to the four core labour rights set out by the International Labour Organization in the eight ILO fundamental Conventions. Likewise, some IFAs contain a commitment of the signatories to uphold and foster human and labour rights encompassed in UN instruments.

An example is the recent 'Global Framework Agreement on Social Dialogue Guidelines', which was concluded in 2013 by the Italian MNE ENEL, IndustriALL, PSI and two national trade union federations (Flaei CISL and Uiltec UIL). In this agreement, the signatory parties reaffirm the importance and their commitment to further the fundamental rights and principles contained in the eight ILO fundamental Conventions and in different UN instrument.[185]

In addition to that, the text of some IFAs contains a commitment of the signatories beyond ILO core labour standards. Some IFAs then include issues such as working conditions, health and safety at the workplace and the establishment of a committee in charge of occupational health and safety, decent work, temporary agency workers, sustainable development (e.g., environmental sustainability). The 2011 'Danone/IUF Agreement on health, safety, working conditions and stress' is an example of an IFA addressing issues other than the ILO core labour rights. This agreement intends to decrease the number of occupational accidents and illnesses in Danone's operations by tackling the underlying causes that give rise to them and involving workers' representatives in safeguarding the respect and compliance of health and safety standards at work. At the same time, the signatory parties draw their attention to the notion of stress as developed by the European Agency for Health and Safety at Work and the occupational risks it may cause.[186]

Unlike IFAs, the chief attention of EFAs' signatories is on issues such as restructuring, anticipation of changes, social dialogue, vocational training, data protection, human resource policies, working conditions and financial participation.[187] An

182. Bronstein (n. 4) 115. See also Telljohann et al., 'European and International Framework Agreements: Practical Experiences and Strategic Approaches' (n. 29) 6.
183. Telljohann et al., 'European and International Framework Agreements: Practical Experiences and Strategic Approaches' (n. 29) 1.
184. Schömann, 'Transnational Company Agreements: Towards an Internationalisation of Industrial Relations' (n. 3) 203.
185. Text available at <http://ec.europa.eu/employment_social/empl_portal/transnational_agreements/enel_gfa_en.pdf> accessed 23 May 2014.
186. Text available at <http://ec.europa.eu/employment_social/empl_portal/transnational_agreements/Danone_H&S%20Stress_EN.pdf> accessed 30 May 2014.
187. Telljohann et al., 'European and International Framework Agreements: New Tools of Transnational Industrial Relations' (n. 119) 512; Telljohann et al., 'European and International Framework Agreements: Practical Experiences and Strategic Approaches' (n. 29) 1.

example is the ‘Agreement on social guarantees for Suez Group employees’ concluded in 2008 by the French MNE Suez, the European Trade Union Confederation (hereinafter: ETUC), the European Confederation of Executives and Managerial Staff (hereinafter: CEC), the European Consultative Committee, and the representative national union organizations. The signatory parties of this agreement have tackled a series of social risks that may follow from the merger plan between SUEZ and GDF.[188]

Besides recognizing the MNEs’ commitment to respect working and labour standards, the text of most IFAs include also a procedural part. This encompasses provisions on three main aspects: a) what actor(s) is/are in charge of the implementation process and how the agreement is implemented; b) what actor(s) is/are in charge of how the implementation of the agreement is monitored; c) how disputes that arise on the implementation and interpretation of the agreement are settled.[189]

As to the first aspect, IFAs usually specify what actor(s) is/are responsible for the implementation process. This differs from text to text depending on the needs and interests of the parties. In some IFAs, the company itself is amongst the actors involved.[190] In others, both parties to the agreement are responsible[191] or the social partners of each country in which the MNE operates.[192] As to how the agreement will be implemented, some IFAs specify that it will be implemented in each business unit.[193]

Regarding the second aspect, the actors in charge of monitoring the implementation of the agreement differ significantly from text to text. Moreover, some texts do not provide any specific information about the monitoring procedures.[194] The following paragraphs will illustrate three examples of IFAs that include a provision on the actor in charge of monitoring the implementation of the agreement and on the monitoring procedure to follow.

First, the ENEL ‘Global Framework Agreement on Social Dialogue Guidelines’ sets up a Global Works Council consisting of employees’ representatives of the

188. Text available at <http://ec.europa.eu/employment_social/empl_portal/transnational_agreements/Suez_Social_guantees_EN.pdf> accessed 30 May 2014.

189. Christian Welz, A Qualitative Analysis of International Framework Agreements: Implementation and Impact’ in Konstantinos Papadakis (ed.), *Shaping Global Industrial Relations – The Impact of International Framework Agreements* (Palgrave Macmillan 2012) 39-42.

190. See, for instance, the ‘Agreement between Fellesforbundet/IndustriAll Global Union and Norske Skogindustrier ASA on the development of good working relations in Norske Skogindustrier’s worldwide operations’, concluded on 11 December 2013. Text available at <http://ec.europa.eu/social/main.jsp?catId=978&langId=en&agreementId=237> accessed 1 June 2014.

191. See, for instance, the agreement ‘UNI-TEL Telecomunicacoes LTDA Code of Conduct’, concluded in March 2009. Text available at <http://ec.europa.eu/social/main.jsp?catId=978&langId=en&agreementId=172> accessed 1 June 2014.

192. See, for instance, ‘A Transparent annual Activity Discussion for mutual Listening (TALK)’, concluded in 2010 by Thales and EMF. Text available at <http://ec.europa.eu/social/main.jsp?catId=978&langId=en&agreementId=174> accessed 1 June 2014.

193. See, for instance, the ‘International Framework Agreement’ concluded in 2005 by EADS, EMF, EWC and IMF. Text available at <http://ec.europa.eu/employment_social/empl_portal/transnational_agreements/EADS_IFA_EN.pdf> accessed on 23 June 2014.

194. See, for instance, the ‘Global Framework Agreement for the Americas Union Network International (UNI) and Banco do Brasil’, concluded in 2011 and renewed in 2013 between Banco do Brasil and Uni Americas. See footnote n. 117.

countries in which the company operates. This body is responsible to oversee the implementation of the agreement and, to that end, it holds an annual meeting with the Coordination Management Committee.[195]

Second, the monitoring procedure of the 'Global framework agreement on social, societal and environmental responsibility between the Renault Group, the Renault Group Works' Council and IndustriALL Global Union' is carried out during the annual meeting of the company's works council. The actors in charge of monitoring the implementation of the agreements are the MNE's management, the members of the company's works council and the representatives of the global union federation (IndustriALL in the case at issue).[196]

Third, the 'Global framework agreement on Human Rights and Working Conditions' concluded in 2012 by Man SE, IMF and the company's works council sets up a system of periodic reporting (in the first quarter of every year) on the status of the IFA's implementation by the group's management.[197]

Concerning the third procedural aspect, a number of IFAs include rules on how conflicts that might arise from the lack or incorrect implementation and/or interpretation of the agreement will be solved. In the same way as for the implementation and monitoring of the agreement, the actor(s) responsible for, and procedure to follow in order to resolve potential conflicts, depend on the texts.

For instance, the 'International Framework Agreement on Social Responsibility and promotion of Employees' Rights' concluded in 2009 by Wilkhan, the company's works council, BWI and a German trade union, establishes that the body responsible for the monitoring of the implementation of the IFA is also responsible for the settlement of disputes that cannot be resolved at local level.[198]

Furthermore, in the 'Global agreement on fundamental social rights' concluded in 2012 between Eurosport, UNI and French trade unions, the signatory GUF will consult as a first step the company's management in order to search for a solution once a dispute has arisen.[199]

[D] Current Practice

The terminology used by the signatories of IFAs varies significantly. There are agreements called 'international framework agreements', but also 'global framework agreement', 'charter', 'agreement', 'global framework protocol', to mention some.

195. See footnote n. 185.
196. Text available at <http://ec.europa.eu/employment_social/empl_portal/transnational_agreements/Renault_ACI_EN.pdf> accessed 21 June 2014.
197. Text available at <http://ec.europa.eu/employment_social/empl_portal/transnational_agreements/MAN_GFA_EN.pdf> accessed 24 May 2014.
198. Text available at <http://ec.europa.eu/employment_social/empl_portal/transnational_agreements/Wilkhahn_FrameworkAgreement_%202008_EN.pdf> accessed 24 May 2014.
199. Text available at <http://ec.europa.eu/employment_social/empl_portal/transnational_agreements/Eurosport_FR.pdf> accessed 24 May 2014.

There is no consistency in the titles used for these agreements. This feature makes it difficult to estimate correctly how many IFAs have been concluded up until now.

Next to that, there is no clear stance as to what agreements fall within the category 'International framework agreements'. In fact, sometimes the category of IFAs has been limited to those 'negotiated instruments between MNEs and global union federations (GUFs), namely international federations of national unions by sector of activity'.[200] In addition to that, IFAs have been regarded as negotiated agreements signed by a GUF and with global scope of application.[201] Moreover, the European Commission has classified TCAs in three categories: 'global' (agreements addressing primarily fundamental rights and applicable throughout all MNE's operations globally), 'mixed' (global text addressing European issues) and 'European' (scope of application limited to the European area).[202] More specifically, according to the European Commission, IFAs are 'a particular type of global text' concluded by global union federations on the employees' side.[203] Finally, the category of IFAs has been widened to include also agreements concluded by "global structures, World Works Councils or employee committees, together with regional structures, such as European Works Councils and European Industry Federations".[204]

For the purpose of this book, IFAs are agreements concluded between *mostly* GUFs and the management of MNEs with *primarily* a global scope of application. The term 'mostly' is used because some agreements have global scope of application but they have been concluded by World Works Council (WWCs), European Works Council (EWCs), European Industry Federations (EIFs) and also other bodies representing employees at company level. In other words, this book embraces a broader definition of IFAs, no longer restricted at agreements concluded by only GUFs.[205]

In addition to that, the term 'primarily' is used because some agreements have been concluded by GUFs but have a regional scope of application.[206] Furthermore, agreements that in the classification of the European Commission are considered as 'mixed agreement' will be included in the category of IFAs because of their global scope of application.[207]

By using this definition, the author has conducted a research in the database of the European Commission on TCAs and in the websites of GUFs in order to determine how many IFAs have been concluded between 1988 and May 2014 (see Table 1 in Annex).

200. Gallin, 'International Framework Agreements: A Reassessment' (n. 83) 20.
201. Telljohann et al., 'European and International Framework Agreements: New Tools of Transnational Industrial Relations' (n. 119) 508.
202. Commission, 'Mapping of transnational texts negotiated at corporate level' (n. 114) 4-5.
203. *Ibid.*, 5.
204. Nikolaus Hammer, 'International Framework Agreements: global industrial relations between rights and bargaining' (Winter 2005) 4(05) Transfer 511, 523.
205. *Ibid.*, 523.
206. For instance the Chiquita agreement, the agreement concluded by Tel Telecomunicacoes LTDA and Ability Tecnologias e Servicos S/A, which are applicable only in Latin America.
207. European Commission, 'Mapping of transnational texts negotiated at corporate level' (n. 114) 4.

Since the conclusion of the first IFA in 1988, the number of IFAs has swiftly expanded, with 145 IFAs concluded until May 2014. As to the pace at which IFAs have been concluded from 1988 to 2014, parties signed only 13 IFAs until the end of 2000. Danone concluded five of these agreements in 1989. When these agreements were signed, their scope of application was limited to Europe; only in 2005, they became applicable in all Danone's operations worldwide.[208]

A considerable number of agreements has been concluded between 2000 and 2007 (68 IFAs), reaching a total number of 81 IFAs at the end of 2007. Afterwards, one has assisted to a slightly slow-down, with 62 agreements concluded until the end of 2013. Only 2 agreements have been concluded in the first 5 months of 2014.

Even though the number of IFAs is still limited considering the number of MNEs currently operating on the labour market, the pace at which parties have concluded these agreements in the last fifteen years shows the growing interest of MNEs and workers' representatives in engaging in such negotiations. Similarly, it displays the willingness of the signatory parties to foster a culture of social dialogue within the enterprise and beyond, which arguably is necessary in times of industrial changes. As the Secretary-General of BWI, Ambet Yuson, notes: "IFAs help affiliates gain access to work sites, and initiate dialogue between management and the subsidiaries, suppliers and subcontractors. IFAs do not replace national legislation or existing collective bargaining but are designed to create a framework within which all workers are guaranteed a minimum level of international labour standards."[209]

The graphs in the next page show the number of IFA concluded per year from 1988 and May 2014 (Figure 1.2) and the pace in the conclusion of IFAs in the same period (Figure 1.3).

208. Telljohann et al., 'European and International Framework Agreements: New Tools of Transnational Industrial Relations' (n. 119) 511.

209. BWI, 'BWI targets Multinational Companies' (2013) 3 <www.bwint.org/pdfs/EN_MNCbooklet.pdf accessed> 14 June 2014.

Figure 1.2 Number of IFAs per year, 1988–May 2014

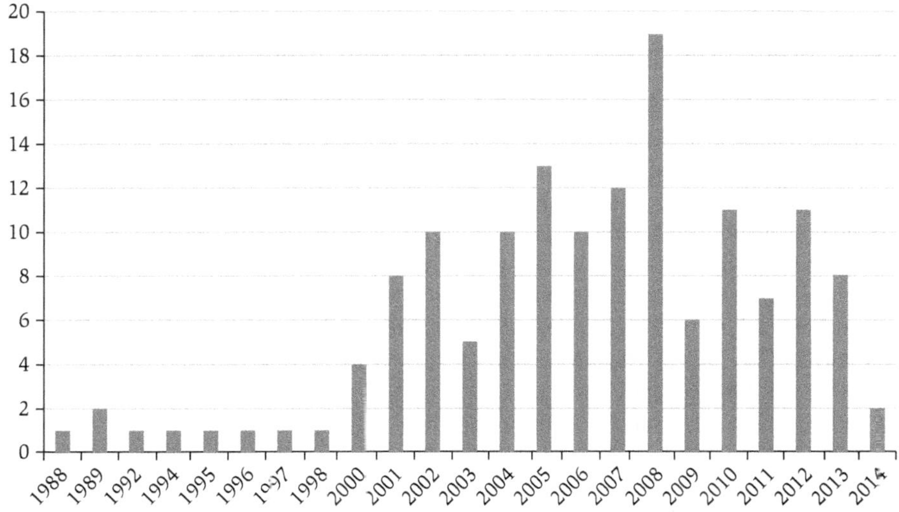

Source: The author.

Figure 1.3 Pace of IFAs, 1988–May 2014

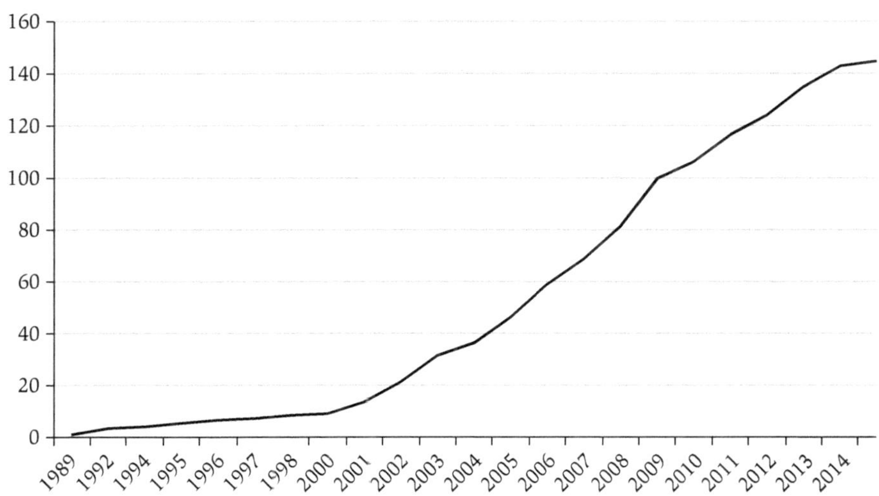

Source: The author.

[E] International Framework Agreements: From a European to a Global Phenomenon?

Chapter 1, §1.01 [F] [3] of the present book has shown that the conclusions of TCAs, irrespective of their classification as IFAs or EFAs, has been, and largely still is, a European phenomenon. More specifically, for the most part TCAs have been signed by companies headquartered in European countries with a long-lasting and stable history of industrial relations (e.g. France and Germany). This section will analyse whether the use of IFAs can also be considered a European phenomenon and therefore aligning with the conclusion in Chapter 1, §1.01 [F] [3].

By examining the 145 IFAs that have been concluded between 1988 and May 2014, one can note that the conclusions of these agreement is still a European-driven phenomenon, with more 80% (118 out of the 145) of the texts signed by enterprises headquartered in the European Union or in the European Economic Area.[210] In particular, companies from France and Germany have been the most active in negotiating and concluding IFAs. Amongst the companies not headquartered in the European Union or in the European Economic Area, the United States of America[211] and Brazil are the forerunners with 6 IFAs/country concluded to date. Switzerland and South Africa follow, with 3 IFAs each one. Four IFAs have been concluded by companies headquartered in Indonesia and Japan, more specifically, two agreements per company. Finally, five companies headquartered in Canada, Malaysia, Russia and New Zealand, Australia have concluded one agreement each one.

This pattern can be explained by the culture of social dialogue spread in Europe between management and workers' representatives, which usually does not characterize labour relations in liberal market economies, such as in the United States of America.

Figure 1.4 displays the geographical distribution of IFAs between 1988 and May 2014 according to the country of origin of the enterprises signatories.

210. In order to identify the country of origin of the MNEs the date of signature of the agreement has been taken as a reference point.

211. The agreement signed by Chiquita was the first agreement concluded by an American multinational company. This IFA does not have a global scope of application, but it is applicable at a regional level since it only applies to Latin America (not to the USA (where the headquarters of the company are located) and not to other parts of the world).

Figure 1.4 Geographical Distribution of IFAs, 1988–May 2014

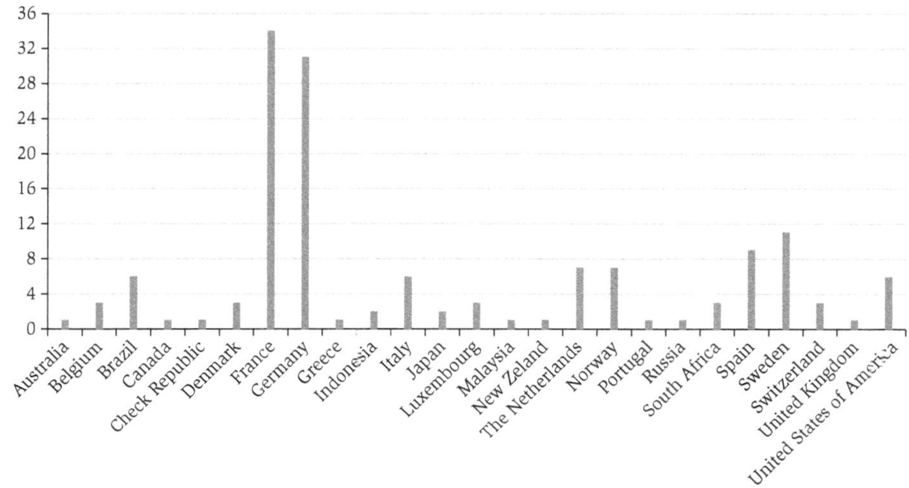

Source: The author.

By examining Figure 1.4, one can observe that IFAs, while global in scope, are still not global in origin. Still few companies headquartered in countries that are not part of the European Union (or the European Economic Area) are willing to engage in transnational negotiations at company level. However, one significant aspect in the conclusion of IFAs by these companies has to be taken into account. If one considers the IFAs concluded before or after 1 January 2007, a specific pattern can be identified. In fact, as from this date, a growing number of MNEs headquartered in countries beyond Europe and the European Economic Area have engaged in negotiations with primarily GUFs to regulate the labour conditions of their workers worldwide (or at regional level in the case of some agreements).

More specifically, MNEs' with headquarters in Brazil, Canada, Indonesia, Japan and Malaysia have concluded their first IFA after 1 January 2007 (1 agreement in the case of Canada and Malaysia, 2 agreements for Japan and Indonesia and 6 agreements in the case of Brazil). For example, Takashimaya is the first Japanese MNE concluding an IFA, followed by Mizuno, a company operating in the textile industry. Both IFAs intend to develop and strengthen the social dialogue between management and workers' representatives and they address the core labour rights contained in the eight ILO fundamental Conventions. In addition to that, 6 Brazilian companies signed respectively 1 IFA each one between 2008 and 2014: Itaú-Unibanco S.A (2014), Banco de Brasil (2011, renewed in 2013). Petrobas (2011) Tecnologia and Tel Telecomunicacoes LTDA (2009). Ability Tecnologias e serviços (2008), Iconom (2008).

Moreover, American, South African and Swiss companies have continued to concluded IFAs but at a different pace. While the number of agreements concluded by MNEs headquartered in the United States of America tripled after 1 January 2007, the pace at which MNEs headquartered in South Africa and Switzerland have concluded agreements has slowed down (only 1 IFA as from 2007).

Finally, companies with headquarters in Australia, New Zealand and Russia did not sign any IFAs after 1 January 2007.

The graph below shows the evolution in the number of IFAs concluded by MNEs that are not headquartered in a country in the European Union or in the European Economic Area. The dark part of the bar represents the IFAs that were concluded after 1 January 2007 and the light grey part represents the IFAs concluded before this date.

Figure 1.5 Number of IFAs Concluded by MNEs' Headquartered outside the Europe Union (or the European Economic Area) before and after 1 January 2007

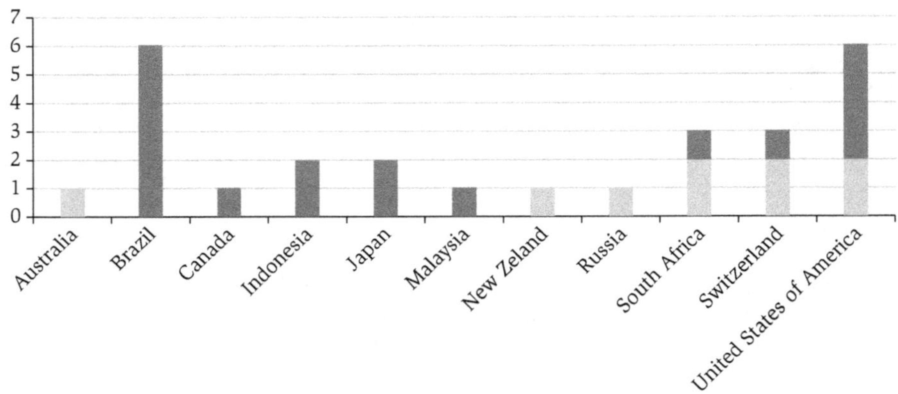

Source: The author.

Although IFAs are for the most part still limited to the European area in terms of the country of origin of the MNEs signatories, the increasing number of IFAs concluded by companies headquartered outside Europe represents a significant development. In fact, the growing involvement of these MNEs illustrates that these agreements have the potential of becoming a global phenomenon and, in the long term, they may represent a form of social dialogue no longer restricted at European level, but on a global level.[212]

§1.03 EUROPEAN FRAMEWORK AGREEMENTS AT COMPANY LEVEL AND TRANSNATIONAL COLLECTIVE BARGAINING AT EUROPEAN LEVEL

[A] Introduction

The present section intends to examine the development of EFAs and the main questions that arise from the conclusion of these agreements. Moreover, the analysis

212. Stevis, 'International framework agreements and global social dialogue: Parameters and prospects' (n. 108) 14. See also Papadakis, 'Introduction' (n. 2) v.

will be conducted by outlining the concept and the outcome of European social dialogue. As Chapter 1, §1.01 has shown, it is argued that transnational collective bargaining takes place not only at European company level but also at European cross-industry and sectoral level. By way of example, Boni uses a broader definition of transnational collective bargaining as 'encompassing all developments in this area, i.e. social dialogue, the coordination of national collective bargaining, European Works Councils'.[213]

[B] European Social Dialogue

The International Labour Organization (hereinafter: ILO) has defined social dialogue as "all types of negotiation, consultation or simply exchange of information between, or among, representatives of governments, employers and workers on issues of common interest relating to economic and social policy".[214] According to the notion elaborated by the ILO, social dialogue has a tripartite dimension, involving not only the social partners in the two different sides of industry but also public authorities.

Differently, according to the European Commission social dialogue encompasses "discussions, consultations, negotiations and joint actions involving organisations representing the two sides of industry (employers and workers)".[215] More specifically, social dialogue at European level do not only takes a tripartite dimension (also known as tripartite concertation according to the social partners)[216] but also a bipartite one. Only as of mid-1980s the importance of social dialogue at European level gained momentum. This was the result of, *inter alia*, the arrival of Jacques Delors as President of the European Commission and, more specifically, of the Val Duchesse talks started in 1985 between three cross-industry European social partners: on the employers' side, the Union of Industrial and Employers' Confederation of Europe (UNICE – currently known as BusinessEurope) and the European Centre of Enterprises with Public Participation and of Enterprises of General Economic Interest (hereinafter: CEEP); on the workers' side, the European Trade Union Confederation (hereinafter: ETUC).[217]

The significant role acquired by European social partners through the *Val Duchesse* talks has been later on formalized in the Social Policy Agreement, which, together with the Social Policy Protocol, constituted the Social Chapter introduced by the Maastricht Treaty in 1992. More specifically, the Social Policy Agreement introduced two provisions, Articles 3 and 4 (now Articles 154 and 155 TFEU), which granted European social partners a role in the EU law-making process and entitled them to

213. Guido Boni, 'Introduction' in Isabelle Schömann et al., *Transnational Collective Bargaining at Company Level – A New Component of European Industrial Relations?* (ETUI aisbl 2012) 8.
214. ILO, 'Social Dialogue Sector' < www.ilo.org/public/english/dialogue/index.htm > accessed 14 July 2014.
215. European Commission, 'Social Dialogue' < http://ec.europa.eu/social/main.jsp?catId = 329&langId = en > accessed 14 July 2014.
216. Eurofound, 'European industrial relations dictionary' < www.eurofound.europa.eu/areas/industrialrelations/dictionary/index.htm > accessed 14 July 2014.
217. Catherine Barnard, *EU Employment Law* (Oxford University Press 2012) 17.

conclude European-wide collective agreements. According to Article 154 TFEU, the representative European social partners[218] are to be consulted by the European Commission in the first stage of the legislative process, more specifically before submitting a proposal, on the possible direction of the European action. After that, if the Commission considers European action advisable, then it initiates a second consultation on the content of the proposal.[219] This can lead to two different results: first, the social partners can give their opinions about the proposal and the Commission continues the legislative process; second, the social partners can decide to start collective negotiations that can lead to a Community-wide collective agreement. This collective agreement can be implemented in two ways: via a national or subnational collective agreement 'in accordance with the procedures and practices specific to management and labour and the Member States' (autonomous agreements); via a Council Decision[220] following the procedures set up in Article 155 TFEU.

In addition to Articles 154 TFEU and 155 TFEU, the entry into force of the Treaty of Lisbon has formally recognized the role of social partners in Article 152 TFEU, according to which "[t]he Union recognises and promotes the role of the social partners at its level, taking into account the diversity of national systems. It shall facilitate dialogue between the social partners, respecting their autonomy".[221]

European social dialogue takes place at three levels: cross-industry, sectoral and company.[222] As to the latter level, social dialogue can take place throughout EWCs[223] and the participation of employees in the Societas Europeae. At the same time, Welz considers IFAs and EFAs as a form of European social dialogue (see Figure 1.6).[224]

218. For the criteria set up by the Commission for identifying the representatives organizations see Commission, 'Communication concerning the application of the agreement on social policy presented by the Commission to the Council and the European Parliament' (Communication) COM(93) 600 final, para. 24. See also Commission, 'Communication from the Commission of 20 May 1998 adapting and promoting the social dialogue at Community level' (Communication) COM (98) 322 final. The list of representative European social partners (88 as of May 2014) that, according to Article 154 TFEU, the European Commission has to consult in the first stage of consultation is available at European Commission, 'Social Dialogue' <http://ec.europa.eu/social/main.jsp?catId=329&langId=en> accessed 14 July 2014.
219. Articles 154 and 155, Consolidated Version of the Treaty on the Functioning of the European Union [2012] OJ C 326/01. See also Manfred Weiss, 'The European Social Dialogue' (2011) 2(2) ELLJ 155, 156; Barnard (n. 217) 67-87.
220. On the concept of 'Decision', see Barnard (n. 217) 75-77.
221. Article 152, Consolidated Version of the Treaty on the Functioning of the European Union [2012] OJ C 326/01.
222. Fernando Rocha and Pere J. Beneyto (n. 102) 130.
223. *Ibid.*, 132.
224. EWCs and the participation of employees in the Societas Europeae are outside the scope of this book.

Figure 1.6 European System of Industrial Relations

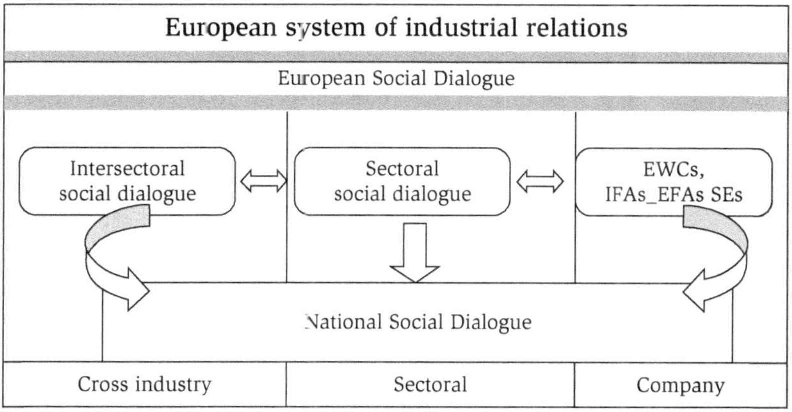

Source: Christian Welz, 'IFAs and EFAs: – 'essai' of a qualitative analysis, Expert Group – transnational company agreements' (Expert Group transnational company agreements, Brussels, 27 November 2009) <http://ec.europa.eu/social/BlobServlet?docId=6369&langId=en> accessed 14 July 2014.[225]

[1] Cross-Industry Social Dialogue

Different social partners are involved in cross-industry social dialogue, which may lead not only to an exchange of views, opinions, and communications but also to European framework agreements. According to Eurofound, "[a] framework agreement is the term used to describe the successful outcome of the European social dialogue. The term 'framework' is intended to highlight the particular nature of the agreement as providing an outline of general principles to be implemented in the Member States 'either in accordance with the procedures and practices specific to management and labour and the Member States or at the joint request of the signatory parties, by a Council decision on a proposal from the Commission'."[226]

More specifically, five cross-industry organizations are involved in this level of social dialogue:[227]

- on the workers' side: ETUC[228] and Eurocadres (the Council of European Professional and Managerial Staff);

225. See also Commission, 'Second Meeting of the Expert Group on TCAs of 27 November 2009' (Minutes) EMPL F2 EP, 9.
226. Eurofound, 'European industrial relations dictionary' <www.eurofound.europa.eu/areas/industrialrelations/dictionary/index.htm> accessed 14 July 2014.
227. European Commission, 'Cross-industry social dialogue' available at <http://ec.europa.eu/social/main.jsp?catId=479&langId=en> accessed 14 July 2014.
228. The European Confederation of Executives and Managerial Staff (CEC) takes part in the European social dialogue as a delegation in ETUC.

- on the employers' side, the Confederation of European Business (BUSINESSEUROPE), CEEP and the European Association of Craft, Small and Medium Sized Enterprises (hereinafter: UEAPME).

Only three Community-wide collective agreements concluded by social partners at cross-industry level have resulted in the adoption of a Council Decision: Council Directive 96/34/EC on parental leave, Council Directive 97/81/EC on part-time work and Council Directive 1999/70/EC on fixed-term work. These Directives can be included in the supranational system of industrial relations outlined in Chapter 1, §1.01 of this book. Four Community-wide agreements have not followed the EU decision-making process leading to a Council Decision and their implementation has been left to "procedures and practices specific to management and labour and the Member States" (Article 155(2) TFEU).[229] These agreements (also called autonomous agreements) cover a broad range of EU social policy fields: telework (2000), work-related stress (2004), harassment and violence at work (2007) and inclusive labour market (2010).[230]

[2] Sectoral Social Dialogue

In addition to the cross-industry level, European social dialogue takes place also at sectoral level through numerous European Sectoral Social Dialogue Committees (hereinafter: ESSDCs), which aim at "improving and harmonizing working conditions and also, in some cases, improving the economic competitive position of the sector concerned".[231] EESDCs were set up by Commission Decision 98/500/EC[232] as a replacement of the six *comités paritaires* established by the same European institution in the period from 1952 to 1974 in the following sectors: mines, agriculture, road transport, navigation, fishery and railways.[233]

ESSDCs are consultative bodies to the European Commission, whose functions, according to Ales, is no longer limited at the consultative level but it has moved towards the negotiation level.[234] The number of ESSDCs has sharply grown over the years insomuch as this bipartite form of European social dialogue covers almost all sectors of industry.[235] As to their composition, representatives of social partners,

229. Bronstein (n. 4) 203. ("These agreements are to be implemented in each EU Member State through national collective bargaining or by other means that rely on social dialogue").
230. These agreements are available at: European Commission, 'Social dialogue texts database' available at http://ec.europa.eu/social/main.jsp?catId=521&langId=en accessed 14 July 2014.
231. Commission, 'Communication from the Commission of 20 May 1998 adapting and promoting the social dialogue at Community level' (n. 218) 9.
232. Commission Decision 98/500/EC on the establishment of Sectoral Dialogue Committees promoting the Dialogue between the Social Partners at European level [1998] OJ l225/27.
233. Edoardo Ales et al., 'Transnational Collective Bargaining: Past, Present and Future' (Final Report – European Commission 2006) 9-10 <http://ec.europa.eu/social/BlobServlet?docId=4641&langId=en> accessed 14 March 2014.
234. *Ibid.*, 12.
235. Currently there are 43 ESSDCs (May 2014). Information available at: Eurofound, 'European industrial relations dictionary' <www.eurofound.europa.eu/areas/industrialrelations/dictionary/index.htm> accessed 14 July 2014.

employers and workers (a maximum of 64 representatives for each category) are part of these consultative bodies.[236]

Moreover, as of May 2014, 15 European sectoral trade union organizations (or European Industry Federations) and 65 European sectoral organizations representing employers meet the criteria to be included in the list of representative social partners that need to be consulted according to Article 154 TEFU.[237]

Table 1.2 List of Representatives of European Sectoral Trade Union Organizations

European Industry Federations Affiliated with ETUC	*European Industry Federations Not Affiliated with ETUC*
European Arts and Entertainment Alliance (EAEA)	European Cockpit Association (ECA)
European Federation of Building and Woodworkers (EFBWW)	European Confederation of Independent Trade Unions (CESI)
European Federation of Journalists (EFJ)	International Federation of Actors (FIA)
European Federation of Public Service Unions (EPSU)	International Federation of Musicians (FIM)
European Federation of Trade Unions in the Food, Agriculture and Tourism Sectors and Allied Branches (EFFAT)	International Federation of Professional Footballers' Associations– Division Europe (FIFPro)
European Trade Union Committee for Education (ETUCE)	International Dockworkers Council (IDC)
Union Network International (UNI) Europa	
European Transport Workers' Federation (ETF)	
IndustriAll European Trade Union[238]	

Source: The author on the basis of European Commission, 'List of European social partners' organisations consulted under Article 154 TFEU' <http://ec.europa.eu/social/BlobServlet?docId=2154&langId=en> accessed 14 July 2014.

As to the outcome of the European sectoral social dialogue, social partners have not only adopted opinions, guidelines, recommendations, but they have also concluded several autonomous agreements and Community-wide agreements that have been transposed into European Directives.[239]

236. European Commission, 'Sectoral Social Dialogue' <http://ec.europa.eu/social/main.jsp?catId=480&langId=en> accessed 14 March 2014.
237. European Commission, 'List of European social partners' organisations consulted under Article 154 TFEU' <http://ec.europa.eu/social/BlobServlet?docId=2154&langId=en> accessed 14 July 2014.
238. This EIF was founded in 2012 following the dissolution of EMCEF, EMF and ETUF-TCL.
239. For example, the Council Directive 2005/47 on the Agreement of 27 January 2004 between the Community of European Railways and the European Transport Workers' Federation on certain aspects of the working conditions of mobile workers engaged in interoperable cross-border

The following sections will provide an in-depth analysis of the development of EFAs as well as the main features of these texts and the main challenges linked to the conclusion of this new form of social dialogue.

[C] European Framework Agreements at Company Level

The conclusion of EFAs, and more in general of TCAs, has represented a significant and promising response to the challenges that result from the process of globalization and the consequent internationalization of economic activities.[240] Together with the autonomous agreements, EFAs seem to show that voluntary initiatives gain more and more importance in the European industrial relations scenario.[241] Moreover, Pulignano, da Costa, Rehfeldt and Telljohann argue that these agreements "are considered crucial for the management of employment relations within multinationals in Europe".[242]

The following sub-section will provide an overview of the development and current status in the conclusion of EFAs.

[1] Overview of the Current Practice

The analysis conducted in Chapter 1, §1.02 on IFAs has shown that it is very difficult to accurately assess how many IFAs have been concluded to date. This applies equally to EFAs because there are also agreements concluded by EIFs and/or EWCs that have a global scope of application.[243] For the purpose of this book, EFAs are those agreements concluded between EIFs and/or EWCs (or other forms of workers'

services in the railway sector; Council Directive 2010/32/EU on preventing injuries and infections to healthcare workers from sharp objects such as needles; Council Directive 2009/13/EC implementing the agreement concluded by the European Community Ship-owners Associations (ECSA) and the European Transport Workers' Federation (ETF) on the Maritime Labour Convention, 2006.

240. Valeria Pulignano et al., 'Local Actors and Transnational Structures – Explaining Trends in Multinational Company-Level Negotiations in Europe' in Peter Fairbrother, Marc-Antonin Hennebert and Christian Lévesque (eds), *Transnational Trade Unionism: Building Union Power* (Routledge 2013) 143. See also Salvo Leonardi, 'Transnational Company Agreements: A Stepping Stone towards a Real Internationalization of Industrial Relations?' in Salvo Leonardi et al., *European Action on Transnational Company Agreements: A Stepping Stone towards a Real Internationalisation of Industrial Relations?* (IRES 2012) 5 ff.
241. Antonio Lo Faro, 'Bargaining in the shadow of 'optional frameworks'? The rise of transnational collective agreements and EU law' (2012) 18(2) European Journal of Industrial Relations 153, 154.
242. Valeria Pulignano et al. (n. 240) 183-202.
243. Two examples are: (1) the Triumph's International's Code of Conduct, which was signed in 2001 by the European Regional Organization of ITGLWF; (2) the CSR Protocol (2009) concluded between ENEL on the company's side and Italian national trade unions, EPSU and EMCEF on the employees' side. Both agreements have been included in the list of IFAs due to their global scope of application.

participation) and/or national trade unions, on the employees' side, and the management of MNEs, on the employer's side. Additionally, these agreements have European scope of application. However, agreements that are applicable to wider-Europe-EMEA have been included in the category of EFAs.

In order to estimate how many EFAs have been signed until May 2014, the author has conducted a research on the database of the European Commission on TCAs. The result of the research conducted has shown that 112 EFAs were concluded between 1996 and May 2014. Table 2 in Annex contains a list of EFAs concluded between 1996 and May 2014.

Whereas the very first EFA was signed in 1996, the years from 1996 to 2000 have witnessed the negotiation and conclusion of only a few EFAs, more specifically between 0 and 4 agreements per year. This pattern has changed as from 2001, when the number of EFAs has rapidly increased, reaching a first peak in 2001, with 10 agreements concluded just in that year. In 2002, MNEs and trade unions and/or workers' representatives signed an equivalent amount of agreements as the previous year. Subsequently, the average number of EFAs negotiated between 2002 and 2006 has decreased to 5/6 agreements per year (in 2005 only 3). After this period, the pace at which EFAs have been concluded has increased, reaching a second peak in 2008 with 9 agreements signed. However, 2010 is the year in which most agreements have been concluded (14). After that, one has assisted to a minor decrease between 2011 and 2013, with only two EFAs concluded in the first 5 months of 2014.

Amongst the texts concluded so far, one should mention that in 2010 an EFA involved, for the first time ever, two companies: Alstom and Schneider Electric. This EFA deals with the acquisition of Areva T&D by the two French companies at issue and, specifically, it sets out certain employment commitments as to how to integrate Areva T&D's employees.[244]

The graphs in the next page display the number of EFA concluded per year from 1996 and May 2014 (Figure 1.7) and the pace that has characterized the signature of EFAs in the same period (Figure 1.8).

244. Linda Rackham, 'An innovative social agreement' (Press Release 2010) <www.emf-fem.org/Press/Press-releases/An-innovative-social-agreement> accessed 14 April 2014.

Figure 1.7 Number of EFAs per year, 1996–May 2014

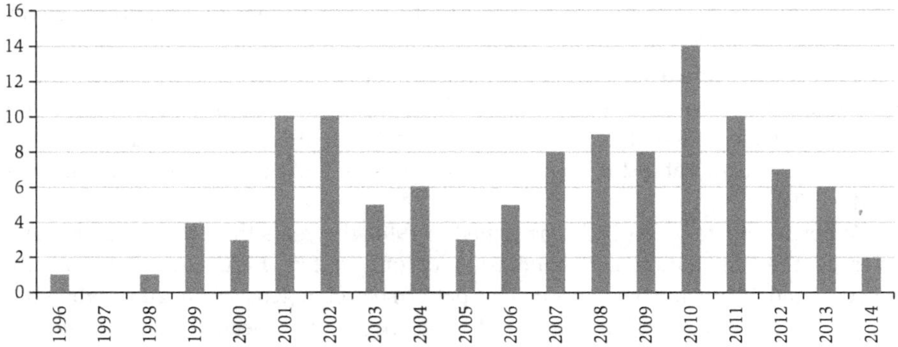

Source: The author.

Figure 1.8 Pace of EFAs, 1988–May 2014

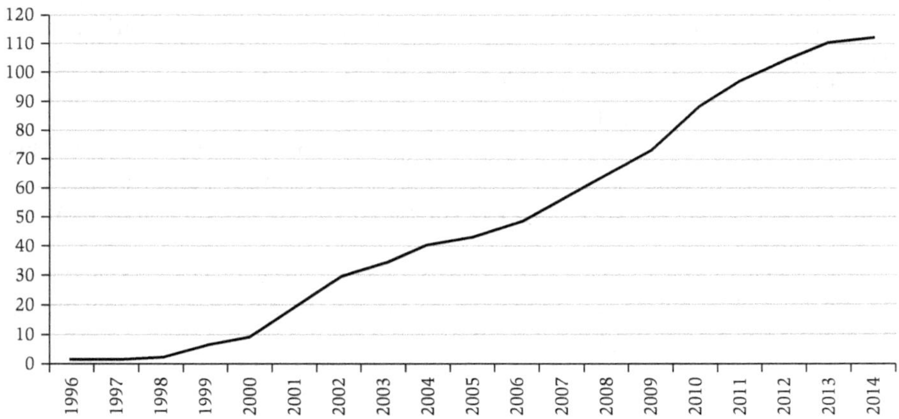

Source: The author.

In addition, in order to identify the country of origin of the MNEs the date of signature of the agreement has been taken as a reference point. In fact, the headquarter of some MNEs has changed over the years (e.g., General Motors Europe) and/or some companies do no longer exist as separate entities because they have been acquired by other companies (e.g., General Electric Plastics).

The vast majority of MNEs are headquartered in the European Union. More specifically, just as for the IFAs, French MNEs are the forerunner in the conclusion of EFAs, followed by German and Belgium MNEs. Furthermore, MNEs headquartered outside the European Union or the European Economic Area (Switzerland and United States of America) concluded only a few EFAs (21 out of 112).

Figure 1.9 shows the results obtained from the analysis of the headquarters of the MNEs signatories of EFAs from 1996 to May 2014.

Figure 1.9 Number of EFAs per Country of Origin of MNEs, 1996–May 2014

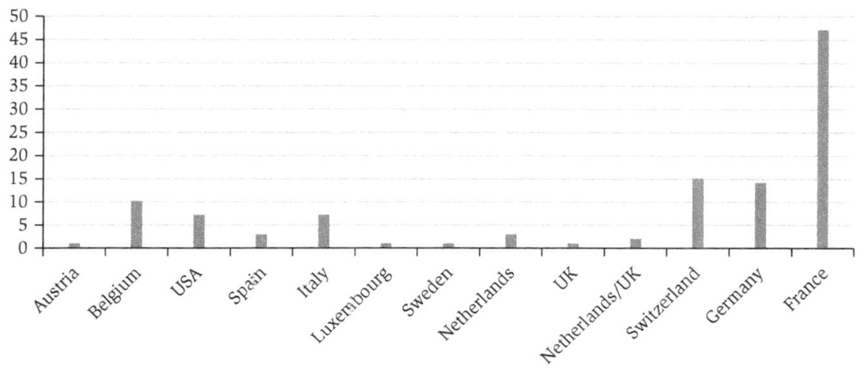

Source: The author.

The following sections will analyse the relation between EWCs and EFAs. More specifically, attention will be paid to whether these transnational bodies are legally entitled to conclude these transnational agreements.

[D] European Works Councils and European Framework Agreements at Company Level[245]

As far as the employee-side signatories of EFAs is concerned, EWCs[246] have had so far the leading role in initiating, negotiating and concluding EFAs.[247] In particular, as of May 2014, these transnational bodies have signed or co-signed more than 70% of the EFAs (81 texts out of 110 as 2 texts were not available and the information could not be retrieved from other sources). Moreover, even when EWCs have not been among the

245. This Chapter examines only the relationship between EWCs and EFAs. However, it must be stressed that a significant number of IFAs have been concluded by EWCs. The involvement of EWCs in the conclusion of these transnational agreements is questionable not only for the reasons that will be explained in the text in relation to EFAs but also because the "EWC is a European body and as such does not have any mandate to negotiate a global agreement that affect workers outside the EU" (see Schömann, 'Transnational Company Agreements: Towards an Internationalisation of Industrial Relations' (n. 3) 200).
246. Telljohann et al., 'European and International Framework Agreements: Practical Experiences and Strategic Approaches' (n. 29) 56.
247. For an analysis of the driving forces behind the conclusion of EFAs by EWCs see Zimmer, 'European Works Councils as Participants in Euro-Wide Collective Agreements: Analysis from a German Perspective' (n. 128) 319-320.

signatories of EFAs, in many cases they still participated in the initiation and negotiation of these agreements as bodies of information and consultation within MNEs.[248] Their role cannot be disregarded.[249] In addition to that, it is worth mentioning that the works councils of SE Allianz have signed two EFAs.[250]

The pie chart (Figure 1.10) shows the relationship between the number of EFAs (co-) signed by EWCs and the amount of EFAs concluded only by other actors on the employees' side (e.g., EIFs, national trade unions, company's representatives).

Figure 1.10 Signatories of EFAs: EWCs and Other Actors, 1996–May 2014

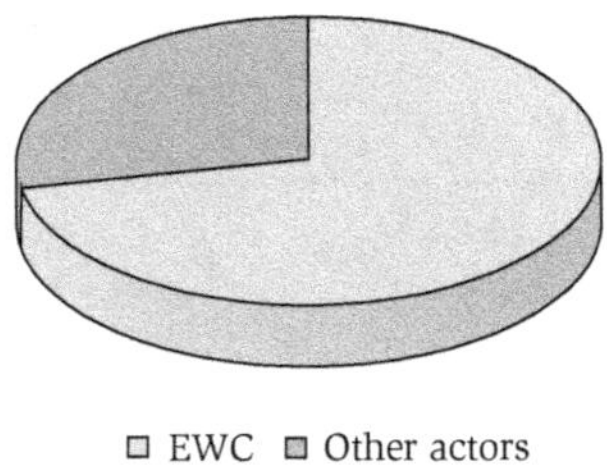

Source: The author.

The graph above displays that EWCs play a significant role in the process of conclusions of EFAs compared to other actors. However, given the composition of EWCs and their mandate, this situation has given rise to many concerns. EWCs are transnational bodies in charge of consultation and information within enterprises meeting specific thresholds.[251] Moreover, EWCs' members are not necessarily linked to trade unions and this aspect brings about problems of representation of workers' interests.[252] For

248. Commission, 'Transnational company agreements: realising the potential of social dialogue' (n. 107) 8.
249. The importance of the involvement of EWCs in the initiation and negotiation of TCAs has been stressed also by the European Parliament. See European Parliament, 'Resolution on cross-border collective bargaining and transnational social dialogue' (2012/2292(INI)) ("7. Considers that European works councils should be fully involved in the negotiations with European trade union federations where applicable, notably since they are able to detect the need/opportunity for a TCA, initiate the process and pave the way for negotiations, and help in ensuring the transparency and dissemination of information concerning the agreements to the workers involved; welcomes the fact that some European trade union federations have designed procedural rules for involving European works councils").
250. Zimmer, 'European Works Councils as Participants in Euro-Wide Collective Agreements: Analysis from a German Perspective' (n. 128) 319 ("Anyway, most of the SE founding agreements for the Works Council do contain the explicit authorisation to negotiate and conclude agreements with management.").
251. For more information, see Council Directive 2009/38/EC of 6 May 2009 on the establishment of a European Works Council or a procedure in Community-scale undertakings and Community-scale groups of undertakings for the purposes of informing and consulting employees [2009] OJ L 122 (European Works Council Recast Directive).
252. Jagodzinski, 'European Works Councils and Transnational Company Agreements – Balancing on the Thin Line between Effective Consultation and Overstepping Competences' (n. 98) 179-180. See also Commission, 'Transnational company agreements: realising the potential of social dialogue' (n. 107) 8.

these reasons, the involvement of EWCs in the conclusion of TCAs is not well perceived by trade unions, which feel deprived of their main competence, namely engaging in collective bargaining in order to represent and defend workers' interests. In particular, trade unions are concerned that the supremacy of EWCs in signing EFAs would consequently impede them to remain involved in company-level negotiations.[253]

The following subsections will consider two issues: first, whether the EWCs are legally entitled to conclude EFAs in the light of Treaty provisions, Directive 94/45/EC and Directive 2009/38/EC (hereinafter: Recast Directive 2009); second, which is the relationship between EWCs and trade unions concerning the involvement in transnational company negotiations.

[1] *Are European Works Councils Entitled to Conclude European Framework Agreements at Company Level?*

The driving question to be examined in this subsection is the following: are EWCs entitled to conclude EFAs? In other words, is the current EU legislation (both treaty law and EU secondary legislation) a sufficient legal basis for allowing EWCs to conclude TCAs? Have these transnational bodies already exceeded the mandate given by the European legislator through the EU Directive 94//45/EC and currently the Recast Directive 2009?[254]

As to the EU Treaty provisions, Jagodzinki has examined in-depth this issue. According to him, Article 28 of the Charter of Fundamental Rights of the European Union does not provide trade unions with the exclusive power to enter and conduct negotiations to trade unions but consider workers' representatives as legitimate transnational bargaining parties.[255]

Moving to EU secondary legislation, it is worth starting analysing the legislation on EWCs, in particular, the EU Directive 94/45/EC and the Recast Directive 2009, which have been paved the way for information and consultation of employees on transnational matters.[256] More specifically, it is important to examine the competences that have been provided to these bodies and how the Recast Directive 2009 has modified the legal framework established by the previous Directive. In fact, although EWCs *de facto* concluded and still conclude the vast majority of EFAs, it is still doubtful whether these bodies are legally entitled to sign these agreements.

Arguably, both Directives have restrained the scope of action of EWCs to information and consultation and the terms used by the two European legislative acts

253. Telljohann et al., 'European and International Framework Agreements: Practical Experiences and Strategic Approaches' (n. 29) 56-58; Lo Faro, 'Bargaining in the shadow of 'optional frameworks'? The rise of transnational collective agreements and EU law' (n. 241) 160-161; Romuald Jagodzinski, 'Involving European Works Councils in Transnational Negotiations – a Positive Functional Advance in their Operation or Trespassing?' (2007) vo. 14(4) Industrielle Beziehungen 316, 329.
254. Jagodzinski, 'Involving European Works Councils in Transnational Negotiations – a Positive Functional Advance in their Operation or Trespassing? (n. 253) 323.
255. Jagodzinski, 'European Works Councils and Transnational Company Agreements – Balancing on the Thin Line between Effective Consultation and Overstepping Competences' (n. 98) 172.
256. For the definition of 'transnational matters' see Article 1(4) Recast Directive 2009.

do not seem to point towards the extension of the competences of these actors. In fact, Directive 94/45/EC stipulates under article 1(a) of the Annex 'Subsidiary requirements' that "[t]he competence of European Works Councils shall be limited to information and consultation (...)".[257] Similarly, according to Article 1 of the same Annex in the Recast Directive 2009, "[t]he competence of the European Works Council shall be determined in accordance with Article 1(3)", according to which "the competence of the European Works Council and the scope of the information and consultation procedure for employees governed by this Directive shall be limited to transnational issues".[258]

Even though it seems that EWCs' mandate is restricted to information and consultation, one could still look at the definition of consultation and consider if it could lay the basis for the involvement of EWCs in concluding EFAs. Compared to Directive 94/45/EC, the Recast Directive 2009 has given a definition of consultation,[259] which is still broad,[260] but more precise than the previous Directive.[261] However, Jagodzinki points out that the definition of consultation enshrined in Article 2(1)(g) of the Recast Directive 2009 "seems not to go beyond an expression of opinion".[262] According to the same scholar, "had the EU legislator considered granting negotiating powers to EWCs, it would have shaped the wording of the new definition of 'consultation' around that used in Directive 2002/14/EC. This sets forth that consultation is done 'with a view to reach an agreement'".[263]

At the same time, Jagodzinski seems to open the possibility to assert that these bodies are entitled to conclude TCAs by claiming that both Directives have not set any limits to the negotiation powers of the EWCs. In other words, they have not explicitly forbidden these bodies to conclude EFAs[264] and therefore it can be asserted that they may be entitled to do so. In other words: 'if it is not forbidden, it is allowed'.

257. Council Directive 94/45/EC of 22 September 1994 on the establishment of a European Works Council or a procedure in Community-scale undertakings and Community-scale groups of undertakings for the purposes of informing and consulting employees [1994] OJ L 254 (European Works Council Directive 94/45/EC).
258. Recast Directive 2009 (n. 251).
259. Article 2(1)(g) Recast Directive 2009 reads that "the establishment of dialogue and exchange of views between employees' representatives and central management or any more appropriate level of management, at such time, in such fashion and with such content as enables employees' representatives to express an opinion on the basis of the information provided about the proposed measures to which the consultation is related, without prejudice to the responsibilities of the management, and within a reasonable time, which may be taken into account within the Community-scale undertaking or Community-scale group of undertakings".
260. Roger Blanpain, 'European Works Councils: The European Directive 2009/38/EC of 6 May 2009' (2010) 1(1) European Labour Law Journal 107, 109.
261. Article 2(1)(f) of European Works Council Directive 94/45/EC defines consultation as "the exchange of views and establishment of dialogue between employees' representatives and central management or any more appropriate level of management".
262. Jagodzinski, 'European Works Councils and Transnational Company Agreements - Balancing on the Thin Line between Effective Consultation and Overstepping Competences' (n. 98) 178.
263. *Ibid.*, 178.
264. *Ibid.*, 178-179.

[2] European Works Councils versus Trade Unions

The issue as to what actors are entitled to conclude TCAs has been and still is much contested in the European context, where EWCs are the leading actors in signing EFAs.[265] EWCs initiate, negotiate and conclude the vast majority of these agreements and this pattern is a matter of concern for trade unions, which reckon that the conclusion of these texts falls within the scope of their competences. This concern is well depicted in a statement of the European Metalworkers' Federation (hereinafter: EMF), according to which:

> [c]ollective bargaining is a core competence of national trade unions and their local representatives, based on national legislation and varying practices in different countries. As mandates rest with the trade unions, the EWCs do not have a mandate for collective bargaining and they should not become counterparts for management in such issues. The area of collective bargaining is, however, not clear-cut. It is in the interest of the EMF and its affiliates to ensure the full involvement of trade unions in any possible bargaining processes also at the European level.[266]

Hence, according to trade unions, the involvement of EWCs in transnational company negotiations may seriously jeopardize their interests. For example, EFAs can address issues that are dealt with by national collective bargaining. However, the vast majority of these transnational agreements is concluded by EWCs, which are bodies not always representative of all the employees of a company.[267]

Pioneered by the EMF in 2006, some EIFs (such as EMCEF and UNI-Europe) have adopted internal procedures for negotiations at multinational company level as a way to solve the lack of an European framework for transnational negotiations and define the status of the relationship between trade unions and EWCs in concluding TCAs.[268]

265. On this topic see Zimmer, 'European Works Councils as Participants in Euro-Wide Collective Agreements: Analysis from a German Perspective' (n. 128) 320 ff.
266. EMF, 'Internal EMF Procedure for negotiations at multinational company level' (2006) 1 <www.emf-fem.org/Areas-of-work/Company-Policy/Adopted-documents-Position-papers-Publications/Position-papers2/Internal-EMF-Procedure-for-negotiations-at-multinational-company-level/2006-12-internal-proc.-nego.-mn.-cny-level-EN> accessed 15 August 2014.
267. Torsten Müller and Hans Wolfgang Platzer and Stefan Rüb, 'European Collective agreements at company level and the relationship between EWCs and trade unions- lessons from the metal sector' (2011) 17(1) Transfer: European Review of Labour and Research 217, 221.
268. ETUC (Executive Committee), 'More and Better European Company Framework Agreements: Enhancing Trade Unions in Transnational Negotiations with Transnational Companies' (Discussion Note 2012) EC198/EN/12. 9-11 <http://collective.etuc.org/sites/default/files/12-EN-More-and-Better-European-Company-Framework-Agreements%20ADOPTED.pdf> accessed 15 August 2014; Anna Alaimo, 'Transnational Company Agreements and Sectoral Social Dialogue: Parallel Lines, No Convergence?' in Salvo Leonardi et al., *European Action on Transnational Company Agreements: A Stepping Stone towards a Real Internationalisation of Industrial Relations?* (IRES 2012) 57-58; Marco Cilento, 'Development of Transnational Negotiations with Multinational Companies in a Trade Union Perspective' in Salvo Leonardi et al., *European Action on Transnational Company Agreements: A Stepping Stone towards a Real Internationalisation of Industrial Relations?* (IRES 2012) 122-123.

In particular, EIFs intend to regain their central role in the conclusion of EFAs and, in addition, to involve EWCs only in the preliminary stage of consultation and information and in the implementation of the signed agreements.[269]

[E] A Legal Framework for Transnational Collective Bargaining at Company Level: Initiatives towards the Introduction of an Optional European Framework for Transnational Negotiations

Over the years EFAs, and more in general TCAs, have emerged without any legal framework neither at international nor at European level.[270] The spread of transnational collective negotiations at company level has gained increased attention at European level and, therefore, the European Commission has taken different steps toward the regulation of this new form of social dialogue. This section intends to outline briefly the main steps undertaken by the Commission and other European actors to define the legal framework for concluding TCAs.[271]

The European Commission undertook the first initiative towards the recognition of the growing importance of transnational collective bargaining in 2004. In the communication 'Partnership for change in an enlarged Europe' (in the section 'Preparing further developments'), this European actor affirmed that:

> In view of the growing number of new generation texts, the Commission considers there to be a need for a framework to help improve the consistency of the social dialogue outcomes and to improve transparency (...). Interest in and the importance of transnational collective bargaining have been increasing in recent years, particularly in response to globalisation and economic and monetary union. EWCs are adopting a growing number of agreements within multinational companies which cover employees in several Member States. There is also a growing interest in cross-border agreements between social partners from geographically contiguous Member States, as well as agreements between the social partners in particular sectors covering more than one Member State.[272]

269. Valeria Pulignano, 'European Integration and Transnational Employment Regulation: The company-level experience of EFAs in the metal sector in Europe' (2010) 1(1) European Labour Law Journal 81, 84. See also Torsten Müller and Hans Wolfganf Platzer and Stefan Rüb, 'European Collective agreements at company level and the relationship between EWCs and trade unions- lessons from the metal sector' (n. 267) 221-222.
270. Zimmer, 'Establish a Legal Frame for Transnational Collective Agreements in Europe: a Difficult Task' (n. 107) 46.
271. For in-depth analysis of the topic see: Dominique Bé, 'A Report on the European Commission Initiative for a European Framework for Transnational Collective Bargaining' in Konstantinos Papadakis (ed.), *Cross-Border Social Dialogue and Agreements: An Emerging Global Industrial Relations Framework?* (International Institute for Labour Studies, 2008); Edoardo Ales and Anne Dufresne, 'Transnational collective bargaining: Another (problematic) fragment of the European multi-level industrial relations system' (2012) 18(2) European Journal of Industrial Relations 95-106; Zimmer, 'Establish a Legal Frame for Transnational Collective Agreements in Europe: a Difficult Task' (n. 107) 46-52.
272. Commission, 'Partnership for change in an enlarged Europe: Enhancing the contribution of European social dialogue' (Communication) COM (04) 557, 11.

Although the European Commission did not focus its attention only on transnational collective bargaining at company level, but also at sectoral level,[273] this intervention marked a decisive step towards the acknowledgment of the importance of TCAs.

Moreover, in order to develop and improve this emerging form of social dialogue, in the Social Agenda 2005-2010, the Commission officially launched an initiative aimed at creating an optional European framework for transnational collective bargaining. This document stated that the introduction of an optional legal framework as a complementary level of collective negotiations at the European level[274] could have been the best means for tackling certain issues. Particularly, the document asserted that:

> providing an optional framework for transnational collective bargaining at either enterprise level or sectoral level could support companies and sectors to handle challenges dealing with issues such as work organization, employment, working conditions, training. It will give the social partners a basis for increasing their capacity to act at transnational level. It will provide an innovative tool to adapt to changing circumstances, and provide cost-effective transnational responses (...).[275]

The European Commission charged a group of experts led by professor Edoardo Ales with the analysis of the status of transnational collective bargaining in Europe, as well as with the assessment of the possibility to introduce the optional framework. The aim pursued was to identify the various features of the optional legal framework.[276] More specifically, the study considered Article 115 TFEU as a legal basis that could justify such a proposal. Pursuant to this Article, "(...) the Council shall, acting unanimously in accordance with a special legislative procedure and after consulting the European Parliament and the Economic and Social Committee, issue directives for the approximation of such laws, regulations or administrative provisions of the Member States as directly affect the establishment or functioning of the internal market".[277] Hence, the smooth functioning of the internal market has been considered a reason that can be used to justify the introduction of an optional framework for European transnational negotiations.[278]

A few years later, the European Commission commissioned other two studies. The first study was commissioned to Professor Van Hoek and Professor Hendricks and it focussed on 'International private law aspects and dispute settlement related to

273. Bé, 'A Report on the European Commission Initiative for a European Framework for Transnational Collective Bargaining' (n. 271) 224.
274. Jagodzinski, 'Involving European Works Councils in Transnational Negotiations – a Positive Functional Advance in their Operation or Trespassing?' (n. 253) 327.
275. Commission, Commission, 'Communication from the Commission on the Social Agenda' (Communication) COM (2005) 33 final, 8.
276. Commission, 'The development of transnational agreements', First approach (March 2006) 4, <http://ec.europa.eu/social/BlobServlet?docId=2895&langId=en> accessed on 14 July 2014.
277. Article 115, Consolidated Version of the Treaty on the Functioning of the European Union [2007] OJ C 326.
278. Ales et al., 'Transnational Collective Bargaining: Past, Present and Future' (n. 233) 34.

transnational company agreements'.[279] The second study was conducted under the direction of Professor Rodriguez and it examined 'the characteristics and legal effects of agreements between companies and workers' representatives'.[280]

In addition to the initiatives undertaken by the European Commission, it is worth mentioning that on 12 September 2013 the European Parliament adopted a Resolution on cross-border collective bargaining and transnational social dialogue. This document, which was welcomed positively by ETUC,[281] proposes "that the Commission might consider whether an optional European legal framework for these European TCAs would be necessary and useful in order to provide greater legal security, greater transparency, and foreseeable and enforceable legal effects for agreements following the framework provisions".[282]

[F] European Framework Agreements at Company Level: No Legal Framework but Legal Context within the European Social Dialogue?

As mentioned in the previous section, doctrine agrees that TCAs have emerged without any legal framework. As Schömann points out, "currently no legal order has explicitly conferred any power on MNCs and trade unions to create such a norm as TCAs, whereby the legal nature of any norm is dependent on the powers given by (labour) law to its actors (their legal capacity)".[283]

Nevertheless, it is still important to consider whether EFAs are somehow developing within a legal context and more specifically, within the European social dialogue as defined by Articles 154 TFEU and 155 TFEU.[284]

In this regard, Leonardi argues that there are certain provisions at both international and EU level that can "legitimatize [TCAs'] existence". More specifically, the

279. Aukje Van Hoek and Frank H R Hendrickx, 'International Private Law Aspects and Dispute Settlement Related to Transnational Company Agreements' (Final Report 2009 - VC/ 2009/0157) <http://ec.europa.eu/social/BlobServlet?docId=4815&langId=en> accessed 14 August 2014.

280. R Rodríguez et al., 'Study on the Characteristics and Legal Effects of Agreements between Companies and Workers' Representatives' (Final Report 2011) <http://ec.europa.eu/social/BlobServlet?docId=7631&langId=en> accessed 14 August 2014.

281. ETUC, 'On the Resolution of the EU Parliament on Cross Border Collective Bargaining and Transnational Social Dialogue letter' (Letter 12 November 2013) <http://www.epsu.org/a/9917> accessed 14 August 2014.

282. European Parliament, 'Resolution on cross-border collective bargaining and transnational social dialogue' (n. 249), para. 2.

283. Schömann, 'Transnational Collective Bargaining: In Search of a Legal Framework' in Isabelle Schömann et al., *Transnational Collective Bargaining at Company Level – A New Component of European Industrial Relations?* (ETUI aisbl 2012) 220.

284. *Ibid.*, 220-221 (the scholar explicitly mentions Article 152 TFEU introduced by the Lisbon Treaty. More specifically, according to Schömann, Article 152 TFEU refers to EU Social Partners, not MNEs).

scholar refers to ILO Conventions No. 87 and 98,[285] Article 155 TFEU[286] and Article 28 of the Charter of Fundamental Rights of the European Union.[287]

Taking into consideration EU law provisions, Leonardi argues that TCAs could be considered as a sub-specie of the autonomous agreements encompassed in Article 155 TFEU. Moreover, particular attention needs to be paid to the first paragraph of Article 155(1), pursuant to which "[s]hould management and labour so desire, the dialogue between them at Community level may lead to contractual relations, including agreements".[288] Even though this Article has been used so far in relation to cross-industry and sectoral social dialogue, one may argue that its broad formulation could be interpreted as to foresee the possibility for parties other than European social partners at cross-industry and sectoral level to enter into negotiations at company level. This interpretation is also upheld by Hendrickx.[289] The dialogue between the management of MNEs and trade unions could then lead to the conclusion of EFAs, which will be encompassed within Article 155 TFEU.[290]

In addition, looking at Article 28 of the Charter of Fundamental Rights of the European Union, this provision reads that "[w]orkers and employers, or their respective organizations, have, in accordance with Community law and national laws and practices, the right to negotiate and conclude collective agreements at the appropriate levels".[291] The Explanations relating to the Charter of Fundamental Rights of the European Union has clarified the reference to the "appropriate levels for conclusion of collective agreements". According to this document, "[t]he reference to appropriate levels refers to the levels laid down by Union law or by national laws and practices, which might include the European level when Union legislation so provides".[292] Even if Union law and national laws do not explicitly mention transnational collective bargaining at company level as a further level of negotiation, the reference to the 'levels laid down in practices' may arguably be considered a sufficient basis to allow the different parties to negotiate and conclude EFAs, when it is deemed necessary and

285. Jagodzinski, 'European Works Councils and Transnational Company Agreements – Balancing on the Thin Line between Effective Consultation and Overstepping Competences' (n. 98) 162 ff.
286. Leonardi, 'Transnational Company Agreements: A Stepping Stone towards a Real Internationalization of Industrial Relations?' (n. 240) 27.
287. *Ibid.*, 27.
288. Consolidated version of the Treaty on the Functioning of the European Union, OJ C 326.
289. Frank H R Hendrickx, 'The Development of Transnational Company Agreements in Europe' (2009) <https://pure.uvt.nl/portal/files/1305894/Hendrickx_Development_of_transnational_company_agreements_110209_postprint_embargo1y.pdf> accessed 11 August 2014.
290. The possible connection between TCAs and European Social Dialogue is addressed also in Van Hoek and Hendrickx (271) 10-11.
291. Article 28, Charter of Fundamental Rights of the European Union [2012] OJ C 326/02.
292. Explanations relating to the Charter of Fundamental Rights [2007] OJ C 303/17. See also Brian Bercusson, *European Labour Law and the EU Charter of Fundamental Rights* (ETUI 2003) 57 (The principle of collective autonomy of the social partners means the reference to 'appropriate levels' leaves it to the unfettered discretion to the parties to the bargaining process to decide which is the most appropriate level to undertake collective bargaining. This may be European, national, territorial, interconfederal, sectoral, national or international group of enterprises or plant level).

appropriate. Jagodzinski also corroborates this view.[293] In fact, the increased use of EFAs by the social partners as a new mode of corporate regulation points out the significance of this practice in the current system of industrial relations.

293. Jagodzinski, 'Involving European Works Councils in Transnational Negotiations – a Positive Functional Advance in their Operation or Trespassing?' (n. 253) 321. Despite this interpretation, one cannot disregard that Article 28 of the Charter of Fundamental Rights speaks about 'collective agreements' and labelling TCAs, and more specifically EFAs, collective agreements is still questionable. On the latter point, see Stefan Clauwaert, 'European Framework Agreements: "Nomina Nuda Tenemus" or What's in the Name? Experiences of the European Social Dialogue' in Isabelle Schömann et al., *Transnational Collective Bargaining at Company Level – A New Component of European Industrial Relations?* (ETUI aisbl 2012) 118-119.

CHAPTER 2

A Comparative Analysis between International Framework Agreements and European Framework Agreements at Company Level

§2.01 INTRODUCTION

This chapter will be devoted to a comparative analysis between IFAs and EFAs by taking into consideration different aspects of these agreements, such as the titles given by the parties, the addressees and the follow-up procedures, among others. In particular, this chapter intends to identify the similarities and differences between IFAs and EFAs. In the light of the analysis of the diverse agreements, one should be able to determine the status of this emerging mode of corporate regulation as well as of its possible future progress.

However, before going more deeply into the details of the analysis, it is necessary from the point of view of practical feasibility (at the time of writing, more than 250 TCAs have been concluded until May 2014) to make a selection of the texts to be examined. One criterion has been used to make such a choice: the number of employees in the MNEs that have signed the text. Specifically, this study will examine only agreements concluded by MNEs[294] with more than 80,000 workers globally in 2013 (unless otherwise stated).[295] This choice can be explained by the fact that the

294. One agreement classified as TCA in the database of the European Commission has been concluded by the UNI and the Universal Postal Union (UPU), a specialized agency of the United Nations. This agreement will not be included in the list of IFAs to analyse even if the number of people employed by UPU is more than 80,000. Only agreements concluded by MNEs are taken into consideration.

295. The number of employees has been retrieved in annual reports, financial reports, companies' website as well as in the database of the European Commission. For a few MNEs, the most

conclusion of TCAs by these companies might have a more significant influence on the evolution of this new form of social dialogue. The selection of IFA and EFAs to analyse in this Chapter is based on the data contained in Table 1 and Table 2 in the Annex.

The following sections will draw a comparative analysis of the main features of IFAs and EFAs with the aim to understand whether it is possible to draw a precise distinction between these two types of of agreements. Tables 2.1 and 2.2 indicate which and how many IFAs (62) and EFAs (76) fulfil the criterion laid out above. However, it is important to underline that the text of 13 out of the 76 EFAs is not available.

Table 2.1 IFAs Concluded by MNEs with More Than 80,000 Employees

Company	*Agreement*	*Date*	*Content*	*Sector*
GDF Suez	Global Health and Safety Agreement of the GDF Suez Group	2014	H&S	Utilities
Itaú-Unibanco S.A.	Framework Agreement between Banco Itaú-Unibanco S.A. and Union Network International for the Americas	2014	Fundamental social rights	Banking
Metro	Joint Statement of Metro Group & UNI Global Union	2013	Relationship between the company and trade unions and workers' representatives	Retail
Renault	Global framework agreement on social, societal and	2013	CSR and respect for fundamental social rights	Automotive industry

recent available data concerning the number of employees date back to 2012. Moreover, some agreements have been concluded by subsidiaries. For the purpose of this book, the number of employees of the parent company has been taken into consideration.

Company	*Agreement*	*Date*	*Content*	*Sector*
	environmental responsibility between the Renault Group, the Renault Group Works' Council and IndustriALL Global Union			
Volkswagen	Charter on Temporary Work	2012	Working conditions temporary work	Automotive industry
ThyssenKrupp AG	Global agreement of an idea management Health & Safety at ThyssenKrupp Elevator Operating Units	2012	H&S	Steel industry
Ford	Global framework agreement	2012	Fundamental social rights	Automotive industry
Inditex	Global agreement on the involvement of unions to monitor the respect of worker's conditions at supplier	2012	Trade union role in the implementation of the IFA in suppliers and external manufacturers	Textile and clothing
Siemens	International Framework Agreement between Siemens AG, the Central Works Council of Siemens AG, the IG Metall and the IndustriALL Global Union	2012	Fundamental social rights	Engineering

Company	*Agreement*	*Date*	*Content*	*Sector*
Banco do Brasil	Global Framework Agreement for the Americas Union Network International (UNI) and Banco do Brasil	2011 (renewed in 2013)	Fundamental social rights, CSR	Banking
Danone	Danone / IUF Agreement on health, safety, working conditions and stress	2011	H&S	Food and drink
Sodexo	International Framework Agreement	2011	Fundamental social rights	Quality of life services
Petrobas	Terms of Understanding of Good Labor Relations	2011	Fundamental social rights	Energy
GDF Suez	Group agreement on fundamental principles regarding health and safety	2010	H&S	Utilities
GDF Suez	Global Agreement on Fundamental Rights, Social Dialogue and Sustainable Development	2010	Fundamental social rights	Utilities
France Telecom (now as Orange S.A.)	Agreement of France Telecom's Worldwide Works Council	2010	Establishment of a Worldwide council	Telecommunications
Shoprite Checkers	Global Framework agreement	2010	Fundamental social rights	Food retailer

Company	*Agreement*	*Date*	*Content*	*Sector*
Volkswagen	Charter on Labour Relations within the Volkswagen Group	2009	Employees' representatives rights	Automotive industry
Inditex	Global agreement for implementation of fundamental labour rights and decent work	2009	Fundamental social rights	Textile and clothing
ArcelorMittal	Agreement on minimum requirements for Plant level Joint H&S Committees	2008	H&S	Steel industry
ArcelorMittal	Terms of reference for a joint global OSH committee in Arcelor Mittal	2008	H&S	Steel industry
G4S	A global Agreement: Ethical Employment Partnership	2008	Fundamental social rights	Security Services
PSA Peugeot	Agreement on the extension of the strategic equal committee	2008	Anticipation of change	Automotive industry
Thyssen-KruppAG	Principles of Social Responsibility in Labor Relations in the ThyssenKrupp Group	2007	Fundamental social rights	Steel industry

Company	*Agreement*	*Date*	*Content*	*Sector*
Siemens	Joint Statement between group management and Siemens Europe Committee concerning Compliance	2007	Compliance	Engineering
Danone	Convention on Diversity	2007	Promotion of diversity and equality of opportunity	Food and drink
Inditex	International Framework Agreement on the Implementation of International Labour Standards throughout the Inditex Supply Chain	2007	Fundamental social rights	Textile and clothing
Suez* (now GDF Suez)	Agreement on Commitment to promoting equality and diversity within the Group	2007	Promotion of equality and non-discrimination	Utilities
Suez* (now GDF Suez)	Group Agreement on Employees Ownership Scheme	2007	Creation of a financial motivation scheme	Utilities
France Telecom*	Worldwide Agreement on Fundamental Labour Rights within the France Telecom Group	2006	Fundamental social rights	Telecommunications

Company	*Agreement*	*Date*	*Content*	*Sector*
PSA Peugeot*	International Framework Agreement on PSA Peugeot Citroën's Social Responsibility	2006 (revised in 2010)	Fundamental human and social rights CSR	Automotive industry
DaimlerChrysler	Occupational Health and Safety Principles of DaimlerChrysler	2006	H&S	Automotive industry
Securitas	Agreement between Securitas AB (publ) and Union Network International and Swedish Transport Workers' Union on the development of good working relations in the Securitas group	2006	Fundamental social rights	Security services, transport
EDF	Agreement on EDF Group Corporate Social Responsibility	2005 (renewed in 2009)	Fundamental social rights CSR	Energy
EADS	International Framework Agreement	2005	Fundamental social rights	Aerospace
Danone	Fundamental Social Principles	2005	Fundamental social rights	Food and drink
Danone	Convention on the setting up of social indicators at group level	2005	Information on social indicators	Food and drink
Coca Cola	Joint Coca-Cola and IUF Statement	2005	Trade union rights	Food and drink

Company	*Agreement*	*Date*	*Content*	*Sector*
BMW	Joint Declaration on Human Rights and on Working Conditions in the BMW Group	2005	Fundamental social rights	Automotive industry
Arcelor	Worldwide Agreement on the Principles of Arcelor's Corporate Social responsibility	2005	Fundamental social rights	Steel industry
Bosch	Basic Principles of Social Responsibility at Bosch	2004	Fundamental social rights	Engineering
Lukoil	Agreement between International Federation of Chemical, Energy, Mine and General Workers' Unions, Russian Oil and Gas Workers Union And Open Joint Stock Company 'Oil Company LUKOIL'	2004	Fundamental social rights	Energy (and Oil)
H&M	Agreement between H & M hennes & Mauritz AB (H &M) and Union Network International (UNI) on Cooperation in order to secure	2004	Fundamental social rights	Retail

Company	*Agreement*	*Date*	*Content*	*Sector*
	and promote fundamental worker's rights at H&M's workplaces worldwide			
Renault	Renault Group employees' fundamental rights declaration	2004	Fundamental social rights	Automotive industry
ISS	Uni – ISS Global Agreement	2003 (replaced in 2008)	Fundamental social rights	Cleaning and maintenance
ENI	Agreement on transnational industrial relations and corporate social responsibility	2002 (updated in 2004 and 2009)	Fundamental social rights	Energy
DaimlerChrysler	Social Responsibility Principles of DaimlerChrysler	2002	Fundamental social rights	Automotive industry
Volkswagen	Declaration on Social Rights and Industrial Relationships at Volkswagen	2002	Fundamental social rights and principles	Automotive industry
Suez (now GDF Suez)	Charter Health and Safety at Work	2002	H&S	Utilities
Telefonica	UNI-Telefonica Code of conduct	2001	Fundamental social rights	Telecommuni-cations
IKEA	Framework agreement between IKEA and the IFBWW	2001	Fundamental social rights	Furniture retail/ manufacturing
Hochtief	Framework agreement between Hochtief and IFBWW	2000	Fundamental social rights	Construction

Company	*Agreement*	*Date*	*Content*	*Sector*
Carrefour	Global Agreement Carrefour – UNI Union Network International	2000	Trade union rights and fundamental social rights	Retail
Suez-Lyonnaise des Eaux	International social charter	1998	Fundamental social rights	Utilities
Danone	Convention applicable in the event of changes in business activities affecting employment or working conditions	1997 (updated in 2005)	Anticipation of change	Food and drink
Vivendi (before 1998 known as Générale des Eaux)	Charter of fundamental social rights	1996	Fundamental social rights	Utilities and communication
Accor	Agreement between the IUF and the Accor Group on Trade Union Rights	1995	Trade union's rights	Hotels
Danone	Convention on trade union rights	1994 (updated in 2005)	Trade union rights	Food and drink
Danone	Convention on skills training	1992 (updated in 2005)	Training programmes	Food and drink
Danone	Convention on economic and social data in Group Danone companies	1989 (updated in 2005)	Information of economic and social data to employees	Food and drink
Danone	Convention for the promotion of equality of men and women in the workplace	1989 (updated in 2005)	Equality at work	Food and drink

Company	*Agreement*	*Date*	*Content*	*Sector*
Danone	Common viewpoint IUF/BSN	1988	Trade union rights, equality, training	Food and drink

* Mixed agreements according to Commission, 'Mapping of transnational texts negotiated at corporate level', EMPL F2 EP/bp 2008 (D) 14511.

Table 2.2 EFAs Concluded by MNEs with More Than 80,000 Workers

Company	*Agreement*	*Date*	*Content*	*Sector*
Michelin*	European framework agreement on social responsibility and sustainable development	2014	CSR	Automotive industry
Air France/KLM	Framework agreement regarding the Air France KLM and Martinair Cargo organization in Europe	2013	Restructuring	Transport
Air France/KLM	Framework agreement regarding the Outstation and commercial organizations in Europe	2013	Restructuring	Transport
Air France/KLM	Social Rights and Ethics Charter	2013	Fundamental social rights	Transport
Allianz SE	Agreement on guidelines concerning Lifelong Learning	2012	Lifelong learning	Finance, insurance

Company	*Agreement*	*Date*	*Content*	*Sector*
Veolia Environment	Letter of commitment from the General Human Resources	2012	H&S	Utilities
	Management and the members of the Bureau of Veolia environment's European Works Council			
Alstom	European agreement on social commitments during the transition period of the Joint-venture between Alstom and Shanghai Electric on Boilers	2012	Joint Venture and social terms and conditions	Energy and transport
GDF Suez	GDF Suez Group European agreement on professional equality between men and women	2012	Equality	Utilities
BNP Paribas	European social charter – employment management agreement	2012	Anticipation of change	Banking
AXA Assistance	European agreement on anticipating changes within AXA Assistance	2011	Anticipation of change	Finance and insurance
AXA Group	European agreement on anticipating changes	2011	Anticipation of change	Finance and insurance

Company	*Agreement*	*Date*	*Content*	*Sector*
Allianz SE	Agreement on guidelines concerning work related stress	2011	H&S	Finance and insurance
Alstom	Agreement on the anticipation of change or developments in Alstom	2011	Anticipation of change	Energy and transport
EADS	Group agreement on the harmonization of the variable remuneration of Senior Managers within the EADS Group	2011	Remuneration	Aerospace
EADS	Agreement for the Implementation of a Success-Sharing Plan within the EADS-NV Group	2011 (this text replaces the text of 2009)	Profit-sharing scheme	Aerospace
Air France/KLM	Framework agreement regarding the Outstations in Europe	2011	Restructuring	Transport
Santander	Joint Declaration of the European Works Council (EWC) and the Central Management of Santander Group regarding the labour relations framework for the provision of financial services	2011	CSR	Banking

Company	*Agreement*	*Date*	*Content*	*Sector*
EADS	Agreement relating to the procedure for labor negotiations at European level	2010	Definition of procedures for negotiation at European level between trade unions and Central Management	Aerospace
Veolia Environment	Veolia Environment European Works Council agreement	2010 (it replaces the text of 2005)	Modus operandi EWC	Utilities
Alstom	European Agreement	2010	Acquisition of undertaking and social commitments	Energy and transport
Schneider Electric	European Agreement	2010	Acquisition of undertaking and social commitments	Energy
Air France / KLM	Framework agreement on sales agencies in airports (ATOs) in Europe between, on the one hand, the management of CDL Europe/North Africa and, on the other, the European Group Council	2010	Anticipation of change	Transport
Adam Opel AG*	Agreement on European restructuring ('Opel Plan for the Future')	2010	Restructuring	Automotive industry

Company	*Agreement*	*Date*	*Content*	*Sector*
GDF Suez	European group agreement relating to the employment and expertise plan	2010	Forward-looking management of jobs and skills	Utilities
ABB	European Appendix to ABB social policy	2009	Social (HR) Policy	Electrical equipment
Axa Group	Agreement on the AXA Group European Works Council	2009	Social dialogue	Finance and insurance
General Motors Europe*	Working time reduction	2009	Working time reduction	Automotive industry
ArcelorMittal	Managing & Anticipating change at ArcelorMittal (V10)	2009	Management of anticipation of change	Steel industry
Unicredit	Joint declaration on 'equal opportunities and non-discrimination'	2009	Equal opportunity and non-discrimination	Banking
Santander	Declaration on Social Rights and Labour Relations in Santander Group	2009	Fundamental social rights	Banking
Unicredit	Joint declaration on 'training, learning and professional development'	2008	Training	Banking
BP	Agreement on 'Business Service Centre (BSC)' Consultation	2008	Restructuring	Oil & Gas
Santander	Joint Declaration to be signed in the meeting on 21.05.2008	2008	Equal treatment	Banking

Company	*Agreement*	*Date*	*Content*	*Sector*
	between the European Works Council and the representatives designated by grupo santander's senior management			
Suez (now GDF Suez)	Agreement on social guarantees for Suez Group employees	2008	Merger and social guarantees	Utilities
Unicredit	Establishment of the Joint Commissions	2008	Establishment of Joint Commissions	Banking
GDF (now GDF Suez)	European agreement on the corporate social responsibility of the Gaz de France group	2008	Fundamental social rights	Utilities
Starwood Lodging	Agreement regarding the transnational transfer of Starwood Employees	2007	Transfer of undertaking	Hotels
Total	European agreement on assistance in creation, purchase or development of small and medium sized businesses	2007 (amended in 2012)	Encouragement of SMEs	Oil & Gas
DaimlerChrysler	Framework Regulation with the European Works Council (EWC) on the	2007	Transfer of undertaking and terms and conditions of employment	Automotive industry

Company	*Agreement*	*Date*	*Content*	*Sector*
	Realignment of the Sales Organization in the European Union			
General Motors (Europe)*	Restructuring at Antwerp	2007	Restructuring	Automotive industry
General Motors (Europe)*	Allocation of next Astra	2007	Restructuring	Automotive industry
Suez (now GDF Suez)	Group agreement – Suez Group's Social Dynamics – section on 'Employment and Expertise Plan'	2007	Employability of employees	Utilities
Schneider Electric	European Agreement on the Anticipation of Change	2007	Management and anticipation of change	Energy
Kraft Foods	European Framework Agreement regarding Project One Europe to be Concluded Between Kraft Foods Europe Management and the Employee Representatives	2007	Restructuring	Food and drink
DaimlerChrysler	Framework agreement for information and consultation with employees and employee representatives in the local European operations of DaimlerChrysler AG	2006	Information and consultation	Automotive industry

Company	*Agreement*	*Date*	*Content*	*Sector*
Allianz SE	Agreement concerning the participation of employees in Allianz SE	2006	Transnational negotiations for the participation of employees in Allianz SE	Finance, insurance
Total	European agreement on equal opportunity Total Group	2005	Principle of non-discrimination and equality of opportunity	Oil & Gas
EADS	Agreement on the European Works Council of EADS N.V. and its derived committees concluded between European Aeronautic Defence and Space Company EADS N.V. and its employees' representatives	2005	Transnational negotiations for the adaptation of the EWC	Aerospace
Philip Morris (Kraft Jacobs)*	Guidelines on information and consultation employment	2005	Information and consultation	Tobacco
Unilever	Agreed joint statement UEWC and Unilever on protection of personal data	2004	Protection of personal data	Food and drink, home and personal care
General Electric Plastics (Europe)	Agreement on Pre-employment screening ('background checks')	2004	Pre-employment screening	Plastics
Total	European agreement – social platform Total Group	2004	Social Dialogue	Oil & Gas

Company	*Agreement*	*Date*	*Content*	*Sector*
Deutsche Bank	Common Standpoint of the Deutsche Bank Group and the EWC	2004	Management of change	Banking
Ford (Europe)*	IOS restructuring: maintenance of jobs, investments, employability	2004	Restructuring	Automotive industry
General Motors (Europe)	Restructuring Framework	2004	Restructuring	Automotive industry
General Electric Plastics (Europe)	Amendment to the GEPE EBR Agreement on the introduction of regulations (including methodology and practice) during negotiations between the GEPE Central Management ('CM') and the GEPE EWC ('EWC')	2003	Bargaining methods	Plastics
Ford (Europe)	Ford of Europe and the Ford European Works Council (FEWC) Agreed upon Social Rights and Social Responsibility Principles	2003	Fundamental social rights	Automotive industry
General Electric Plastics (Europe)	GEPE Agreement on use of electronic communication systems	2002	Use of electronic communication systems	Plastics

Company	*Agreement*	*Date*	*Content*	*Sector*
General Motors (Europe)	General Motors Europe and the European Employee Forum agree on Principles of Social Responsibility	2002	Fundamental social rights	Automotive industry
Philip Morris (Kraft Jacobs)*	Processing key HR data (part of EWC agreement)	2002	Processing HR data	Tobacco
ENI	Agreement report	2002	Training programme for workers	Energy
Kraft Foods*	Framework understanding concerning the protection and processing of employment related personal data of employees of Kraft Foods International in EU/EEA Countries	2002	Processing HR data	Food and drink
Danone	Joint opinion on the applicable social standards for all the undertakings concerned by the restructuring programme of the Biscuits Pole in Europe presented on 29 March 2001	2001	Social standards in case of restructuring	Food and drink
Bouygues	European Social Charter of the Bouygues Group	2001	CSR	Construction & telecoms/media

Company	*Agreement*	*Date*	*Content*	*Sector*
Unilever	Responsible Restructuring	2001	Restructuring	Food and drink, home and personal care
General Motors (Europe)	European framework, dated 5 March 2001 at 20:30 ('The following framework agreement is in relation of GM's current restructuring initiatives')	2001	Restructuring	Automotive industry
Philip Morris (Kraft Jacobs)*	Agreement on the use of data recorded by sales forces	2001	Use of data	Tobacco
Philip Morris (Kraft Jacobs)	Agreement by the EU Assembly for the workforce of Philip Morris tobacco companies in the European regions of Philip Morris on the protection of personal data processed by ITSC Europe S.A.R.L.	2001	Protection of personal data	Tobacco
General Motors (Europe)	Framework 'regarding "Project Olympia" initiatives'	2001	Restructuring	Automotive industry
General Motors (Europe)	Framework	2000	GM/Fiat Alliance	Automotive industry
Ford (Europe)*	Joint Venture CFT: maintenance of Ford contracts, investments	2000	Joint Venture	Automotive industry

Company	*Agreement*	*Date*	*Content*	*Sector*
Ford	Agreement governing the separation of the Ford Visteon organization	2000 (reneg-otiated in 2003)	Sale of Visteon: transfer of employees, terms and conditions of employment, employees' representation	Automotive industry
Vivendi (before 1998 known as Générale des Eaux)	Charter on the safety at the workplace in the Group	1999	H&S	Utilities
Philip Morris (Kraft Jacobs)*	Principles on the introduction of euro	1999	Introduction of euro	Tobacco
Philip Morris (Kraft Jacobs)*	Code of conduct smoking at the workplace	1998	Smoking at the workplace	Tobacco
ENI	Agreement	1996 (updated in 2004)	H&S	Energy

* Text not available.

§2.02 TITLES

The title is one of the main characteristics of IFAs and EFAs that can show how the signatory parties perceive these texts. Different names are given to IFAs and EFAs and it is still not clear if there is a connection between the title of the agreement and the main issues addressed. From the analysis of the IFAs listed in Table 2.1, the following titles have been identified:

- Agreement: 11
- Charter: 4
- Code of Conduct: 1
- Common viewpoint: 1
- Convention: 7
- Declaration: 2
- Framework Agreement: 3
- Global Framework Agreement: 4
- Global Agreement: 8

- Group Agreement: 2
- International Framework Agreement: 5
- International Social Charter: 1
- Joint Statement: 3
- Joint Declaration: 1
- Principles: 5
- Terms of Understanding: 1
- Terms of Reference: 1
- Worldwide Agreement: 2

From the analysis of the EFAs listed in Table 2.2, the following titles have been identified:

- Agreement: 18
- Agreed Joint Statement: 1
- Agreement Report: 1
- Amendment: 1
- Code of Conduct: 1
- Common Standpoint: 1
- European Framework agreement: 2
- European Agreement: 10
- European Framework: 1
- European Group Agreement: 1
- European Appendix: 1
- (European Social) Charter: 4
- EWC Agreement: 1
- Framework: 3
- Framework Agreement: 5
- Framework Regulation: 1
- Framework Understanding: 1
- Guidelines: 1
- Group Agreement: 2
- Group European Agreement: 1
- Joint Opinion: 1
- (Joint) Declaration: 5
- Letter of Commitment: 1
- Principles: 1
- Title corresponding with the content of the agreement: 11

In the following subsections, a detailed study of the just mentioned agreements will try to find out whether there is a connection between the title of the agreement and the issues covered.

[A] International Framework Agreements

The majority of IFAs analysed in Table 2.1 address CSR and fundamental social rights and health and safety (see Figure 2.5).

By analysing the agreements that cover CSR and fundamental social rights and their title, it can be argued that there is not a clear symmetry between these two features. In fact, while the majority of IFAs are named 'Global Framework Agreement', 'Global Agreement' and 'International Framework', there are also IFAs with very different titles (e.g., 'Agreement', 'Code of Conduct', 'Joint Declaration', 'Terms of Understanding'). Moreover, the signatory parties of IFAs addressing other topics, such as trade unions' rights and trade unions' role, have used these titles too. For example, the IFA concluded by Inditex and ITGLWF in 2012 deal with the trade union's role in the implementation of the IFAs in suppliers and external manufactures. 'Global agreement' is the title given by the signatory parties to this IFA.

Concerning the issues of health and safety, the same conclusion can be reached. The signatories have given a wide range of titles to these IFAs, from 'Global Agreement' to 'Principles' and 'Terms of reference'.

[B] European Framework Agreements at Company Level

Section §2.02 of this Chapter has shown that the signatory parties of EFAs have given different titles to these agreements. It is now important to analyse whether there is a connection between the choice of the title and the issues addressed by the EFAs.

First of all, the topics dealt with by European agreements at company level are related for the most part to the phenomena of restructuring, transfer of undertakings, mergers, acquisitions and anticipation of changes. Some texts deal with CSR and fundamental social rights, even though this topic still remains largely addressed in IFAs.

Considering the data included in Figure 2.3 in relation to the content of the agreements and the titles of the agreements, it can be argued that there is not a strict correlation between the topic of restructuring and the title given to the agreement. However, the range of titles chosen by the parties revolve around the word 'Agreement' (e.g., 'Framework Agreement', 'Agreement' and 'European Framework Agreement') and the title of some EFAs correspond to the content of the agreement (e.g., Unilever - 'Responsible Restructuring').

Furthermore, EFAs dealing with transfer of undertaking, mergers, acquisitions and anticipation of changes follow a similar pattern. In fact, the great majority of EFAs dealing with these issues contain in their title the word 'agreement' (for instance, 'framework agreement', 'European agreement' or merely 'agreement') or have a title that correspond with the content of the agreements (e.g., ArcelorMittal - Managing & Anticipating change at ArcelorMittal (V10). Two exceptions are the EFAs concluded by BNP Paribas ('European Social Charter') and Deutsche Bank ('Common Standpoint').

On the contrary, when looking at the EFAs dealing with CSR and fundamental social rights, equal opportunities and social dialogue, the titles used by the signatories are diverse and do not appear to follow a certain pattern. By way of example, some EFAs on CSR and fundamental social rights are called 'Charter' (AirFrance/KLM 'Social Rights and Ethics Charter'). Others EFAs are named 'Declaration' (Santander 'Declaration on Social Rights and Labour Relations in Santander Group'), 'European Social Charter' (Bouygues 'European Social Charter of the Bouygues Group') or 'European

Agreement' (GDF 'European agreement on the corporate social responsibility of the Gaz de France Group'). Moreover, EFAs dealing with equality are also given different titles, namely 'European agreement' and 'Joint Declaration'.

§2.03 SIGNATORY PARTIES ON THE EMPLOYEES' SIDE

As Chapter 1, §1.01 has outlined, next to the scope of application, another significant difference between IFAs and EFAs concerns the signatory parties of these agreements. In fact, on the employer's side, both types of agreement at company level are signed on behalf of the MNEs either by the enterprise's President or by the enterprise's CEO or the Head of human resources (on behalf of the company's executive committee), among other actors. On the employees' side, IFAs and EFAs are different. Whilst GUFs have usually concluded IFAs (many of them by the Secretary General of the GUFs), EIFs and/or EWCs have usually been the leading actors in the conclusion of EFAs.

In order to compare the IFAs and the EFAs in this domain, it is opportune to focus the attention on the data contained in Table 1 and Table 2 in Annex regarding the signatory parties on the employees' side in MNEs with more than 80,00 employees.

[A] International Framework Agreements

In light of the information contained in Table 1 in Annex, in IFAs concluded by MNES with more than 80,000 employees it is possible to categorize the following employees' side signatories:

- GUFs
  a. BWI
  b. PSI
  c. Uni Global Union
     - Uni Americas
  d. IMF
  e. ITGLWF
  f. IUF
  g. ICEM
  h. IFBWW
  i. IFME (International Federation of Municipal Engineering)
- EIFs
  a. IndustriALL
  b. EMF
  c. EPSU
  d. ETUC
  e. CEC
- EWC
- National trade unions
- Special Negotiating Group composed of national trade unions
- Other forms of employees' representation

Figure 2.1 shows the number of IFAs concluded by the different actors. The dark grey (part of the) bar represents the agreements that have been signed only by one actor, while the light grey (part of the) bar represents the agreements that have been co-signed by multiple actors. Finally, the black part of the bar represents the agreement(s) in which a GUF has played an advisory role.

Figure 2.1 Signatory Parties of IFAs on the Employees' Side

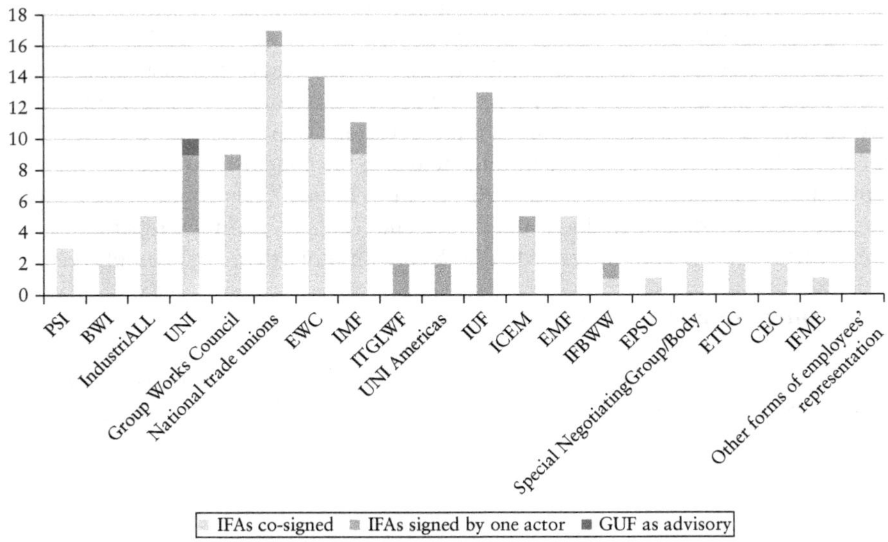

Source: The author.

Figure 2.1 shows that the IFAs listed in Table 2.1 in this Chapter have been signed by a wide range of parties on the employees' side, usually by the GUFs in the industrial sector where the MNEs operate. In particular, the GUF that has concluded most agreements so far is IUF, followed by IMF and UNI Global Union. This can be regarded as a sign of the positive attitude of the MNEs active in this sector towards this new mode of governance at company level as well as an indication of the growing power of these GUFs to encourage MNEs to negotiate and conclude IFAs.

Despite the involvement of GUFs, EWCs and national trade unions play the most important role in the conclusion of these agreements. Whilst the involvement of EWCs raises the concerns explained in Chapter 1, §1.03, the involvement of national trade unions may have significant consequence on the legal status of these agreements, which may acquire the status of national collective agreements and legally binding effects. By looking at Figure 2.1, one can readily observe that national trade unions are the actors more involved in the conclusion of these agreements, even though, they have always been among the parties that co-signed the IFAs but in one case.

Two further situations merit closer attention: first, with the exception of IUF, the other GUFs have for the most part co-signed the IFAs; secondly, in one IFA, UNI Global Union has played 'merely' the role of advisor.

However, not only GUFs are involved in IFAs, but also EIFs, which nevertheless have never been the only signatory party. Finally, yet importantly, other forms of employees' representation have been involved in the conclusion of IFAs.

[B] European Framework Agreements at Company Level

The employees' side signatories of EFAs differ from those involved in the conclusion of IFAs and, more specifically, EIFs and EWCs have concluded the majority of these agreements. In light of the information contained in Table 2 in Annex, in EFAs concluded by MNES with more than 80,000 employees it is possible to categorize the following employees' side signatories:

- EWC
- European Industry Federations
  a. CEC
  b. EMF
  c. EMCEF
  d. EPSU
  e. IndustriALL
  f. FECEC
  g. FECCIA
  h. UNI-Europa
  i. FECER
  j. EFFAT
- ETUC
- Global Union Federations
  a. UNI (UNI Europa)
  b. IUF
- National Trade Unions
- Special Negotiation Body/Group represented by national trade unions
- Other Forms of employees' representation

Figure 2.2 shows the number of EFAs concluded by the different actors. The dark grey (part of the) bar represents the agreements that have been signed only by one actor, while the light grey (part of the) bar represents the agreements that have been co-signed by multiple actors.

Figure 2.2 Party Signatories of EFAs on the Employees' Side

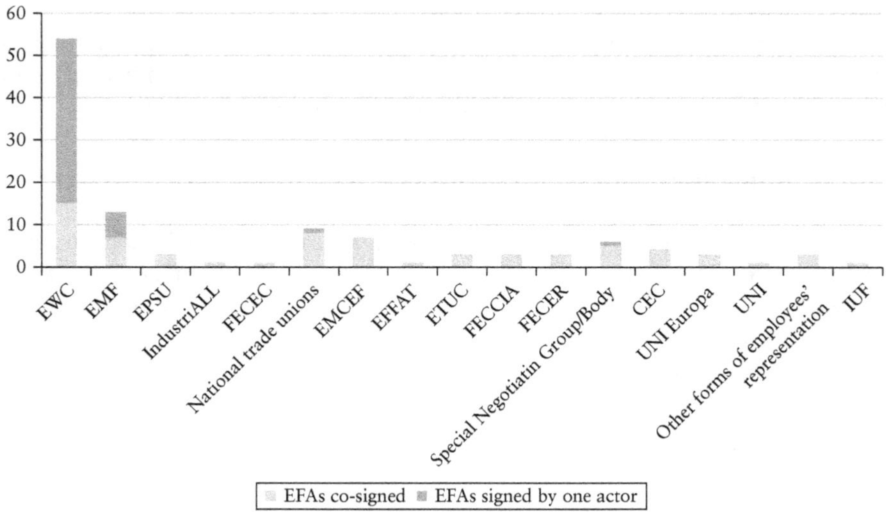

Source: The author.

Examining the signatory parties of the EFAs concluded by MNEs with more than 80,000 employees, one can notice that EWCs are the foremost actors involved in such agreements. In particular, EWCs have signed or co-signed 54 out of the 75 EFAs listed.[296] This significant number shows the leading role that this actor has in the conclusion of transnational agreements at European level. Interesting is that these transnational bodies have been the sole party in the great majority of EFAs concluded (39 EFAs).

In addition to that, national trade unions have also been much involved in the conclusion of EFAs so far, two times even signing the agreements alone. Finally, EMF has been the forerunner among EIFs in the conclusion of EFAs, followed by EMCEF.

§2.04 SECTORS

This section analyses in what sector the MNEs signing TCAs operate and, in particular, it examines whether enterprises doing business in specific sector are more inclined to engage into negotiations with trade unions and/or workers' representatives at company level. The nomenclature used in this section builds upon what is used by the European Commission.[297]

296. The text of one EFAs is not available and this information could not be found in any other source.
297. Commission, 'Mapping of transnational texts negotiated at corporate level' (n. 113).

[A] International Framework Agreements

Looking at the IFAs listed in Table 2.1, these agreements have been concluded by MNEs operating in the following sectors:

- Aerospace
- Automotive industry
- Banking
- Cleaning and maintenance
- Construction
- Engineering
- Energy and transport
- Food and drink
- Quality of life services
- Hotels
- Retail
- Security services
- Steel industry
- Textile and clothing
- Telecommunications
- Utilities[298]

Figure 2.3 Sectors of IFAs

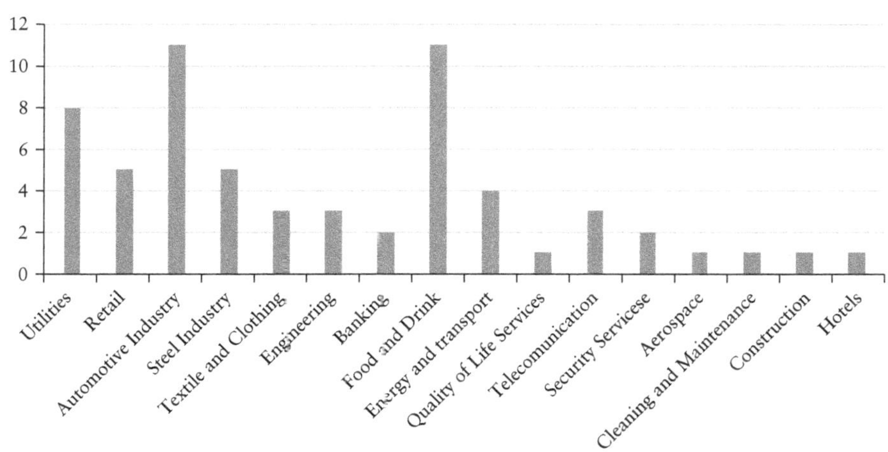

As it can be observed from Figure 2.3, the food and drink and automotive industry sectors account for the most significant number of agreements signed (11 IFAs for each sector, together almost one third of the texts concluded until May 2014 by MNEs with more than 80,000 employees). With the exception of the utilities industry, the

298. The EFA concluded by Vivendi in 1996, the 'Charter of fundamental social rights', falls within the broader sector 'Utilities and Communication'.

difference with other sectors is of note because only a few enterprises involved in sectors such as hotels, aerospace and cleaning and maintenance have concluded IFAs.

[B] European Framework Agreements at Company Level

Concerning the EFAs listed in Table 2.2, the MNEs that signed these agreements operate in the subsequent sectors:

- Aerospace
- Automotive industry
- Banking
- Construction & telecoms/media
- Electrical equipment
- Energy and Transport
- Food and drink, home and personal care
- Finance and Insurance
- Hotel
- Oil and Gas
- Plastics
- Steel Industry
- Tobacco
- Utilities

Figure 2.4 Sectors in EFAs

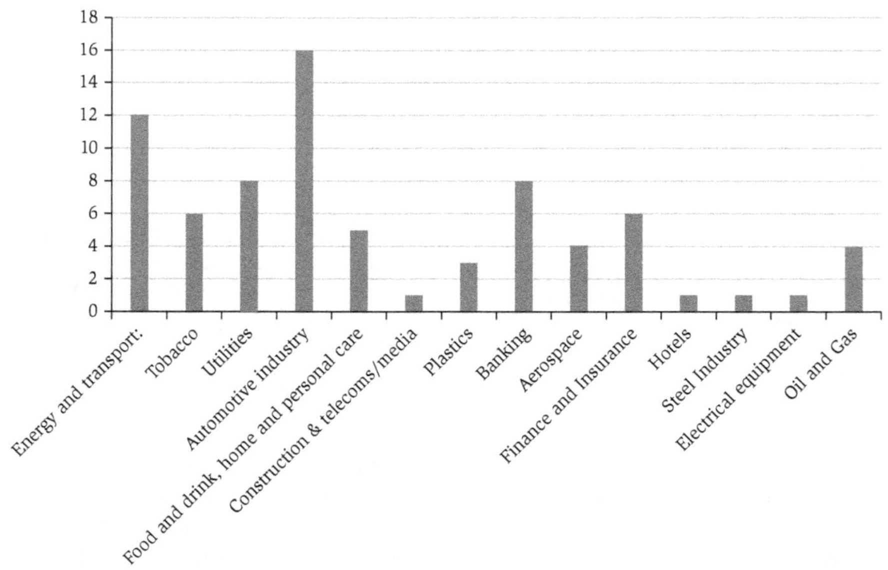

Just like IFAs, the automotive industry has been one of the most important contributors in signing EFAs (16 agreements). The reason behind the choice of MNEs operating in this sector to sign these agreements can be found in the characteristics of the European labour market. As will be examined in the section §2.05 of this book, restructuring is the most covered issue by EFAs as well as the phenomenon that has involved and is currently still involving the automotive sector in Europe.

More specifically, between 2007 and 2014 MNEs operating in the automotive sector have concluded a great number of EFAs on restructuring, social commitments, management and anticipation of changes. This can be explained by the need to mitigate the negative consequences on the level of employment stemming from the economic crisis that has characterized the labour market in the past few years.[299] For this reason, one can observe a strong link between the sector involved, the automotive sector, and the issues dealt with by EFAs concluded by MNEs operating in this field.

Other sectors have also been quite involved in the conclusion of these European texts: MNEs active in the energy and transport industry (e.g., Alstom, Schneider Electric but also Air France / KLM) have concluded almost an equivalent number of agreements compared to the automotive industry (12). MNEs involved in utilities, tobacco, banking, finance and insurances follow. On the contrary, MNEs operating in sectors such as hotels and steel industry have not been much inclined to engage in this emerging mode of social dialogue.

§2.05 CONTENT

The issues covered by TCAs vary depending on the needs and interests of MNEs and trade unions and workers' representatives. The scope of application of the agreement play an important role too. In fact, the content of these agreements at company level is to some extent different for IFAs and EFAs, which deal with different aspects of the labour relations.

In particular, while IFAs are mostly devoted to the acknowledgment of ILO core labour standards, such as the abolition of forced labour, the elimination of child labour, freedom of association and the rights to collective bargaining, among others, EFAs for the most part address restructuring process, anticipation of change and social dialogue issues.

Additionally, IFAs are usually not detailed agreements because they tend to set up frameworks of guidelines and principles that signatories and other addressees of the agreement should respect.[300] On the contrary, EFAs frequently represent a tool used by MNEs and social partners to regulate in a specific way certain phenomena within the enterprise, such as social terms and conditions following mergers, acquisitions and transfers. In other words, the range of issues dealt with by EFAs is much broader compared to IFAs.

In the following two subsections, a detailed analysis and comparison of the content of the IFAs and EFAs listed in Tables 2.1 and 2.2 will be carried out.

299. Konstantinos Papadakis, 'Restructuring Enterprises through social dialogue and labour management agreements: Social responsibility practices in time of crisis' (International Labour Office 2010) 1ff, < www.ilo.org/public/libdoc/jobcrisis/download/restructuring_enterprises.pdf > accessed 23 May 2014.

300. Telljohann et al., 'European and International Framework Agreements: Practical Experiences and Strategic Approaches' (n. 29) 7.

[A] International Framework Agreements

The analysis of the content of the IFAs in Table 2.1 has led to the following list of issues:

- Fundamental social rights and CSR
- H&S
- Equality
- Anticipation of change
- Information on economic and social data to employees
- Temporary work
- Training
- Rights of trade unions and workers representatives
- Trade unions' role
- Establishment of World Works Council
- Compliance
- Financial motivation scheme
- Information on social indicators

Figure 2.5 shows the number of IFAs concluded on the issues listed below.

Figure 2.5 Content of IFAs Signed by MNEs with More Than 80,000 Employees

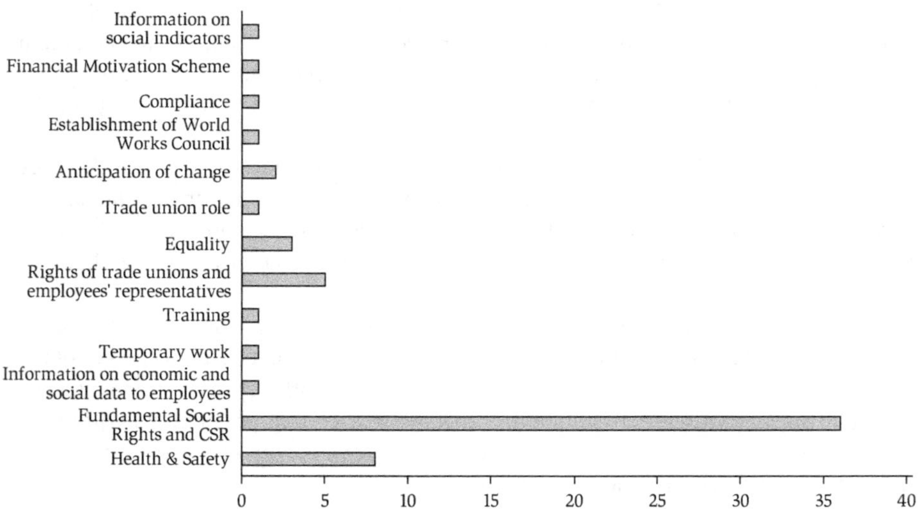

From Figure 2.5, one can note that the overwhelming majority of IFAs deals with fundamental social rights and CSR issues (36 out of 62). More specifically, many IFAs recall and reaffirm the importance of the fundamental labour rights set forth in the eight ILO fundamental Conventions as well as in ILO Declaration 1998. Moreover, the more recent texts refer to the ten principles addressed in the UN Global Compact. Some of these texts focus also on issues such as wages, decent living, remuneration, social dialogue as well as ethical and environmental standards.

Next to fundamental social rights and CSR, the second most discussed issue in IFAs is health and safety and related issues, such as stress at work and working conditions. These texts intend to set a framework to prevent and deal with occupational risks and illnesses.

In contrast, much less attention is paid to issues such as equality, temporary work and training. A few texts deal with issues typically addressed by EFAs, namely management and anticipation of changes as well as terms and conditions that must be guaranteed in case of restructuring of enterprises.

[B] European Framework Agreements at Company Level

In terms of content, EFAs listed in Table 2.2 cover the following issues:

- Restructuring
- Fundamental social rights and CSR
- Forecast employment skills' needs
- Information and consultation
- Assistance to SMEs
- Use, protection and possession of data
- Pre-employment screening
- Lifelong learning
- Human resources
- H&S
- Social dialogue
- Anticipation of change
- Working time reduction
- Merger, acquisition, transfer, sale
- Joint venture and social terms
- Use of electric communication systems
- Equality
- Training
- Remuneration
- Profit-Sharing scheme
- Definition of procedures for negotiation
- Introduction of euro
- Smoking at workplace
- Framework for transnational negotiations

Figure 2.6 shows the number of EFAs concluded on the issues listed above.

Figure 2.6 Content of EFAs Signed by MNEs with More Than 80,000 Employees

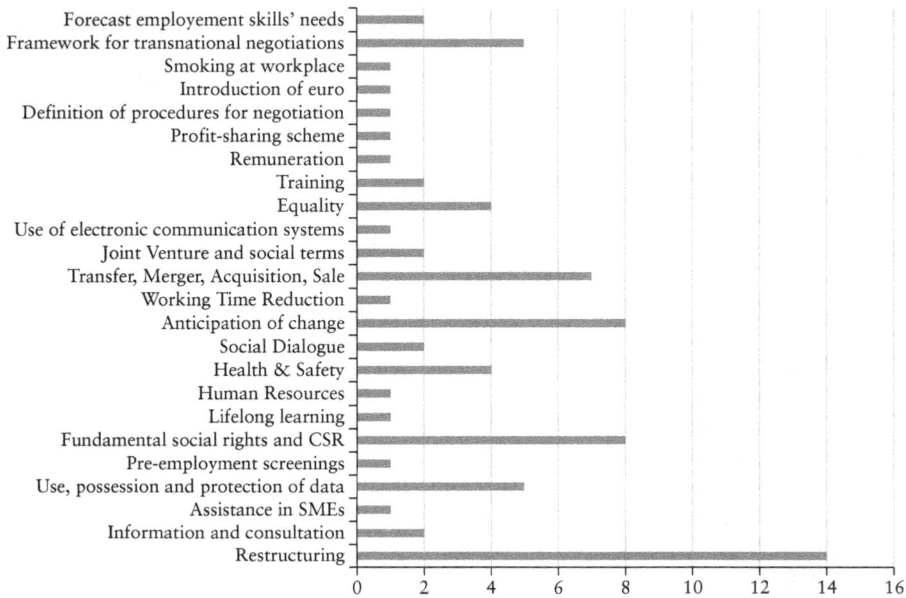

One of the biggest differences between IFAs and EFAs can be found in the content of these agreements at company level. The reason behind this dissimilarity can be found in the features of the European industrial relations system, which led MNEs, trade unions and workers' representatives to cope with matters particularly sensitive at European level, such as significant enterprises' restructuration as well as anticipation and management of changes. More specifically, just below half of the EFAs listed in Table 2.2 (29) deal with these topics.

In addition, the long-standing culture of dialogue in many European countries (for instance France and Germany) has been the main reason for which MNEs and EIFs and/or EWCs have decided to deal with topics related to social dialogue and trade unions rights. The aim pursued by these actors is to further promote and encourage the exchange of views and opinions between the two sides of industry.

Despite this main difference, many EFAs cover issues related to fundamental social rights and CSR (8 out of 76). This fact may reflect an increasing concern by MNEs to business ethics issues also at the European level, although IFAs have usually addressed these topics at global level.

§2.06 ADDRESSEES

Identifying who are the addressees of IFAs and EFAs is one of the most important issues that need to be discussed, especially because TCA's impact on the system of industrial relations and on the protection of fundamental social rights is strictly connected to their scope of application.[301]

It is therefore significant to examine how the IFAs and the EFAs listed in Tables 2.1 and 2.2 deal not only with subsidiaries but also with business partners, such as suppliers, contractors and subcontractors.

[A] International Framework Agreements

First of all, it is important to stress that amongst the 62 IFAs listed in Table 2.1, 8 of them do not contain any statement as to the addressees of the agreements besides the signatory parties.[302] On the contrary, all the remaining IFAs make reference to the addressees. It is therefore important to examine two main addressees: first, subsidiaries; second, suppliers, contractors and subcontractors.

As far as the subsidiaries are concerned, 47 IFAs out of 54 IFAs[303] specify that the agreement is addressed also to these legal entities. However, a distinction has to be made between two groups: first, IFAs addressing subsidiaries on terms that are more general; second, IFAs addressing subsidiaries by referring to the degree of control and/or influence the parent company holds over them.[304]

Concerning the first group, 36 IFAs specify that the company's commitments extend to the entire group.[305] These agreements are highlighted in light grey in Table 3 in Annex. Amongst them, on the one hand, some agreements do not indicate that subsidiaries are within the scope of application of the agreement but they refer to the group as a whole. On the other hand, other agreements clearly point out that they are applicable also to subsidiaries. Some examples will be provided in the following paragraphs.

The Volkswagen 'Charter on Labour Relations within the Volkswagen Group' (2009) stipulates:

> This Charter shall apply for all companies and sites represented on the Volkswagen Group's European Group Works Council and Group Global Works Councils.[306]

301. Peter Wilke and Kim Schütze, 'Background Paper on International Framework Agreements for a Meeting of the Restructuring Forum devoted to Transnational Agreements at Company Level' (2008) 9 <http://ec.europa.eu/social/BlobServlet?docId=4969&langId=en> accessed 17 May 2014.
302. DaimlerChrysler 2002, Coca Cola 2005, DaimlerChrysler 2006, Siemens 2007, PSA Peugeot 2008, two IFAs concluded by ArcelorMittal in 2008 and Itaú-Unibanco S.A. 2014.
303. As mentioned at the beginning of the section, 8 IFAs do not contain any reference neither to subsidiaries nor to suppliers, contractors and subcontractors.
304. Wilke and Schütze (n. 301) 9.
305. One of these IFAs, the 'Social Responsibility Principles' concluded by DaimlerChrysler, the Company World Employee committee and IMF in 2002, does not refer explicitly to the Group but states that the principles contained in the IFA need to be implemented by DaimlerChrysler worldwide. Moreover, the IFA concluded by H&M is applicable in all H&M's workplaces worldwide.
306. Text available at <http://ec.europa.eu/employment_social/empl_portal/transnational_agreements/Volkswagen_LabourRelationsCharter_EN.pdf> accessed on 18 May 2014.

The ISS 'Uni – ISS Global Agreement' (2003-2008) reads:

> This global agreement is between UNI Global Union and ISS. "Union" refers to UNI Global Union and its affiliate unions and "ISS" refers to ISS A/S and its subsidiaries.[307]

One interesting example of IFA addressing its subsidiaries is the agreement concluded by Shoprite Checkers, according to which a specific and different condition has to be met for extending the agreement to these legal entities.

The Shoprite Checkers 'Global Framework agreement' (2010) states:

> The principles set out in this global agreement will apply to all Shoprite Checkers operations and its subsidiaries where Shoprite Checkers formally recognises UNI Global Union alliance members.[308]

Moving to the second group, 11 IFAs explicitly declare that the agreements apply only to the subsidiaries that are under direct control or (dominant) influence of the parent company. These agreements are highlighted in dark grey in Table 3 in Annex.

The France Telecom 'Worldwide Agreement on Fundamental Labour Rights' (2006) reads:

> The present agreement applies to companies directly controlled by the France Telecom Group, i.e. companies in which France Telecom Group holds the majority of the capital or a majority of voting rights or in which it appoints more than half the members of the administrative, management or monitoring bodies.[309]

The Arcelor 'Worldwide Agreement on the Principles of Arcelor's Corporate Social responsibility' (2005) stipulates:

> This agreement applies to the entities over which the Group exercises a dominant influence, be it through direct ownership, financial participation or governance rules.
> When an entity leaves the perimeter of the Group as defined above, this agreement ceases to apply to it. Conversely, when an entity enters its perimeter, the signatory parties undertake to carry out all necessary steps to integrate this company within the effective implementation of the agreement.[310]

The GDF Suez 'Global Agreement on Fundamental Rights, Social Dialogue and Sustainable Development' (2010) reads:

307. Text available at <http://ec.europa.eu/employment_social/empl_portal/transnational_agreements/ISS_IFA_EN.pdf> accessed on 18 May 2014.
308. Text available at <http://ec.europa.eu/employment_social/empl_portal/transnational_agreements/Shoprite-IFA_EN.pdf> accessed on 18 May 2014.
309. Text available at <http://ec.europa.eu/employment_social/empl_portal/transnational_agreements/FranceTelecom_Fundamentalright_En.pdf> accessed 18 May 2014.
310. Text available at <http://ec.europa.eu/employment_social/empl_portal/transnational_agreements/Arcelor_IFA_EN.pdf> accessed 18 May 2014.

> This agreement applies to all present and future GDF Suez companies fully consolidated within GDF Suez Group's scope of consolidation and those in which the Group has dominant influence.[311]

Regarding suppliers, contractors and subcontractors, the content of the clauses referring to these legal entities differ significantly from text to text. Within the IFAs listed in Table 2.1, more than half of the texts (42 out of 54)[312] address this issue, although a distinction has to be made among three groups of IFAs.

The first group comprises IFAs that consider the compliance with the standards set forth in the agreement as a 'criterion for being chosen and maintained as a supplier or subcontractor [or contractor]'.[313] Moreover, the agreements specify different levels of commitments of the parties in relation to the business relationships with suppliers, contractors and sub-contractors. This is reflected in the use of language used in the text. Some texts use verbs such as 'endeavour' and 'strive' in relation to the relationship between the company and business partners, while others make use of 'shall' or 'will not work'. Some examples are provided below:

The Bosch 'Basic Principles of Social Responsibility at Bosch' (2004) reads:

> Bosch will not work with any suppliers who have demonstrably failed to comply with basic ILO labor standards.[314]

The Shoprite Checkers 'Global Framework agreement' (2010) stipulates:

> Shoprite Checkers will strive, in its dealing with suppliers, to engage with those that share its commitment to the principles of good governance.[315]

The Inditex 'Global agreement for implementation of fundamental labour rights and decent work' (2009) reads:

> The undertaking shall not knowingly use for its commercial network the services of third parties who violates the principles of this Global Agreement.[316]

The Renault 'Renault Group employees' fundamental rights declaration' (2004) reads:

> As provided by ILO convention No. 138 on the minimum working age, Renault agrees not to employ people younger than the mandatory school-leaving age in the relevant country or, in any event, below the age of fifteen. Suppliers and service providers must comply with this policy in order to work with Renault.[317]

---

311. Text available at <http://ec.europa.eu/employment_social/empl_portal/transnational_agreements/GDFSUEZ_IFA_EN.pdf> accessed 18 May 2014.
312. The 'Global agreement on the involvement of unions to monitor the respect of worker's conditions at supplier' concluded by Inditex and ITGLWF is specifically about the role of trade unions in the implementation of the IFA between Inditex and ITGLWF within the supply chain.
313. Wilke and Schütze (n. 301) 10.
314. Text available at <http://ec.europa.eu/employment_social/empl_portal/transnational_agreements/Bosch_IFA_EN.pdf> accessed 20 May 2014.
315. See footnote n. 308.
316. Text available at <http://ec.europa.eu/employment_social/empl_portal/transnational_agreements/Inditex_LabourRights_EN.pdf> accessed 20 May 2014.
317. Text available at <http://ec.europa.eu/employment_social/empl_portal/transnational_agreements/Renault_IFA_EN.pdf> accessed 20 May 2014.

The second group covers IFAs according to which the MNE has to inform, circulate and/or communicate the agreement to its suppliers and/or contractors and subcontractors. Moreover, some companies encourage them to respect the standards laid down in the agreement and/or introduce equivalent principles in their business policies.[318]

As the examples below show, the signatory parties seem to undertake different commitments when concluding these IFAs. Similar to what is described in the first group of IFAs, the language used mirrors the diverse approach the signatory parties take (some parties use verbs such as 'encourage', while others prefer stronger verbs such as 'request').

In addition, some of the IFAs at issue consider the compliance with the content of the agreement a strong basis for business relationships, thus belonging to both the first group and the second group of IFAs. Some examples will explain all these differences.

The Renault 'Renault Group employees' fundamental rights declaration' (2004) reads:

> Renault informs its suppliers of the contents of this declaration and the Global Compact and urges them to consider adhering to it. It encourages them to introduce and implement equivalent principles in their own companies.[319]

The BMW 'Joint Declaration on Human Rights and on Working Conditions in the BMW Group' (2005) reads:

> The BMW Group's partners and suppliers will be encouraged to introduce comparable principles in their corporate structures and to apply them in the context of their own corporate policy. The BMW Group expects them to use these principles as a basis in their mutual dealings and regards them as a suitable criterion for lasting business relationships.[320]

The PSA Peugeot 'International Framework Agreement on PSA Peugeot Citroën's Social Responsibility' (2006-2010) stipulates:

> Without replacing its suppliers', sub-contractors', industrial partners' and distribution networks' legal responsibility, PSA PEUGEOT CITROËN undertakes to communicate this agreement to these companies and request that they apply the previously mentioned ILO international conventions.
>
> PSA PEUGEOT CITROËN requests from its suppliers a similar commitment in respect of their own suppliers and sub-contractors.[321]

Furthermore, the EADS 'International Framework Agreement' (2005) stipulates:

> Compliance with EADS standards serves as a criterion for selecting suppliers. EADS therefore expects all its suppliers to recognize and apply the principles of

318. Wilke and Schütze (n. 301) 10.
319. See footnote n. 317.
320. Text available at <http://ec.europa.eu/employment_social/empl_portal/transnational_agreements/BMW_IFA_EN.pdf> accessed 20 May 2014.
321. Text available at <http://ec.europa.eu/employment_social/empl_portal/transnational_agreements/PSA_IFA_EN.pdf> accessed 20 May 2014.

> this framework agreement and encourages them to introduce and implement equivalent principles in their own companies.[322]

Finally, the last and third group covers IFAs whose scope of application extends also to business partners. Among the 42 IFAs that deal with this issue, only 3 IFAs explicitly make reference to this aspect.

The GDF Suez 'Global Health and Safety Agreement of the GDF Suez Group' (2013) reads:

> To the fullest extent possible it is also applicable to sites and operations within the GDF Suez's sphere of influence, without any geographical restrictions.[323]

In this regard, the Hochtief 'Framework agreement between Hochtief and IFBWW' (2000) reads:

> HOCHTIEF, one of the world's biggest construction groups, today signs an agreement committing it to observe – in its building activities anywhere in the world – the social standards of the International Labour Organization (ILO). The agreement imposes the same obligation on all HOCHTIEF's subcontractors.[324]

Furthermore, the Arcelor 'Worldwide Agreement on the Principles of Arcelor's Corporate Social responsibility' (2005) sets forth:

> In accordance with Article 8 of this agreement, companies in which the ARCELOR Group has a significant presence, albeit without exercising a dominant influence there, along with contractors and suppliers also fall within the scope of this agreement.[325]

[B] European Framework Agreements at Company Level

As far as the addressees of EFAs are concerned, only 63 out of the 76 EFAs listed in Table 2.2 have been taken into consideration due to the unavailability of the texts. Nevertheless, some interesting results have come up from the analysis of these EFAs.

Particularly, in 20 cases out of 63 the signatory parties have not referred neither to subsidiaries nor to suppliers, contractors and subcontractors. In addition to that, a considerable number of texts (10) does not explicitly mention the subsidiaries but refer to the 'sites', 'brands', 'plants' of the company, thus making it difficult to understand whether subsidiaries are amongst the addressees of the agreement. These agreements are not highlighted in Table 4 in Annex.

If now one examines whether the subsidiaries are regarded as addressees of EFAs two groups of agreements can be identified. This situation is akin to what has been already discussed about the IFAs in the previous subsections.

322. See footnote n. 193.
323. Text available at <http://www.world-psi.org/sites/default/files/documents/research/accord_mondial_sante_securite_may._13_2014_-en1.pdf> accessed 20 June 2014.
324. Text available at <http://ec.europa eu/employment_social/empl_portal/transnational_agreements/Hochtief_FrameworkAgreement_EN.pdf> accessed 20 May 2014.
325. See footnote n. 310.

In 25 EFAs (highlighted in light grey in Table 4 in Annex), the signatory parties have indicated that the agreement addresses the whole Group without any reference to the degree of control of the parent company over the subsidiary. For example, the BNP Paribas 'European social charter – employment management agreement' (2012) reads:

> The present agreement applies to all BNP Paribas-controlled branches and fully-integrated subsidiaries within the geographical remit of the European Works Council.[326]

Moreover, the Total 'European agreement – social platform Total Group' (2004) reads:

> This agreement applies to all the Total Group's legally autonomous entities mentioned in the 1st article of the agreement concerning the European Works Council (EWC) of Total dated 20 March 2001, provided that they have a personnel representation body.[327]

In 8 EFAs (highlighted in dark grey in Table 4 in Annex) the agreement applies to subsidiaries when the parent company has controlling interests over them or exercises a certain degree of control or dominant influence over them.

For example, the GDF 'European agreement on the corporate social responsibility of the Gaz de France group' (2008) reads:

> This agreement applies, on a European scale, to the fully integrated and monitored entities, namely:
>
> a) companies in which Gaz de France holds directly or indirectly, a fraction of the capital which gives it a majority of the voting rights in the meeting of these companies;
> b) companies over which Gaz de France, by virtue of voting rights, held either directly or indirectly, has the possibility of ensuring that its point of view takes precedence at general meetings;
> c) companies in which Gaz de France is, directly or indirectly, either associated or a shareholder and thus has the power to appoint or abrogate the majority of the members constituting the administrative, managerial or regulatory bodies of this company.[328]

In addition, the GDF Suez 'European group agreement relating to the employment and expertise plan' (2010) reads:

> This agreement applies to a GDF Suez and its subsidiaries which are globally integrated in the GDF Suez consolidation scope in Europe, or which are more than 50% owned, subject to compliance with the criterion of dominant influence.[329]

---

326. Text available at <http://ec.europa.eu/employment_social/empl_portal/transnational_agreements/BNP%20Paribas%20European%20Social%20Charter_EN.pdf> accessed 14 May 2014.
327. Text available at <http://ec.europa.eu/employment_social/empl_portal/transnational_agreements/Total_socialplatform_EN.pdf> accessed 14 May 2014.
328. Text available at <http://ec.europa.eu/employment_social/empl_portal/transnational_agreements/GDF_CSRagreement_EN.pdf> accessed 21 May 2014.
329. Text available at <http://ec.europa.eu/employment_social/empl_portal/transnational_agreements/GDF%20SUEZ_GPEC_EN.pdf> accessed 21 May 2014.

Finally, the Veolia Environment 'Veolia Environment European Works Council agreement' (2010) stipulates that:

> ARTICLE 2. SCOPE
> The Veolia Environnement European Works Council encompasses Veolia Environnement S.A. and all its subsidiaries or sub-subsidiaries within the European Union and in Member States of the European Economic Area in which it has a controlling interest, in accordance with the provisions of Article L.2343-2 of the French Labour Code.[330]

Moving now to the suppliers, contractors and subcontractors, the signatory parties of EFAs have rarely asserted that the agreements at issue apply to these actors.

In fact, only 5 out of 63 EFAs explicitly refer to suppliers and/or contractors and/or subcontractors as the addressees of the texts.[331] A common pattern that can be identified among these texts is that they all address issues such as fundamental social rights, CSR and equality. Moreover, the distinction made in the previous subsection among three different groups of IFAs addressing these business partners becomes partially meaningless since it is not possible to identify texts that belong to the third category.

More specifically, 4 EFAs fall within the first and second categories identified in relation for the IFAs. First, the EFA concluded by Ford (Europe) and EWC in 2003 ('Ford of Europe and the Ford European Works Council (FEWC) Agreed upon Social Rights and Social Responsibility Principles') reads:

> Ford of Europe will encourage business partners throughout its value chain to adopt and enforce similar policies to those contained in these Principles, as the basis for establishing mutual and durable business relationships. The Company will seek to identify and utilize business partners who aspire in the conduct of their business to standards that are consistent with this document.[332]

Second, the EFA concluded by General Motors (Europe), EMF and the EWC in 2002 seems containing a stronger commitment to ensure the respect of fundamental social rights by business partners. In particular, the text of this EFA ('General Motors Europe and the European Employee Forum agree on Principles of Social Responsibility') stipulates:

> We support and encourage the application of these principles by those with whom we do business.
> The principles will be shared with our business partners as a solid basis for a sustainable business relationship. They shall comply with all applicable laws and regulations that relate to wages, hours & conditions of employment, discrimination and occupational health & safety. Under contracts with GME, our suppliers

330. Text available at <http://ec.europa.eu/employment_social/empl_portal/transnational_agreements/Veolia_EWC_EN.pdf> accessed 21 May 2014.
331. In one EFA, the 'Agreement on Pre-employment screening ("background checks") concluded by General Electric Plastics in 2004, an external supplier is charged with performing the background checks in compliance with international legal requirements. This agreement has not been included amongst the 5 EFAs mentioned in the text.
332. Text available at <http://ec.europa.eu/employment_social/empl_portal/transnational_agreements/Ford_SocialRights_EN.pdf> accessed 21 May 2014.

> represent and signify that they will not utilize forced or involuntary labor in the supply of goods or provision of services to GME.[333]

Third, the EFA concluded by GDF in 2008 ('European agreement on the corporate social responsibility of the Gaz de France group') establishes a strong mechanism in case the suppliers or subcontractors do not comply with the standards laid down in the agreement. The EFA at issue indeed sets up corrective measures when these actors behave inconsistently with the principles declared in the text. This fact is remarkable because it shows that MNEs are aware of the commitments undertaken by signing these agreements and, in addition, they strictly sanction the partners that are not in line with the direction taken by the company. In particular, this EFA reads:

> The Gaz de France Group's suppliers and subcontractors will be informed of this agreement. Relations with suppliers and subcontractors should not generally cause situations to arise in which the Group's ethical commitments and those described in this agreement are brought into question. All Gaz de France companies expect their suppliers to observe the current international laws and agreements. Any disregard for Human Rights will be made the subject of corrective measures further to a warning issued by the Group's companies. Non-observance of these rights will lead to cessation of the commercial partnerships.[334]

Fourth and finally, the 'Social Rights and Ethics Charter' concluded by Air France / KLM and EWC in 2013 stipulates:

> Companies of the AIR FRANCE KLM Group (see Appendix 2) will be particularly attentive to ensuring that these principles and fundamental social rights are respected by all subcontractors with whom they maintain relations anywhere in the world, in the respect of the Procurement principles defined in the Sustainable Development Charter, described in Appendix 3. The contact person at the Procurement Division will attentively monitor the situation, particularly in case of specific problems.[335]

The Sustainable Development Charter mentioned in the text above is a document containing the commitment of Air France / KLM to the principles contained in the UN Global Compact and a reminder for its suppliers to comply with a number of principles specified in the Charter (fundamental social principles and labour standards, environmental principles). Importantly, by entering into a contract with Air France / KLM, the suppliers "agree that Air France and/or KLM may carry out audits to verify application of the principles of this Charter".[336]

Finally, 1 EFA falls within the second category: the 'GDF Suez Group European agreement on professional equality between men and women' concluded by GDF Suez, IndustriALL, CEC, EPSU and a Special Negotiating Body (SNB) in 2012. In this

333. Text available at <http://ec.europa.eu/employment_social/empl_portal/transnational_agreements/GM_PrinciplesSocialResponsibility_EN.pdf> accessed 21 May 2014.
334. See footnote n. 328.
335. Text available at <http://ec.europa.eu/employment_social/empl_portal/transnational_agreements/charte_sociale_AFKL_EN.pdf> accessed 21 May 2014.
336. *Ibid.*

agreement the company encourages business partners to respect and comply with the principles set forth in the text. According to Article 13 of this EFA:

> In compliance with the global agreement on fundamental rights, social dialogue and sustainable development, the company is committed to ensuring that its suppliers and subcontractors comply with the principles of equality between women and men.[337]

§2.07 DURATION, RENEWAL, TERMINATION AND REVISION

Duration, renewal, termination and revision of TCAs are aspects often addressed by the signatory parties of these agreements. However, even though the parties often introduce in the texts of IFAs and EFAs provisions concerning duration (indefinite or limited), the same cannot be argued for renewal, revision and termination of the agreements. The texts of TCAs rarely cover the latter issues.

[A] International Framework Agreements

From the analysis of the data contained in Table 2.3, it is possible to observe that 31 IFAs do specify neither explicitly nor implicitly the duration of the agreement. In addition to that, these agreements do not include any information on termination, revision and renewal. These data are particularly relevant as 31 agreements are half of the total number of IFAs examined in the present Chapter. Moreover, a pattern can be identified: most of the agreements that do not include this information were concluded at the outset of this mode of corporate governance, namely between 1988 and 2002 (with the exception of Telefonica).

On the contrary, all the remaining IFAs identify at least one of the aspects analysed. In particular, concerning the duration, 9 of them foresee that the agreements will last for an indefinite period, while just in 15 cases, a fixed-term period is established (between 1 and 5 years). Interesting are the cases of the 'Global Agreement: Ethical Employment Partnership' concluded by G4S and the 'International Framework Agreement' concluded by Sodexo. These agreements will continue as long as the parties deem it appropriate and necessary.

Concerning the renewal of the IFAs under examination, the great majority of texts analysed (51 out of 62) do not deal with this aspect. In the remaining IFAs the phrasing used by the parties for the aspect of renewal is nevertheless very different. Some texts can be tacitly and automatically renewed unless terminated by the signatories; others need to be beforehand reviewed before being renewed. One agreement explicitly excludes tacit renewal (the 'Group Agreement on Employees Ownership Scheme' concluded by Suez in 2007).

337. Text available at <http://ec.europa.eu/employment_social/empl_portal/transnational_agreements/GDFSUEZ_equality_EN.pdf> accessed 13 May 2014.

Just like the renewal, also the termination of IFAs is a characteristic that has not attracted much attention by the signatory parties, which have regulated this issue in only 17 out of 62 IFAs. In these agreements, a common pattern can be identified: most of the IFAs establish that each party can terminate the agreement with notice of termination variable between 60 days to 6 months. Two agreements (Inditex and ArcelorMittal) have introduced a mechanism to avoid that the parties give notice of termination just before the agreement terminates. Accordingly, they prescribe that each party can give notice of termination at least respectively 3 and 6 months prior to the expiry of the agreement. Finally, interesting is the agreements concluded by Securitas, in which the signatory parties do not need to give notice of termination in cases of breach of the contract.

As far as the revision of the IFAs is concerned, only a few of the agreements analysed (less than one third of the total – 18 out of 62) introduce a provision about this aspect. In particular, according to the majority of the IFAs at issue, the signatory parties will meet to assess the status of the implementation of the agreement and, afterwards, carry out its revision if necessary. Moreover, in some of the text, renegotiation of the agreement is possible after one of the party has given notice to the other. Finally, one has to observe that 3 IFAs concluded by a French MNE (2 of Suez and 1 of GDF Suez) contain an express reference to national law, in particular the French employment code, whose provisions will be complied with in case of revision of the agreement.

This analysis and the detailed information contained in Table 2.3 shows that whereas, on the one hand, the signatories of IFAs are still quite reluctant to introduce provisions concerning renewal, termination and revision, on the other hand, they are more inclined to define their duration. The main reason behind this situation can be found in the still not so developed practice of concluding such agreements at company level. Arguably, the further evolution of these agreements and the establishment of a framework for transnational negotiations at company level may lead the signatory parties to specify in detail all the features of the IFAs.

Table 2.3 includes information retrieved in the text of the agreements and using the database of the European Commission on TCAs.

Table 2.3 Duration, Renewal, Termination and Revision in the IFAs Concluded by MNEs with More Than 80,000 Employees

Company	*Agreement*	*Date*	*Duration*	*Renewal*	*Termination*	*Revision*
GDF Suez	Global Health and Safety Agreement of the GDF Suez Group	2014	Indefinite	Not defined	With advance notice of 6 months by both parties. In case of termination, the parties will meet within 6 months trying to replace the agreement	In accordance with GDF Management and at least two Global Unions
Itaú-Unibanco	Framework Agreement between Banco Itaú-Unibanco S.A. and Union Network International for the Americas	2014	24 months	Not defined	By either party at any time by a simple formal notice, without any penalties and responsibilities	Not defined
Metro	Joint Statement of Metro Group & UNI Global Union	2013	Not defined	Not defined	Not defined	The parties agree to evaluate the working relationship regularly and determine whether

Company	*Agreement*	*Date*	*Duration*	*Renewal*	*Termination*	*Revision*
						a revision of this statement would be necessary
Renault	Global framework agreement on social, societal and environmental responsibility between the Renault Group, the Renault Group Works' Council and IndustriALL Global Union	2013	Not defined	Not defined	Not defined	Review meeting every year and global review every 3 years
Volkswagen	Charter on Temporary Work	2012	Not defined	Not defined	Not defined	This agreement can be amicably adjusted, when both sides wish to do so
ThyssenKrupp AG	Global agreement of an ideamanage-ment Health & Safety at Thys-senKrupp Elevator Operating Units	2012	5 years	A further 3 years unless terminated more than 3 months before the expiration of these five years	Not defined	Not defined

Company	*Agreement*	*Date*	*Duration*	*Renewal*	*Termination*	*Revision*
Ford	Global framework agreement	2012	Not defined	Not defined	Not defined	Not defined
Inditex	Global agreement on the involvement of unions to monitor the respect of worker's conditions at supplier	2012	Not defined	Not defined	Not defined	Not defined
Siemens	International Framework Agreement between Siemens AG, the Central Works Council of Siemens AG, the IG Metall and the IndustriALL Global Union	2012	Not defined	Not defined	Not defined	Not defined
Banco do Brasil	Global Framework Agreement for the Americas Union Network International	2011 (renewed 2013)	2 years	Not defined	Either signatory may withdraw from this agreement at any time, provided it	Not defined

Company	*Agreement*	*Date*	*Duration*	*Renewal*	*Termination*	*Revision*
	(UNI) and Banco do Brasil				gives a simple formal notice, being in this case, exempt from any penalties and responsibilities	
Danone	Danone / IUF Agreement on health, safety, working conditions and stress	2011	Not defined	Not defined	Not defined	Not defined
Sodexo	International Framework Agreement	2011	It shall remain effective for as long as 'Sodexo' and 'IUF' deem it 'Appropriate'"	Not defined	It may be terminated by either party upon giving the other party at least three months' written notice	It may be renegotiated by either party upon giving the other party at least three months' written notice
Petrobas	Terms of Understanding of Good Labor Relations	2011	2 years	Can be extended for 2 years	The parties can exercise their right to renounce the present terms as long as it	The parties will review the points of these terms at joint meetings which will have to be scheduled in

Company	*Agreement*	*Date*	*Duration*	*Renewal*	*Termination*	*Revision*
					is communicated within six months	advance. The object of these meetings will be to discuss only the questions covered by these terms
GDF Suez	Group agreement on fundamental principles regarding health and safety	2010	Indefinite	Not defined	Not defined	The Agreement may be revised in accordance with the applicable provisions of the Labour Code
GDF Suez	Global Agreement on Fundamental Rights, Social Dialogue and Sustainable Development	2010	3 years	Unless terminated for another 3 years	It may be terminated with advance notice from any party six months prior to its expiration	Not defined
France Telecom (now Orange S.A.)	Agreement of France Telecom's WorldWide Works Council	2010	Indefinite	Not defined	Unilaterally, with 6 months' notice: by Central Management or by a 2/3 majority vote of members,	Modifications may be proposed every 2 years after a review is made with employee representatives

Company	*Agreement*	*Date*	*Duration*	*Renewal*	*Termination*	*Revision*
					requested by the incumbents or the signatories of this agreement	and will be negotiated by a delegation appointed by the Worldwide Works Council and ratified by the latter
Shoprite Checkers	Global Framework agreement	2010	Not defined	Not defined	At any time by one party giving the other 60 days written notice of termination	Not defined
Volkswagen	Charter on Labour Relations within the Volkswagen Group	2009	Not defined	Not defined	Not defined	If so desired by both sides, this Agreement may be consensually modified
Inditex	Global agreement for implementation of fundamental labour rights and decent work	2009	Indefinite	Not defined	Either of two sides may terminate it with a period of notice of at least six months	Either of two sides may request renegotiation with a period of notice of at least six months

Company	*Agreement*	*Date*	*Duration*	*Renewal*	*Termination*	*Revision*
ArcelorMittal	Agreement on minimum requirements for Plant level Joint H&S Committees	2008	4 years	It shall be tacitly renewed for periods of 4 (four) years, unless terminated	By one of the signatories by notification of the others, by registered letter, at least 6 (six) months before the end of the four year period	Throughout its duration this agreement may be revised by the Joint Global H&S Committee by means of addenda to adapt it, particularly if the perimeter of the group changes
ArcelorMittal	Terms of reference for a joint global OSH committee	2008	Not defined	Not defined	Not defined	Not defined
G4S	A global Agreement: Ethical Employment Partnership	2008	For as long as UNI, the GMB and G4S deem it appropriate	Not defined	Subject to three months' written notice of termination	Subject to three months' written notice of renegotiation
PSA Peugeot	Agreement on the extension of the strategic equal committee	2008	Indefinite	Not defined	Not defined	Not defined
ThyssenKrupp AG	Principles of Social Responsibility in Labor Relations in the ThyssenKrupp Group	2007	4 years	Not defined	Not defined	Not defined

Company	*Agreement*	*Date*	*Duration*	*Renewal*	*Termination*	*Revision*
Siemens	Joint Statement between group management and Siemens Europe Committee concerning Compliance	2007	Not defined	Not defined	Not defined	Not defined
Danone	Convention on Diversity	2007	Not defined	Not defined	Not defined	Not defined
Inditex	International Framework Agreement on the Implementation of International Labour Standards throughout the Inditex Supply Chain	2007	1 year	It shall be deemed to be automatically extended for further periods of one year unless termination	Notice to the other at least three months in advance of its expiry date or date of expiry of its extensions	Not defined
Suez (now GDF Suez)	Agreement on Commitment to promoting equality and diversity within the Group	2007	Indefinite	Not defined	Not defined	The agreement may be revised in accordance with the relevant provisions of the Employment Code

Company	*Agreement*	*Date*	*Duration*	*Renewal*	*Termination*	*Revision*
Suez (now GDF Suez)	Group Agreement on Employees Ownership Scheme	2007	3 years	May not be renewed by tacit agreement	Not defined	The agreement may be revised in accordance with the relevant provisions of the Employment Code
France Telecom	Worldwide Agreement on Fundamental Labour Rights within the France Telecom Group	2006	Indefinite	Not defined	By either of the parties at three months' notice	Not defined
PSA Peugeot	International Framework Agreement on PSA Peugeot Citroën's Social Responsibility	2010 (revision of a text of 2006)	Indefinite	Not defined	Not defined	Every three years, the parties agree to meet to carry out an overall review of the actions undertaken and to plan for the required adjusting measures through amendments to the agreement, in particular in

Company	*Agreement*	*Date*	*Duration*	*Renewal*	*Termination*	*Revision*
						respect of legislative and regulatory changes
DaimlerChrysler	Occupational Health and Safety Principles of DaimlerChrysler	2006	Not defined	Not defined	Not defined	Not defined
Securitas	Agreement between Securitas AB (publ) and Union Network International and Swedish Transport Workers' Union on the development of good working relations in the Securitas group	2006	2 years	Successive periods of 1 year, unless termination	Written notice no less than 6 months prior to the expiration date. Moreover, after the negotiation a party may also terminate this agreement with immediate effect upon any material breach of contract by the other party	Not defined
EDF	Agreement on EDF Group Corporate Social Responsibility	2005, 2009	4 years	Possible renewal subject to a review by the parties	Each signatory party may revoke his/her signature to this Agreement	Not defined

Company	*Agreement*	*Date*	*Duration*	*Renewal*	*Termination*	*Revision*
					by registered letter with return receipt, with six months prior notice	
EADS	International Framework Agreement	2005	Not defined	Not defined	Not defined	Not defined
Danone	Fundamental Social Principles	2005	Not defined	Not defined	Not defined	Not defined
Danone	Convention on the setting up of social indicators at group level	2005	Not defined	Not defined	Not defined	Not defined
Coca Cola	Joint Coca-Cola and IUF Statement	2005	Not defined	Not defined	Not defined	Not defined
BMW	Joint Declaration on Human Rights and on Working Conditions in the BMW Group	2005	Not defined	Not defined	Not defined	Not defined
Arcelor	Worldwide Agreement on the Principles of	2005	3 years	Not defined	It can be terminated by any of the signatory	It can be revised, by means of an amendment, in

Company	*Agreement*	*Date*	*Duration*	*Renewal*	*Termination*	*Revision*
	Arcelor's Corporate Social responsibility				parties by registered letter, subject to an advance notice of three months	order to adapt it, in particular in the event of a change in the perimeter of the Group
Bosch	Basic Principles of Social Responsibility at Bosch	2004	Not defined	Not defined	Not defined	Not defined
Lukoil	Agreement between International Federation of Chemical, Energy, Mine and General Workers' Unions, Russian Oil and Gas Workers Union And Open Joint Stock	2004	1 year	Renewal is subject to review	Not defined	Not defined
	Company 'Oil Company LUKOIL'					
H&M	Agreement between H & M hennes & Mauritz	2004	Not defined	Not defined	Not defined	Not defined

Company	*Agreement*	*Date*	*Duration*	*Renewal*	*Termination*	*Revision*
	AB (H &M) and Union Network International (UNI) on Cooperation in order to secure and promote fundamental worker's rights at H&M's workplaces worldwide					
Renault	Renault Group employees' fundamental rights declaration	2004	Not defined	Not defined	Not defined	Not defined
ISS	Uni – ISS Global Agreement	2003, 2008	Indefinite	Not defined	It may be terminated by either party upon giving the other party at least three months' written notice of termination	It may be renegotiated by either party upon giving the other party at least three months' written notice of termination

Company	*Agreement*	*Date*	*Duration*	*Renewal*	*Termination*	*Revision*
ENI	Agreement on transnational industrial relations and corporate social responsibility	2002, 2004, 2009	4 years	it shall be revised and/or confirmed for an equivalent period	Not defined	The parties may agree in advance to the modifications or additions to be made to its contents
DaimlerChrysler	Social Responsibility Principles of DaimlerChrysler	2002	Not defined	Not defined	Not defined	Not defined
Volkswagen	Declaration on Social Rights and Industrial Relationships at Volkswagen	2002	Not defined	Not defined	Not defined	Not defined
Suez (now GDF Suez)	Charter Health and Safety at Work	2002	Not defined	Not defined	Not defined	Not defined
Telefonica	UNI-Telefonica Code of conduct	2001	5 years	Will be evaluated and may be prolonged for a new period	Not defined	Not defined

Company	*Agreement*	*Date*	*Duration*	*Renewal*	*Termination*	*Revision*
IKEA	Framework agreement between IKEA and the IFBWW	2001	Not defined	Not defined	Not defined	Not defined
Hochtief	Framework agreement between Hochtief and IFBWW	2000	Not defined	Not defined	Not defined	Not defined
Carrefour	Global Agreement Carrefour – UNI Union Network International	2000	Not defined	Not defined	Not defined	Not defined
Suez-Lyonnaise des Eaux	International social charter	1998	Not defined	Not defined	Not defined	Not defined
Danone	Convention applicable in the event of changes in business activities affecting employment or working conditions	1997, 2005 (update)	Not defined	Not defined	Not defined	Not defined

Company	Agreement	Date	Duration	Renewal	Termination	Revision
Vivendi (Veolia Générale des Eaux)	Charter of fundamental social rights	1996	Not defined	Not defined	Not defined	Not defined
Accor	Agreement between the IUF and the Accor Group on Trade Union Rights	1995	Not defined	Not defined	Not defined	Not defined
Danone	Convention on trade union rights	1994, 2005 (update)	Not defined	Not defined	Not defined	Not defined
Danone	Convention on skills training	1992, 2005 (update)	Not defined	Not defined	Not defined	Not defined
Danone	Convention on economic and social data in Group Danone companies	1989, 2005 (update)	Not defined	Not defined	Not defined	Not defined
Danone	Convention for the promotion of equality of men and women in the workplace	1989, 2005 (update)	Not defined	Not defined	Not defined	Not defined
Danone	Common viewpoint IUF/BSN	1988	Not defined	Not defined	Not defined	Not defined

[B] European Framework Agreements at Company Level

The situation described in the previous subsection in relation to IFAs is akin to what can be asserted for EFAs. Indeed, by analysing the data contained in Table 2.4, it is possible to observe that more than half of the EFAs analysed (33 out of 63 of the available texts) do not explicitly specify any of the aspects connected to the duration of the agreement. More specifically, similarly to IFAs, the majority of EFAs that do not include this information are those concluded between the first EFA in 1996 and 2002.

Just like the international texts, the party signatories are more inclined to specify the duration of the EFAs compared to renewal, termination and revision. However, one striking difference between IFAs and EFAs is that the European texts contain a significant number of provisions on the possibility to review the texts. This aspect will be explained later in the text.

Moving to the duration of the EFAs analysed, almost half of the texts contained such information. More particularly, 13 EFAs have been concluded for a fixed-term of time, ranging from a specific expiration date to a period of 2 to 3 years from the date of the signatures or the date the agreement comes into force. In addition to that, 13 EFAs have been concluded for an unlimited period of time, unless, as specified in some agreements, the parties decide to terminate it.

Furthermore, almost all the EFAs examined do not foresee the possibility to renew the agreement, with the exception of 9 of them. Similarly to the IFAs, the parties have used different formulations in the texts displaying the different interests they intend to achieve by concluding these agreements. For instance, in some texts, only after an assessment of the implementation of the text the parties can decide to extend the duration of the agreement. Quite differently, some texts establish that the agreement will be automatically and tacitly extended unless one of the parties gives notice of termination.

In addition, in 20 EFAs, the signatory parties have introduced a provision concerning the possible termination of the agreement. A common pattern can be identified: almost all the agreements prescribe a notice period of termination (in writing) between 3 months to 1 year, at times depending on the length of time that has elapsed since the agreement has entered into force. No notice of termination is required if one of the parties breach a clause of the agreement, as prescribed by the Philips Morris agreement of 2001. Interesting are some agreements according to which the party who gives notice of termination (in writing) has to simultaneously submit a draft of a new agreement that will be subject to renegotiation. This can be explained by the need to ensure continuity in this form of social dialogue.

A difference can be found between IFAs and EFAs in relation to the possibility to revise the agreement. Unlike the international texts, more than a third of the texts (22 out of 63) contain a reference to the possibility to revise partially or totally the text, at the request of each party or via a joint proposal, respecting a notice period or at any time. More specifically, in some agreements the parties specify what reasons can be brought forward in order to request a revision of the text: for instance, changes in the geographical scope or in the legislation as well as amendments in order to improve the outcome the parties want to reach via concluding the agreements. In addition to that, some agreements prescribe that revision is possible after an assessment of the implementation of the texts. Similarly to IFAs, some texts refer to the revision procedures laid down in national codes.

To conclude, with the exception of the issue of revision, it can be argued that the signatories of TCAs, both IFAs and EFAs, have gone and are still going in the same direction as far as the duration, renewal and termination are concerned.

Table 2.4 includes information retrieved in the text of the agreements and using the database of the European Commission on TCAs.

Table 2.4 Duration, Renewal, Termination and Revision in the EFAs Concluded by MNEs with More Than 80,000 Employees

Company	*Agreement*	*Date*	*Duration*	*Renewal*	*Termination*	*Revision*
Michelin	European framework agreement on social responsibility and sustainable development	2014	Text not available	Text not available	Text not available	Text not available
Air France/KLM	Framework agreement regarding the Air France KLM and Martinair Cargo organization in Europe	2013	Until 1 April 2014	Not defined	The agreement will end on the 1st of April 2014	Changes in this framework can only be made by mutual agreement and will only be effective after a written and signed revised document
Air France/KLM	Framework agreement regarding the Outstation and commercial organizations in Europe	2013	Until 1 April 2013	Not defined	The agreement will end on the 1st of April 2013	Changes in this framework can only be made by mutual agreement and will only be effective after a

Company	*Agreement*	*Date*	*Duration*	*Renewal*	*Termination*	*Revision*
						written and signed revised document
Air France/KLM	Social Rights and Ethics Charter	2013 (replace one of 2008)	This Charter is applicable for an unlimited duration and replaces the former Social Rights and Ethics Charter, effective as of March 1st, 2008	Not defined	Not defined	If necessary, a revision of this text can be initiated by agreement of the signatories of the present document
Allianz SE	Agreement on guidelines concerning Lifelong Learning	2012	Not defined	Not defined	It may be terminated in writing by either side subject to a period of notice of one year to take effect at the end of a calendar year	Not defined
Veolia Environment	Letter of commitment from the General Human Resources Management and the members of	2012	Not defined	Not defined	Not defined	Not defined

Company	*Agreement*	*Date*	*Duration*	*Renewal*	*Termination*	*Revision*
	the Bureau of Veolia environnement's European Works Council					
Alstom	European agreement on social commitments during the transition period of the Joint-venture between Alstom and Shanghai Electric on Boilers	2012	End of the transition period (31/12/2014)	Not defined	End of the transition period (31/12/2014)	Not defined
GDF Suez	GDF Suez Group European agreement on professional equality between men and women	2012	The agreement is concluded for an initial fixed term until 30 June 2016	The parties will meet in the 1st half of 2016 to make an overall evaluation of the agreement, check the achievement of overall objectives	30 June 2015	The parties will meet in the 1st half of 2016 to make an overall evaluation of the agreement, check the achievement of overall objectives. Following this evaluation, it can

Company	*Agreement*	*Date*	*Duration*	*Renewal*	*Termination*	*Revision*
				Following this evaluation, it can be renewed or revised by agreement between the parties		be renewed or revised by agreement between the parties. The signing parties may revise this agreement in accordance with the provisions of the articles L. 2222-5, L. 2261-7 and L. 2261-8 of the French Labour Code
BNP Paribas	European social charter – employment management agreement	2012	It comes into force with effect from 1 September 2012 for a fixed term of 3 years	It may be renewed by tacit agreement for a period of three years, unless notice of termination is given by one of the signatories at least 6 months prior to the end of the three year period	3 years as from 1 September 2012	Whilst this agreements is in force, it may be modified by written amendment

Company	*Agreement*	*Date*	*Duration*	*Renewal*	*Termination*	*Revision*
AXA Assistance	European agreement on anticipating changes within AXA Assistance	2011	3 years from the date of the signature	It may be renewed by tacit agreement for a period of three years, unless notice of termination is given by one of the signatories at least 6 months prior to the end of the three year period	It may be renewed by tacit agreement for a period of three years, unless notice of termination is given by one of the signatories at least 6 months prior to the end of the three year period	Whilst this agreements is in force, it may be modified by written amendment, especially in case of changes in the geographical scope of application
AXA Group	European agreement on anticipating changes	2011	3 years	It may be renewed by tacit agreement for a period of three years, unless notice of termination is given by one of the signatories at least 6 months prior to the end of the three year period	It may be renewed by tacit agreement for a period of three years, unless notice of termination is given by one of the signatories at least 6 months prior to the end of the three year period	Whilst this agreements is in force, it may be modified by written amendment

Company	*Agreement*	*Date*	*Duration*	*Renewal*	*Termination*	*Revision*
Allianz SE	Agreement on Guidelines Concerning Work Related Stress	2011	Not defined	Not defined	It may be terminated in writing by either side subject to a period of notice of one year to take effect at the end of a calendar year	Not defined
Alstom	Agreement on the anticipation of change or developments in Alstom	2011	3 years	The parties can mutually agree to renew it	Not defined	Not defined
EADS	Group agreement on the harmonization of the variable remuneration of Senior Managers within the EADS Group	2011	Not defined	Not defined	By one of the signatories parties anytime, who must simultaneously submit a new draft agreement. In this case, renegotiation must be undertaken within 6 months following receipt	It can be modified any time at the request of one of the signatory parties with 6 months notice. It remains applicable until the revised version is signed

Company	*Agreement*	*Date*	*Duration*	*Renewal*	*Termination*	*Revision*
					of the termination notice. The provisions of this agreement remain applicable throughout the duration of the renegotiation and in case of failure to reach an agreement for a period of twelve months from the statement of disagreement	Adaptations of the agreements may be suggested following the assessment of its implementation
EADS	Agreement for the Implementation of a Success-Sharing Plan within the EADS-NV Group	2011 (this text replaces the text of 2009)	Indefinite time	Not defined	Not defined	It can be modified at any time on request of EADS Central Management or on request of the two-third majority of the European Negotiating

Company	*Agreement*	*Date*	*Duration*	*Renewal*	*Termination*	*Revision*
						Group's signatory members under a notice period of six months. As an exception to this rule, the split between EADS (70 %) and the Division (30 %) for the calculation of the economic envelope and the principle of operational objective(s) setting are considered as fundamental elements of this agreement. Accordingly they cannot be amended within five years except in the event of an exceptional circumstance

Company	*Agreement*	*Date*	*Duration*	*Renewal*	*Termination*	*Revision*
						confirmed by a joint decision of EADS Central Management and the two-third majority of the European Negotiating Group's signatory members
Air France/KLM	Framework agreement regarding the Outstations in Europe	2011	The agreement will end on 1/4/2013	Not defined	The agreement will end on 1/4/2013	Changes in this framework can only be made by mutual agreement and will only be effective after a written and signed revised document
Santander	Joint Declaration of the European Works Council (EWC) and the Central Management of Santander Group	2011	Not defined	Not defined	Not defined	Not defined

Company	*Agreement*	*Date*	*Duration*	*Renewal*	*Termination*	*Revision*
	regarding the labour relations framework for the provision of financial services					
EADS	Agreement relating to the procedure for labor negotiations at European level	2010	Indefinite	Not defined	Not defined	The signatories agree to meet at any time if necessary in order to modify the provisions of this agreement either due to changes in legislation or simply to improve the effectiveness of this agreement
Veolia Environment	Veolia Environment European Works Council agreement	2010	This Agreement is entered into for an undetermined period running from its signature. It supersedes and replaces the	Not defined	Not defined	To guarantee the ongoing adaptation of this Agreement, a follow-up committee composed of the 7 (seven) members

Company	*Agreement*	*Date*	*Duration*	*Renewal*	*Termination*	*Revision*
			Agreement dated 10 October 2005			of the Bureau has been set up. At the end of the term of office, in the 12 (twelve) months prior to the renewal of the Veolia Environnement European Works Council, the follow-up committee may make proposals for changes to this Agreement, which, after discussion, may give rise to amendments. In this case, the follow-up committee and Management will set a timetable for negotiations and may decide to set

Company	*Agreement*	*Date*	*Duration*	*Renewal*	*Termination*	*Revision*
						up an enlarged Bureau to carry out this review. (for the article on renegotiations, see clause 8.2 of the agreement)
Alstom	European Agreement	2010	Not defined	Not defined	Not defined	Not defined
Schneider Electric	European Agreement	2010	Not defined	Not defined	Not defined	Not defined
Air France/KLM	Framework agreement on sales agencies in airports (ATOs) in Europe between, on the one hand, the management of CDL Europe/North Africa and, on the other, the European Group Council	2010	Until 1 April 2012	Not defined	Until 1 April 2012	Amending is possible if both parties agree and will apply only after the written amendment of the document is duly signed
Adam Opel AG	Agreement on European	2010	No text available	No text available	No text available	No text available

Company	*Agreement*	*Date*	*Duration*	*Renewal*	*Termination*	*Revision*
	restructuring ('Opel Plan for the Future')					
GDF Suez	European group agreement relating to the employment and expertise plan	2010	Indefinite	Not defined	Not defined	Pursuant to Article L. 2222-5 of the Labour Code, this agreement may be revised at the request of Management or of one or several trade union organizations that are signatories of this agreement or having later on subscribed to it as per the provisions of Articles L.2261-7 et seq. of the Labour Code
ABB	European Appendix to ABB social policy	2009	Not defined	Not defined	Not defined	Not defined

Company	*Agreement*	*Date*	*Duration*	*Renewal*	*Termination*	*Revision*
Axa Group	Agreement on the AXA Group European Works Council	2009	Indefinite	Not defined	It can be totally or partly terminated at any time, by registered letter by the first party to take action addressed to the other signatory parties, with six months' notice	Not defined
General Motors Europe	Working time reduction	2009	Text not available	Text not available	Text not available	Text not available
ArcelorMittal	Managing & Anticipating change at ArcelorMittal (V10)	2009	This Agreement enters into force as from its signature for an indeterminate duration, except for chapter 1. Article 1.3. 'Maintaining Purchasing Power', which is valid for the	Not defined	This Agreement can, however, be terminated by either of the two parties with an advanced notice of 3 months during the first year and 6 months after, sent by registered mail with an acknowledgement	In the event that any change occurs which would disrupt the balance of commitments prevailing between the signatory partners at the date of signature of this Agreement,

Company	*Agreement*	*Date*	*Duration*	*Renewal*	*Termination*	*Revision*
			duration of 1 year after signing the agreement, period which by mutual agreement can be extended		of receipt addressed to the other party	either ArcelorMittal or the EMF could ask to modify it. The party who will take the initiative of the request will submit to the other party a draft of a modifying text
Unicredit	Joint declaration on 'equal opportunities and non-discrimination'	2009	Not defined	Not defined	Not defined	Not defined
Santander	Declaration on Social Rights and Labour Relations in Santander Group	2009	Not defined	Not defined	Not defined	Not defined
Unicredit	Joint declaration on 'training, learning and professional development'	2008	Not defined	Not defined	Not defined	Not defined

Company	*Agreement*	*Date*	*Duration*	*Renewal*	*Termination*	*Revision*
BP	Agreement on 'Business Service Centre (BSC)' Consultation	2008	Not defined	Not defined	Not defined	Not defined
Santander	Joint Declaration to be signed in the meeting on 21.05.2008 between the European Works Council and the representatives designated by grupo santander's senior management	2008	Not defined	Not defined	Not defined	Not defined
Suez	Agreement on social guarantees for Suez Group employees	2008	Indefinite time	Not defined	Not defined	It can be revised annually
Unicredit	Establishment of the Joint Commissions	2008	Not defined	Not defined	Not defined	Not defined

Company	*Agreement*	*Date*	*Duration*	*Renewal*	*Termination*	*Revision*
GDF	European agreement on the corporate social responsibility of the Gaz de France group	2008	This agreement has been reached for an initial duration of three years starting from the date it comes into force	At the end of this term, the parties will compile a general report on the actions and the progress accomplished. Depending on this report, the parties may decide to renew the agreement for a determine period of time	If either of the parties fails to serve notice of renewal of the agreement to the other part by registered letter with a receipt of acknowledgment before the end of the initial three year term, the agreement shall immediately cease to be in effect and as a matter of right shall no longer be in force	The agreement may be revised during annual assessment meeting to take into account any changes in the scope of the Gaz de France Group, in accordance with the conditions set out in the labour code
Strawood Lodging	Agreement regarding the transnational transfer of Starwood Employees	2007	This agreement is valid for 2 years and will be extended by one year each time it arrives at its end date, unless it is	This agreement is valid for 2 years and will be extended by one year each time it arrives at its end date, unless it is	This agreement is valid for 2 years and will be extended by one year each time it arrives at its end date, unless it is	Not defined

Company	*Agreement*	*Date*	*Duration*	*Renewal*	*Termination*	*Revision*
			terminated through provision of three months' notice	terminated through provision of three months' notice	terminated through provision of three months' notice	
Total	European agreement on assistance in creation, purchase or development of small and medium sized businesses	2007 (amended in 2012)	At the end of the 36 months set for the experimental period, the Total Group's general management and the European Federations of Trade Unions will meet to study the follow-ups which are advisable to give to the agreement. Negotiations will be undertaken in order to extend or adapt, by additional clauses, the text of the European agreement	At the end of the 36 months set for the experimental period, the Total Group's general management and the European Federations of Trade Unions will meet to study the follow-ups which are advisable to give to the agreement. Negotiations will be undertaken in order to extend or adapt, by additional clauses, the text of the European agreement	Not defined	At the end of the 36 months set for the experimental period, the Total Group's general management and the European Federations of Trade Unions will meet to study the follow-ups which are advisable to give to the agreement. Negotiations will be undertaken in order to extend or adapt, by additional clauses, the text of the European agreement

Company	*Agreement*	*Date*	*Duration*	*Renewal*	*Termination*	*Revision*
DaimlerChrysler	Framework Regulation with the European Works Council (EWC) on the Realignment of the Sales Organization in the European Union	2007	Not defined	Not defined	Not defined	Not defined
General Motors (Europe)	Restructuring at Antwerp	2007	Text not available	Text not available	Text not available	Text not available
General Motors (Europe)	Allocation of next Astra	2007	Text not available	Text not available	Text not available	Text not available
Suez	Group agreement – Suez Group's Social Dynamics – section on 'Employment and Expertise Plan'	2007	Indefinite	Not defined	Not defined	The agreement may be revised in accordance with the relevant provisions of the Employment Code
Schneider Electric	European Agreement on the Anticipation of Change	2007	Indefinite	Not defined	This agreement may also be terminated by the General	The signatories may jointly propose the revision of any

Company	*Agreement*	*Date*	*Duration*	*Renewal*	*Termination*	*Revision*
					Management or by the EMF. The agreement shall cease to apply after a three-month notice period when revoked either by the General Management or the EMF	part of this agreement, or of the entire agreement. The proposed revisions shall replace the previous text as soon as they are agreed by Management and the EMF
Kraft Foods	European Framework Agreement regarding Project One Europe to be Concluded Between Kraft Foods Europe Management and the Employee Representatives	2007	Not defined	Not defined	Not defined	Not defined

Company	*Agreement*	*Date*	*Duration*	*Renewal*	*Termination*	*Revision*
DaimlerChrysler	Framework agreement for information and consultation with employees and employee representatives in the local European operations of DaimlerChrysler AG	2006	Not defined	Not defined	Not defined	Not defined
Allianz SE	Agreement concerning the participation of employees in Allianz SE	2006	Indefinite	If agreement is not terminated, it shall be extended for one-year periods, unless terminated subject to a prior notice period of at least 6 months prior to the expiration of the respective extension period	Yes, in writing by both side subject to a prior notice of 1 year, at the first time 6 years after its entry into force	Not defined

Company	*Agreement*	*Date*	*Duration*	*Renewal*	*Termination*	*Revision*
Total	European agreement on equal opportunity Total Group	2005	Not defined	Not defined	Not defined	Not defined
EADS	Agreement on the European Works Council of EADS N.V. and its derived committees concluded between European Aeronautic Defence and Space Company EADS N.V. and its employees' representatives	2005	Indefinite	Not defined	By both parties, any time, with 6 months notice period. Proposal for a new agreement must be submitted by the terminating party	Possibility to amend it if parties deem it necessary for changes in European legislation. Moreover, possibility to renegotiate the agreement at any time if both parties jointly decide it
Philip Morris (Kraft Jacobs)	Guidelines on information and consultation employment	2005	Text not available	Text not available	Text not available	Text not available

Company	*Agreement*	*Date*	*Duration*	*Renewal*	*Termination*	*Revision*
Unilever	Agreed joint statement UEWC and Unilever on protection of personal data	2004	Not defined	Not defined	Not defined	Not defined
General Electric Plastics (Europe)	Agreement on Pre-employment screening ('background checks')	2004	Not defined	Not defined	Not defined	Not defined
Total	European agreement – social platform Total Group	2004	Not defined	Not defined	Not defined	Not defined
Deutsche Bank	Common Standpoint of the Deutsche Bank Group and the EWC	2004	Not defined	Not defined	Not defined	Not defined
Ford (Europe)	IOS restructuring: maintenance of jobs, investments, employability	2004	Text not available	Text not available	Text not available	Text not available

Company	*Agreement*	*Date*	*Duration*	*Renewal*	*Termination*	*Revision*
General Motors (Europe)	Restructuring Framework	2004	Not defined	Not defined	Not defined	Not defined
General Electric Plastics (Europe)	Amendment to the GEPE EBR Agreement on the introduction of regulations (including methodology and practice) during negotiations between the GEPE Central Management ('CM') and the GEPE EWC ('EWC')	2003	Not defined	Not defined	Not defined	It will be subject of review procedure established in the GEPE EWC agreement
Ford (Europe)	Ford of Europe and the Ford European Works Council (FEWC) Agreed upon Social Rights and Social Responsibility Principles	2003	Not defined	Not defined	Not defined	Not defined

Company	*Agreement*	*Date*	*Duration*	*Renewal*	*Termination*	*Revision*
General Electric Plastics (Europe)	GEPE Agreement on use of electronic communication systems	2002	Not defined	Not defined	Not defined	Not defined
General Motors (Europe)	General Motors Europe and the European Employee Forum agree on Principles of Social Responsibility	2002	Not defined	Not defined	Not defined	Not defined
Philip Morris (Kraft Jacobs)	Processing key HR data (part of EWC agreement)	2002	Text not available	Text not available	Text not available	Text not available
ENI	Agreement report	2002	Not defined	Not defined	Not defined	Not defined
Kraft Foods	European Framework Agreement regarding Project One Europe to be Concluded between Kraft Foods Europe Management and	2002	Text not available	Text not available	Text not available	Text not available

Company	Agreement	Date	Duration	Renewal	Termination	Revision
	the Employee Representatives					
Danone	Joint opinion on the applicable social standards for all the undertakings concerned by the restructuring programme of the Biscuits Pole in Europe presented on 29 March 2001	2001	Not defined	Not defined	Not defined	Not defined
Bouygues	European Social Charter of the Bouygues Group	2001	Not defined	Not defined	Not defined	Not defined
Unilever	Responsible Restructuring	2001	Not defined	Not defined	Not defined	Not defined
General Motors (Europe)	European framework, dated 5 March 2001 at 20:30 ('The following framework agreement is in	2001	Not defined	Not defined	Not defined	Not defined

Company	*Agreement*	*Date*	*Duration*	*Renewal*	*Termination*	*Revision*
	relation of GM's current restructuring initiatives')					
Philip Morris (Kraft Jacobs)	Agreement on the use of data recorded by sales forces	2001	Text not available	Text not available	Text not available	Text not available
Philip Morris (Kraft Jacobs)	Agreement by the EU Assembly for the workforce of Philip Morris tobacco companies in the European regions of Philip Morris on the protection of personal data processed by ITSC Europe S.A.R.L	2001	The present agreement shall come into force immediately after it is signed for an indefinite term and will remain in force as long as one of the parties does not terminate it in writing with a three months notice	Not defined	Should the provider blatantly break the clauses of the present agreement on the protection of data, the client is authorized to terminate the agreement without notice. Should the case arise, all data stored and processed shall immediately be sent back to the client	Not defined

Company	*Agreement*	*Date*	*Duration*	*Renewal*	*Termination*	*Revision*
General Motors (Europe)	Framework 'regarding "Project Olympia" initiatives'	2001	Not defined	Not defined	Not defined	Not defined
General Motors (Europe)	Framework	2000	Not defined	Not defined	Not defined	Not defined
Ford (Europe)	Joint Venture CFT: maintenance of Ford contracts, investments	2000	Text not available	Text not available	Text not available	Text not available
Ford	Agreement governing the separation of the Ford Visteon organization	2000	Not defined	Not defined	Not defined	Not defined
Vivendi (known as from 2003 as Veolia)	Charter on the safety at the workplace in the Group	1999	Not defined	Not defined	Not defined	Not defined
Philip Morris (Kraft Jacobs)	Principles on the introduction of Euro	1999	Text not available	Text not available	Text not available	Text not available

Company	*Agreement*	*Date*	*Duration*	*Renewal*	*Termination*	*Revision*
Philip Morris (Kraft Jacobs)	Code of conduct smoking at the workplace	1998	Text not available	Text not available	Text not available	Text not available
ENI	Agreement	1996	Not defined	Not defined	Not defined	Not defined

§2.08 FOLLOW-UP PROCEDURES

Follow-up procedures are very important because they intend to ensure that TCAs become effective instruments used by MNEs, trade unions and workers' representatives for regulating the labour relations within an enterprise.

In particular, different steps have to be taken for ensuring the effectiveness of IFAs and EFAs: first, dissemination; second, implementation; third, monitoring; last, dispute resolution. These diverse stages will be analysed in the following subsections by giving examples of TCAs that contain provisions on these issues. This analysis will show whether the mechanisms set up by the signatory parties are similar in IFAs and EFAs.

[A] Dissemination, Implementation, Monitoring and Dispute Settlement in International Framework Agreements

In order to assess whether the IFAs listed in Table 2.1 can be regarded as effective instruments at the disposal of MNEs and workers' representatives, it is opportune to verify which follow-up procedures are covered by these agreements.

To that end, Table 2.5 shows which agreements set forth dissemination, implementation, monitoring and dispute settlement mechanisms. More information can be found in the texts of the agreements and in the database of the European Commission on TCAs.

Table 2.5 Follow-Up Procedures in IFAs Signed by MNEs with More Than 80,000 Employees

Company	*Agreement*	*Date*	*Dissemination*	*Implementation*	*Monitoring*	*Dispute Resolution*
GDF Suez	Global Health and Safety Agreement of the GDF Suez Group	2014	X	X	X	
Itaú-Unibanco S.A.	Framework Agreement between Banco Itaú-Unibanco S.A. and Union Network International for the Americas	2014	X	X	X	X
Metro	Joint Statement of Metro Group & UNI Global Union	2013			X	

Company	*Agreement*	*Date*	*Dissemination*	*Implementation*	*Monitoring*	*Dispute Resolution*
Renault	Global framework agreement on social, societal and environmental responsibility between the Renault Group, the Renault Group Works' Council and IndustriALL Global Union	2013	X	X	X	X
Volkswagen	Charter on Temporary Work	2012		X	X	X
ThyssenKrupp AG	Global agreement of an idea management Health & Safety at ThyssenKrupp Elevator Operating Units	2012		X	X	X
Ford	Global framework agreement	2012			X	X
Inditex	Global agreement on the involvement of unions to monitor the respect of worker's conditions at supplier	2012		X		
Siemens	International Framework Agreement between Siemens AG, the Central Works Council of Siemens AG, the IG Metall and the IndustriALL Global Union	2012	X	X	X	X
Banco do Brasil	Global Framework Agreement for the Americas Union Network International (UNI) and Banco do Brasil	2011, 2013	X	X	X	X
Danone	Danone/IUF Agreement on health, safety, working conditions and stress	2011	X	X	X	X
Sodexo	International Framework Agreement	2011	X	X	X	X
Petrobas	Terms of Understanding of Good Labor Relations	2011	X		X	X

Company	*Agreement*	*Date*	*Dissemination*	*Implementation*	*Monitoring*	*Dispute Resolution*
GDF Suez	Group agreement on fundamental principles regarding health and safety	2010	X	X	X	X
GDF Suez	Global Agreement on Fundamental Rights, Social Dialogue and Sustainable Development	2010	X	X	X	X
France Telecom (now Orange S.A.)	Agreement of France Telecom's Worldwide Works Council	2010			X	X
Shoprite Checkers	Global Framework agreement	2010	X	X		X
Volkswagen	Charter on Labour Relations within the Volkswagen Group	2009	X	X	X	X
Inditex	Global agreement for implementation of fundamental labour rights and decent work	2009	X	X	X	X
ArcelorMittal	Agreement on minimum requirements for Plant level Joint H&S Committees	2008		X		X
ArcelorMittal	Terms of reference for a joint global OSH committee in Arcelor Mittal	2008				
G4S	A global Agreement: Ethical Employment Partnership	2008	X	X	X	X
PSA Peugeot	Agreement on the extension of the strategic equal committee	2008	X			
ThyssenKrupp AG	Principles of Social Responsibility in Labor Relations in the ThyssenKrupp Group	2007	X	X	X	X

Company	*Agreement*	*Date*	*Dissemination*	*Implementation*	*Monitoring*	*Dispute Resolution*
Siemens	Joint Statement between group management and Siemens Europe Committee concerning Compliance	2007		X	X	
Danone	Convention on Diversity	2007	X	X	X	X
Inditex	International Framework Agreement on the Implementation of International Labour Standards throughout the Inditex Supply Chain	2007	X	X	X	X
Suez	Agreement on Commitment to promoting equality and diversity within the Group	2007	X	X	X	X
Suez	Group Agreement on Employees Ownership Scheme	2007	X		X	X
France Telecom	Worldwide Agreement on Fundamental Labour Rights within the France Telecom Group	2006	X	X	X	X
PSA Peugeot	International Framework Agreement on PSA Peugeot Citroën's Social Responsibility	2006	X	X	X	X
DaimlerChrysler	Occupational Health and Safety Principles of DaimlerChrysler	2006				
Securitas	Agreement between Securitas AB (publ) and Union Network International and Swedish Transport Workers' Union on the development of good working relations in the Securitas group	2006	X	X	X	X
EDF	Agreement on EDF Group Corporate Social Responsibility	2005, 2009	X	X	X	X

Company	*Agreement*	*Date*	*Dissemination*	*Implementation*	*Monitoring*	*Dispute Resolution*
EADS	International Framework Agreement	2005	X	X	X	X
Danone	Fundamental Social Principles	2005				
Danone	Convention on the setting up of social indicators at group level	2005				
Coca Cola	Joint Coca-Cola and IUF Statement	2005			X	
BMW	Joint Declaration on Human Rights and on Working Conditions in the BMW Group	2005	X	X	X	
Arcelor	Worldwide Agreement on the Principles of Arcelor's Corporate Social responsibility	2005	X	X	X	X
Bosch	Basic Principles of Social Responsibility at Bosch	2004	X	X		X
Lukoil	Agreement between International Federation of Chemical, Energy, Mine and General Workers' Unions, Russian Oil and Gas Workers	2004	X	X	X	
	Union And Open Joint Stock Company 'Oil Company LUKOIL'					
H&M	Agreement between H&M hennes & Mauritz AB (H &M) and Union Network International (UNI) on Cooperation in order to secure and promote fundamental worker's rights at H&M's workplaces worldwide	2004		X		

Company	*Agreement*	*Date*	*Dissemination*	*Implementation*	*Monitoring*	*Dispute Resolution*
Renault	Renault Group employees' fundamental rights declaration	2004	X	X	X	
ISS	Uni – ISS Global Agreement	2003, 2008	X		X	X
ENI	Agreement on transnational industrial relations and corporate social responsibility	2002, 2004, 2009	X	X	X	X
DaimlerChrysler	Social Responsibility Principles of DaimlerChrysler	2002	X	X	X	X
Volkswagen	Declaration on Social Rights and Industrial Relationships at Volkswagen	2002	X	X	X	
Suez	Charter Health and Safety at Work	2002	X		X	
Telefonica	UNI-Telefonica Code of conduct	2001	X	X		X
IKEA	Framework agreement between IKEA and the IFBWW	2001		X	X	X
Hochtief	Framework agreement between Hochtief and IFBWW	2000	X	X	X	X
Carrefour	Global Agreement Carrefour – UNI Union Network International	2000				
Suez-Lyonnaise des Eaux	International social charter	1998	X		X	
Danone	Convention applicable in the event of changes in business activities affecting employment or working conditions	1997, 2005		X		

Company	*Agreement*	*Date*	*Dissemination*	*Implementation*	*Monitoring*	*Dispute Resolution*
Vivendi (Veolia Générale des Eaux)	Charter of fundamental social rights	1996	X			X
Accor	Agreement between the IUF and the Accor Group on Trade Union Rights	1995				X
Danone	Convention on trade union rights	1994, 2005		X		
Danone	Convention on skills training	1992, 2005				
Danone	Convention on economic and social data in Group Danone companies	1989, 2005				
Danone	Convention for the promotion of equality of men and women in the workplace	1989, 2005		X		
Danone	Common viewpoint IUF/BSN	1998				

This subsection will be divided into four parts: first, the dissemination of IFAs will be analysed; second, attention will be paid to the implementation procedures set up by the signatory parties and, especially, to the bodies in charge of this task; third, monitoring mechanisms will be addressed; fourth and last, the different modes of dispute resolution will be examined.

Concerning the first issue, the dissemination of the texts of IFAs is the first important step to be taken after the conclusion of these agreements. More than half of the IFAs analysed (39 out of 62) contained a clause on this issue. More specifically, different methods have been set up in order to promote the spread of the IFAs' content among all the parties involved, be it employees, trade unions' affiliated organizations, the management of the company's offices around the world, the company's subsidiaries and at times also business partners.

For instance, the distribution of the text of the agreement is a good vehicle for disseminating its content. In many agreements, either the company or the signatory on the employees' side or both parties ensure the distribution of the agreements to all companies of the group and/or to all the employees and /or affiliated unions. More specifically, the ways of dissemination vary from text to text, e.g. internal means of communication, publication in the website of the company.

By way of example, the Lukoil 'Agreement between International Federation of Chemical, Energy, Mine and General Workers' Unions, Russian Oil and Gas Workers Union And Open Joint Stock Company "Oil Company LUKOIL" (2004)' reads:

> ICEM will distribute copies of the Agreement to all its member unions, including those that organise employees in LUKOIL companies around the world, and will broadly publicise the existence of the Agreement and explain its implications to the unions organising workers within LUKOIL. LUKOIL will in the same manner distribute copies of the Agreement to all LUKOIL offices in the relevant local languages of the countries concerned.[338]

The EDF 'Agreement on EDF Group Corporate Social Responsibility' (2005-2009) stipulates:

> All the signatories agree to convey this Agreement to the employees of the Group via their own vectors of communication. EDF Group shall organise specific communication for its managers so they may lead and support the implementation of this Agreement for their teams.
>
> EDF Group shall communicate the existence of this text to its subcontractors, in particular the principles concerning them.[339]

In addition, the texts of IFAs are often translated in relevant national languages where the MNE operates. This is an important tool in order to ensure a proper understanding of the agreements by all parties involved.

The PSA Peugeot 'International Framework Agreement on PSA Peugeot Citroën's Social Responsibility' (2006-2010) sets forth:

> PSA PEUGEOT CITROËN undertakes to disseminate information widely about the content of this agreement to the employees of the Group. This text is therefore broadcast throughout the Group through internal communication tools and translated into all languages.[340]

Finally, two IFAs concluded by (GDF) Suez in 2007 and 2010, respectively the 'Group agreement on fundamental principles regarding health and safety' and the 'Group Agreement on Employees Ownership Scheme', prescribe a specific mean of dissemination by filing the agreement at the registry of the relevant court. Both the agreements read that:

> The Agreement shall be filed at the Paris Departmental Directorate for Labour and Employment ("DDTE") and the registry of the Paris Industrial Court ("Conseil de Prud'hommes").[341]

338. Text available at <http://ec.europa.eu/employment_social/empl_portal/transnational_agreements/Lukoil_Agreement_EN.pdf> accessed 25 May 2014.
339. Text available at <http://ec.europa.eu/employment_social/empl_portal/transnational_agreements/EDF_IFA_EN.pdf> accessed 25 May 2014.
340. See footnote n. 321.
341. Text of the EFAs available at <http://ec.europa.eu/employment_social/empl_portal/transnational_agreements/GDF%20SUEZ%20_%20H&SAgreement_EN.pdf> and <http://ec.europa.eu/employment_social/empl_portal/transnational_agreements/Suez_Association_EN.pdf> accessed 20 June 2014.

Moving to the second aspect, namely the implementation of IFAs, 42 out of 62 IFAs analysed deal with this issue. In particular, different actors are in charge of carrying it out, often at local and site level. Moreover, the implementation of the agreement often occur through regular dialogue between the signatory parties.

Different actors are in charge of ensuring the correct and effective implementation of IFAs: the company, senior managers, heads of each business, trade unions and/or works councils.

For example, the Arcelor 'Worldwide Agreement on the Principles of Arcelor's Corporate Social responsibility' (2005) reads:

> ARCELOR undertakes to implement the procedures and principles defined in this agreement and to integrate them in its subsidiaries' policies at the various national and local levels within a reasonable timescale. On the other hand, the Trade Union Federations undertake to contribute to the success of this approach by encouraging the trade union organisations represented within ARCELOR to participate constructively with the personnel in seeking and implementing the means to achieve the objectives referred to in this agreement and to respect the company's people and assets.[342]

The EADS 'International Framework Agreement' (2005) stipulates:

> The head of each business is responsible for ensuring compliance with these principles and will take appropriate measures to ensure their implementation (...). Trade unions or works council representatives may inform central management orally or in writing of any breach of one or more terms of the aforementioned provisions.[343]

The Bosch 'Basic Principles of Social Responsibility at Bosch' (2004) reads:

> Responsibility for their implementation lies with the senior management of the respective divisions, regional subsidiaries and company locations.[344]

The PSA Peugeot 'International Framework Agreement on PSA Peugeot Citroën's Social Responsibility' (2006-2010) reads:

> Each subsidiary undertakes to negotiate with the trade union organisations, the implementation of actions which meets the principles and undertakings of this chapter, in particular in respect of training, professional development and safety in the workplace (...). In the main countries, the implementation work gives rise to the drawing up of a work programme.[345]

As to the monitoring procedures, this follow-up instrument represents the most important stage for ensuring the effectiveness and compliance with the IFAs. Two third of the IFAs examined (42 out of 62) address this issue. Specifically, some agreements set up a system of joint assessment of the implementation of the agreement by the signatory parties and sometimes via a body composed of their representatives. In

342. See footnote n. 310.
343. See footnote n. 193.
344. See footnote n. 314.
345. See footnote n. 321.

addition, monitoring committees are established with the end of periodically verify the correct implementation of the IFAs by the parties and the addressees involved. These review committees are generally composed of employees and management's representatives and, at times, by representatives of local trade unions. Some examples will be provided in the following paragraphs.

The Itaú-Unibanco S.A 'Framework Agreement between Banco Itaú-Unibanco S.A. and Union Network International for the Americas' reads:

> The parties, in accordance with the laws of each country, will be responsible for carrying out this framework agreement, maintaining an ongoing dialogue, and meeting at the end of each year of its duration to assess its implementation.[346]

The Danone 'Danone / IUF Agreement on health, safety, working conditions and stress' (2011) reads that:

> Danone and IUF agree to the establishment of joint monitoring of this Agreement in the Group companies. This monitoring shall consist of at least one annual specified meeting of the IUF/Danone Steering Committee to analyse the following indicators which will be included in the annual report of financial and social indicators to all the CIC members (...).[347]

The Securitas 'Agreement between Securitas AB (publ) and Union Network International and Swedish Transport Workers' Union on the development of good working relations in the Securitas group;' (2006) reads:

> In order to fulfil the implementation of the Code the parties agree to set up an implementation group (...). The Implementation Group will meet annually to review the implementation of this Agreement and any reported breaches of its terms (...). The parties accept that effective local monitoring of this Agreement must involve the local management, the employees and their representatives, health and safety representatives and local trade unions.[348]

The GDF Suez 'Group Agreement on fundamental principles regarding health and safety' (2010) stipulates:

> The Health and Safety Management Committee is responsible for monitoring the Agreement in accordance with the conditions laid down in Article 2.3. It shall be up to the Health and Safety Management Committee to define the indicators as well as the terms to monitor and control.[349]

Finally, the last follow-up instrument is the establishment of mechanisms of dispute resolution to be used in case of IFAs' infringements by the parties and addressees involved. Here, 38 out of 62 IFAs include a provision on dispute resolution, which

346. Text available at <http://ec.europa.eu/employment_social/empl_portal/transnational_agreements/ITAU_EN.pdf> accessed 24 May 2014.
347. See footnote n. 186.
348. Text available at <http://ec.europa.eu/employment_social/empl_portal/transnational_agreements/Securitas_IFA_EN.pdf> accessed 26 May 2014.
349. See footnote n. 341.

specifies the actors who are entitled to solve any disagreement concerning the interpretation of the content of the agreement and/or its application.

For instance, the Petrobas 'Terms of Understanding of Good Labor Relations' (2011) establishes that both the signatory parties will jointly examined issues arisen. According to this IFA:

> Petrobras and ICEM agree that they will both be available continuously to administer and inform on any problem encountered in the application of the present terms and to develop the solutions. The parties agree that any divergence based on the interpretation in the application of the present terms will be examined jointly in order to be explained.[350]

Furthermore, in the GDF Suez 'Group agreement on fundamental principles regarding health and safety' (2010), the monitoring committee is in charge of solving disputes. According to this agreement:

> Questions relating to the interpretation of this agreement are the sole prerogative of the above-mentioned monitoring committee.[351]

In addition, in some IFAs, national courts or arbitrators are in charge of resolving disputes that arise between the signatory parties. By way of example, the Arcelor 'Worldwide Agreement on the Principles of Arcelor's Corporate Social Responsibility' (2005) reads:

> Any disputes will fall within the exclusive competence of the Luxembourg courts.[352]

Further, the EADS 'International Framework Agreement' (2005) reads:

> In a situation of conflict, the arbitration process will be mutually agreed by the EADS head of Human Resources and the European Works Council.[353]

Next to the actor in charge of dispute resolution, it is interesting to observe that some IFAs establish a complex procedure in order to solve the dispute arisen between the signatory parties. This procedure is sometimes based on the principle of subsidiarity; in other words, before the complaint is brought to the attention of the management at local level and only if it is not solved at this level the central management will be made

350. Text available at <http://ec.europa.eu/employment_social/empl_portal/transnational_agreements/Petrobras_%20GFA_EN.pdf> accessed 26 May 2014.
351. See footnote n. 341. In addition, also the Interpretation Committee has been regarded as a body in charge of solving disputes. See the Danone 'Danone/IUF Agreement on health, safety, working conditions and stress' (2010). According to this IFA: "The application of this Agreement in one or several Danone companies shall not override pre-existing situations that are more favourable to employees, whether derived from national laws, the application of a collective agreement at national or any other level, or pre-existing custom at the site. Any dispute on this point shall be referred to the Interpretation Committee."
352. See footnote n. 310.
353. See footnote n. 193.

aware of the issue.[354] An example of this multifaceted procedure is given by the G4S 'A global Agreement: Ethical Employment Partnership' (2008), according to which:[355]

> In the event of a dispute arising between a UNI affiliate and G4S management regarding the interpretation or application of this agreement, the following procedures will apply:
>
> a) Complaint by UNI affiliates
>   i. The complaints should first be raised with the local management;
>   ii. If the complaint is still unresolved with the local management, it may be referred to the Country Manager by the appropriate trade union where recognized or UNI if recognition has yet not been established;
>   iii. If still unresolved, the complaint will be referred to the agreed representatives of UNI who may raise the matter with the Company's Director of Employee Relations;
>   iv. Where infringements are confirmed, the Director of Employee Relations will raise these with the responsible member of management who will ensure corrective steps are taken;
>   v. Disputes that cannot be solved in this way, or which related directly to the terms of this agreement should be referred to the Review meeting for discussion and resolution;
>
> b) Complaints by G4S companies or managers
>   i. The complaints should first be raised with the local union;
>   ii. If the complaint is not resolved with the local union, it may be referred to the national office by the company or manager(s) concerned;
>   iii. If still unresolved, the complaint will be referred to the Company's Director of Employee Relations who may raise the matter with the agreed representatives of UNI;
>   iv. Where infringements are confirmed, UNI will raise these with the responsible UNI affiliate who will ensure corrective steps are taken;
>   v. Disputes that cannot be solved in this way, or which related directly to the terms of this agreement should be referred to the Review meeting for discussion and resolution;
>
> In the event that parties are unable to resolve a dispute concerning the application of this agreement after discussion at the Review Meeting, by mutual agreement the matter may be referred to a neutral arbiter to find a mediated solution.[356]

The procedures mentioned in this section can be considered as a good way to ensure the effectiveness of IFAs, which hence need strong follow-up instruments in order to be regarded as an effective vehicle of regulating the labour relations at company level.

354. Sobczak, 'Ensuring the effective implementation of transnational company agreements' (n. 98) 146.
355. Just like the IFA concluded by G4S, also the ISS IFA establishes a similar procedure. For the text of the latter see footnote n. 307.
356. Text available at <http://ec.europa.eu/employment_social/empl_portal/transnational_agreements/G4S-GlobalAgreement_EN.pdf> accessed 26 May 2014.

However, despite the fact that most of the IFAs examined contain follow up instruments, it is still very difficult to find out whether and how often these procedures have been used.[357]

[B] Dissemination, Implementation, Monitoring and Dispute Settlement in European Framework Agreements at Company Level

This subsection is devoted to the analysis of the follow-up procedures established in the EFAs listed in Table 2.2. The aim pursued is to identify similarities and differences existing between IFAs and EFAs on this aspect.

Table 2.6 shows the EFAs that include provisions related to the communication and notification of these agreements as well as the procedures to implement, monitor and solve the disputes arisen with regard to the EFAs at issue.

Table 2.6 Follow-Up Procedures in EFAs Signed by MNEs with More Than 80,000 Employees

Company	*Agreement*	*Date*	*Dissemination*	*Implementation*	*Monitoring*	*Dispute Resolution*
Michelin	European framework agreement on social responsibility and sustainable development	2014	Text not available	Text not available	Text not available	Text not available
Air France/KLM	Framework agreement regarding the Air France KLM and Martinair Cargo organization in Europe	2013			X	
Air France/KLM	Framework agreement regarding the Outstation and commercial organizations in Europe	2013		X	X	

357. On this topic, see Sobczak, 'Ensuring the effective implementation of transnational company agreements' (n. 97) and Welz, 'A Qualitative Analysis of International Framework Agreements: Implementation and Impact' (n. 189) 38-60.

Company	*Agreement*	*Date*	*Dissemination*	*Implementation*	*Monitoring*	*Dispute Resolution*
Air France/KLM	Social Rights and Ethics Charter	2013	X	X	X	
Allianz SE	Agreement on guidelines concerning Lifelong Learning	2012		X	X	
Veolia Environment	Letter of commitment from the General Human Resources Management and the members of the Bureau of Veolia environment's European Works Council	2012	X		X	
Alstom	European agreement on social commitments during the transition period of the Joint-venture between Alstom and Shanghai Electric on Boilers	2012			X	
GDF Suez	GDF Suez Group European agreement on professional equality between men and women	2012	X	X	X	X
BNP Paribas	European social charter – employment management agreement	2012		X	X	
AXA Assistance	European agreement on anticipating changes within AXA Assistance	2011		X	X	
AXA Group	European agreement on anticipating changes	2011		X	X	

Company	*Agreement*	*Date*	*Dissemination*	*Implementation*	*Monitoring*	*Dispute Resolution*
Allianz SE	Agreement on Guidelines Concerning Work Related Stress	2011		X	X	
Alstom	Agreement on the anticipation of change or developments in Alstom	2011	X	X	X	
EADS	Group agreement on the harmonization of the variable remuneration of Senior Managers within the EADS Group	2011				
EADS	Agreement for the Implementation of a Success-Sharing Plan within the EADS-NV Group	2011			X	
Air France/KLM	Framework agreement regarding the Outstations in Europe	2011		X	X	
Santander	Joint Declaration of the European Works Council (EWCs) and the Central Management of Santander Group regarding the labour relations framework for the provision of financial services	2011	X			
EADS	Agreement relating to the procedure for labor negotiations at European level	2010				

Company	*Agreement*	*Date*	*Dissemination*	*Implementation*	*Monitoring*	*Dispute Resolution*
Veolia Environment	Veolia Environment European Works Council agreement	2010				X
Alstom	European Agreement	2010		X	X	
Schneider Electric	European Agreement	2010		X	X	
Air France/KLM	Framework agreement on sales agencies in airports (ATOs) in Europe between, on the one hand, the management of CDL Europe/North Africa and, on the other, the European Group Council	2010			X	
Adam Opel AG*	Agreement on European restructuring ('Opel Plan for the Future')	2010	Text not available	Text not available	Text not available	Text not available
GDF Suez	European group agreement relating to the employment and expertise plan	2010	X	X	X	X
ABB	European Appendix to ABB social policy	2009		X	X	X
Axa Group	Agreement on the AXA Group European Works Council	2009	Not relevant	Not relevant	Not relevant	Not relevant
General Motors (Europe)*	Working time reduction	2009	Text not available	Text not available	Text not available	Text not available
ArcelorMittal	Managing & Anticipating change at ArcelorMittal (V10)	2009	X		X	X

Company	*Agreement*	*Date*	*Dissemination*	*Implementation*	*Monitoring*	*Dispute Resolution*
Unicredit	Joint declaration on 'equal opportunities and non-discrimination'	2009		X	X	
Santander	Declaration on Social Rights and Labour Relations in Santander Group	2009	X			
Unicredit	Joint declaration on 'training, learning and professional development'	2008			X	
BP	Agreement on 'Business Service Centre (BSC)' Consultation	2008		X		X
Santander	Joint Declaration to be signed in the meeting on 21.05.2008 between the European Works Council and the representatives designated by grupo santander's senior management	2008				
Suez	Agreement on social guarantees for Suez Group employees	2008	X		X	X
Unicredit	Establishment of the Joint Commissions	2008				
GDF	European agreement on the corporate social responsibility of the Gaz de France group	2008	X	X	X	X

Company	*Agreement*	*Date*	*Dissemination*	*Implementation*	*Monitoring*	*Dispute Resolution*
Strawood Lodging	Agreement regarding the transnational transfer of Starwood Employees	2007			X	
Total	European agreement on assistance in creation, purchase or development of small and medium sized businesses	2007 (amended in 2012)	X	X	X	
DaimlerChrysler	Framework Regulation with the European Works Council (EWC) on the Realignment of the Sales Organization in the European Union	2007		X		
General Motors (Europe)*	Restructuring at Antwerp	2007	Text not available	Text not available	Text not available	Text not available
General Motors (Europe)*	Allocation of next Astra	2007	Text not available	Text not available	Text not available	Text not available
Suez	Group agreement – Suez Group's Social Dynamics – section on 'Employment and Expertise Plan'	2007	X	X	X	X
Schneider Electric	European Agreement on the Anticipation of Change	2007	X	X	X	X
Kraft Foods	European Framework Agreement regarding Project One Europe to be Concluded Between Kraft Foods Europe Management and the Employee Representatives	2007				

Company	*Agreement*	*Date*	*Dissemination*	*Implementation*	*Monitoring*	*Dispute Resolution*
DaimlerChrysler	Framework agreement for information and consultation with employees and employee representatives in the local European operations of DaimlerChrysler AG	2006		X		
Allianz SE	Agreement concerning the participation of employees in Allianz SE	2006	Not relevant	Not relevant	Not relevant	Not relevant
Total	European agreement on equal opportunity Total Group	2005	X	X	X	
EADS	Agreement on the European Works Council of EADS N.V. and its derived committees	2005	Not relevant	Not relevant	Not relevant	Not relevant
	concluded between European Aeronautic Defence and Space Company EADS N.V. and its employees' representatives					
Philip Morris (Kraft Jacobs)*	Guidelines on information and consultation employment	2005	Text not available	Text not available	Text not available	Text not available
Unilever	Agreed joint statement UEWC and Unilever on protection of personal data	2004		X	X	

Company	*Agreement*	*Date*	*Dissemination*	*Implementation*	*Monitoring*	*Dispute Resolution*
General Electric Plastics (Europe)	Agreement on Pre-employment screening ('background checks')	2004		X		
Total	European agreement – social platform Total Group	2004	X		X	X
Deutsche Bank	Common Standpoint of the Deutsche Bank Group and the EWC	2004				
Ford (Europe)*	IOS restructuring: maintenance of jobs, investments, employability	2004	Text not available	Text not available	Text not available	Text not available
General Motors (Europe)	Restructuring Framework	2004		X		
General Electric Plastics (Europe)	Amendment to the GEPE EBR Agreement on the introduction of regulations (including methodology and practice) during negotiations between the GEPE Central Management ('CM') and the GEPE EWC ('EWC')	2003				
Ford (Europe)	Ford of Europe and the Ford European Works Council (FEWC) Agreed upon Social Rights and Social Responsibility Principles	2003	X	X	X	

Company	*Agreement*	*Date*	*Dissemination*	*Implementation*	*Monitoring*	*Dispute Resolution*
General Electric Plastics (Europe)	GEPE Agreement on use of electronic communication systems	2002				
General Motors (Europe)	General Motors Europe and the European Employee Forum agree on Principles of Social Responsibility	2002	X	X	X	X
Philip Morris (Kraft Jacobs)*	Processing key HR data (part of EWC agreement)	2002	Text not available	Text not available	Text not available	Text not available
ENI	Agreement report	2002				
Kraft Foods	European Framework Agreement regarding Project One Europe to be Concluded Between Kraft Foods Europe Management and the Employee Representatives	2002	Text not available	Text not available	Text not available	Text not available
Danone	Joint opinion on the applicable social standards for all the undertakings concerned by the restructuring programme of the Biscuits Pole in Europe presented on 29 March 2001	2001	X	X	X	X
Bouygues	European Social Charter of the Bouygues Group	2001	X	X	X	
Unilever	Responsible Restructuring	2001				

Company	*Agreement*	*Date*	*Dissemination*	*Implementation*	*Monitoring*	*Dispute Resolution*
General Motors (Europe)	European framework, dated 5 March 2001 at 20:30 ('The following framework agreement is in relation of GM's current restructuring initiatives')	2001		X		
Philip Morris (Kraft Jacobs)*	Agreement on the use of data recorded by sales forces	2001	Text not available	Text not available	Text not available	Text not available
Philip Morris (Kraft Jacobs)	Agreement by the EU Assembly for the workforce of Philip Morris tobacco companies in the European regions of Philip Morris on the protection of personal data processed by ITSC Europe S.A.R.L.	2001			X	
General Motors (Europe)	Framework 'regarding "Project Olympia" initiatives'	2001		X		
General Motors (Europe)	Framework	2000		X		X
Ford (Europe)*	Joint Venture CFT: maintenance of Ford contracts, investments	2000	Text not available	Text not available	Text not available	Text not available
Ford	Agreement governing the separation of the Ford Visteon organization	2000		X	X	X
Vivendi	Charter on the safety at the workplace in the Group	1999	X	X	X	

Company	*Agreement*	*Date*	*Dissemination*	*Implementation*	*Monitoring*	*Dispute Resolution*
Philip Morris (Kraft Jacobs)*	Principles on the introduction of euro	1999	Text not available	Text not available	Text not available	Text not available
Philip Morris (Kraft Jacobs)*	Code of conduct smoking at the workplace	1998	Text not available	Text not available	Text not available	Text not available
ENI	Agreement	1996 (the text was updated in 2004)				

Like in the previous subsection, this analysis will be divided in four parts, which will take into account the different follow up instruments introduced by the parties of the EFAs at issue.

First and foremost, not all the EFAs examined contain provisions regarding the mode of dissemination of the agreements. In fact, only less than half of the European texts (20 out of 60)[358] set up mechanisms to communicate and notify the agreements to employees and subsidiaries, among others. The ways introduced to spread the knowledge of the EFAs are, however, akin to those contained in the IFAs; for instance the distribution of copies of the agreement, the notification to the parties in accordance with national practices and the translation of the text of the agreement in different languages in order to facilitate its understanding. In addition to that, a further way to disseminate the agreements has been introduced especially in EFAs signed by MNEs headquartered in France: the registration of the agreement with the competent authorities[359] and/or its delivery to the relevant labour court. Moreover, two EFAs, the Vivendi 'Charter on the safety at the workplace in the Group' (1999) and the Total 'European agreement on equal opportunity Total Group' (2005), prescribe respectively that the agreement is lodged to the competent bodies of the ILO and is filed with the European Commission.

358. The text of 13 EFAs is not available and the texts of 3 EFAs is not relevant.
359. Text of the Air France/KLM 'Social and Ethics Charter' (2013), according to which: "This Charter will be registered with the competent authorities as stipulated by French Law, applicable to the present text".

The GDF SUEZ 'GDF Suez Group European agreement on professional equality between men and women' (2012) reads:

> This agreement will be filed in accordance with the provisions in articles L. 2231-6 and D. 2231- 4 et seq. of the French Labour Code, in the territorial unit of Paris (DIRECCTE– Ile-de- France).
> A copy will also be filed with the labour tribunal in Paris, whose jurisdiction the GDF SUEZ head offices fall within.[360]

The ArcelorMittal 'Managing & Anticipating change at ArcelorMittal (V10)' (2009) stipulates:

> This agreement will be communicated to all workers of ArcelorMittal, following national practice and traditions. This Agreement will be translated into all languages of the countries included in the scope of this Agreement.[361]

The second issue that needs to be addressed pertains to the procedures set up in EFAs in order to implement the agreements. Just like IFAs, more than half of the EFAs listed in Table 2.2 (35) specify the appropriate way to put into practice the agreement, the parties entitled to carry out this task (usually local management and social partners) and the level in which the agreement has to be implemented (generally at the local level).

The General Motors 'Restructuring Framework' (2004) reads:

> Implementation of the initiatives will start immediately in the respective countries with the inclusion of national unions and/or employee representation bodies according to national legislation and practice. Implementation of this framework shall occur on the national level. According to European legislation and national laws Management and Employee representatives will ensure that the agreed provisions will become legally binding for individual employees as well as negotiating partners.[362]

The Schneider Electric 'European Agreement on the Anticipation of Change' (2007) reads:

> It is agreed that all of the provisions of this agreement must be implemented in the year after it comes into force. The European Committee members from the country concerned will be informed by the national management of the measures taken for implementation of this agreement in the country concerned regardless of the unit they work for. The social partners of each country represented within the European Committee shall sign this agreement at the relevant level with a view to ensuring its effective application at local level.[363]

360. See footnote n. 337.
361. Text available at <http://ec.europa.eu/employment_social/empl_portal/transnational_agreements/ArcelorMittal_Anticipation_EN.pdf> accessed 27 May 2014.
362. Text available at <http://ec.europa.eu/employment_social/empl_portal/transnational_agreements/GM_RestructuringFramework_EN.pdf> accessed 27 May 2014.
363. Text available at <http://ec.europa.eu/employment_social/empl_portal/transnational_agreements/SchneiderElectric_Anticipation_EN.pdf> accessed 27 May 2014.

As to the monitoring mechanisms established to ensure the effective implementation of EFAs, the signatories of 38 out of 60 of these agreements have introduced provisions similar to those included in IFAs. Hence, for instance there are provisions related to the establishment of monitoring committees, usually composed of management and employees' representatives, and sometimes also EWCs. These bodies are in charge of evaluating whether the responsible parties have correctly implemented the agreement and, in order to do so, they will set periodical meeting.

The AirFrance / KLM 'Social Rights and Ethics Charter' (2013) reads:

> Monitoring its effective application will be the responsibility of the AFKL EWC, consulting with but not substituting itself for the representative bodies in the countries concerned. In this way, the Select Committee of AIR FRANCE KLM European Works Council will be in a position to alert the appropriate personnel representatives and divisions so as to ensure application of the Charter. All procedures which could guarantee the monitoring of the Charter application are described in Appendix 4. Once a year, the agenda of the AFKL EWC will include a report on the application of the Charter.[364]

The Schneider Electric 'European Agreement on the Anticipation of Change' (2007) stipulates:

> A monitoring commission shall be established, comprising an EMF delegation including the European Committee Bureau. This commission will meet once a year, in connection with a European Committee Bureau meeting, to review the implementation of the agreement within the group's various entities. It is agreed that, when making this evaluation, a list will be drawn up of the actions that could have been undertaken in respect of each of the areas of the present agreement and that this will lead to discussion and the setting up of a "good practices" database which will be made available to all the Group's entities. On the basis of this examination, recommendations could be made for improving the application of the agreement.[365]

Finally, as to the last follow-up instrument, only 15 out of 60 EFAs analysed contain a provision related to the settlement of disputes. This issue has not attracted the same attention as in IFAs, where it is addressed in more than half of the agreements.

However, the dispute resolutions mechanisms set up in EFAs are akin to those existing in global texts. Monitoring committees, conciliation bodies, management and trade unions are indeed the main parties involved in the resolution of the matters arisen in the interpretation of the agreements and in their correct implementation. For instance, the ArcelorMittal 'Managing & Anticipating change at ArcelorMittal (V10)' (2009) reads:

> A conciliation body with equal representation on both sides was established at the ArcelorMittal headquarters in order to conciliate in any potential disputes resulting from the interpretation or implementation of this agreement.
> Only this conciliation body can settle such a dispute and its decision is final. It is made up of negotiating teams of this Agreement. Where a member leaves the

364. See footnote n. 335.
365. See footnote n. 363.

> conciliation body, he/she will be replaced by his side, with respect of the balance in the conciliation body.
> Before submitting the dispute to the conciliation body, management and trade unions should first address it through national follow up committees, following national practices and traditions.[366]

Furthermore, the Suez 'Group agreement – Suez Group's Social Dynamics' – section on 'Employment and Expertise Plan' (2007) stipulates:

> Questions of interpretation relating to the agreement are the sole prerogative of the monitoring committee.[367]

§2.09 CONCLUSIONS

The analysis of the different features of IFAs and EFAs signed by MNEs with more than 80,000 employees has led to different results. Even though IFAs and EFAs are similar in many aspects, a comparison of these agreements has shown that there are some differences. The outcome of the analysis carried out in this chapter will be summarized in the following sub-sections.

[A] Titles

First of all, there is no uniformity in the titles given by the signatories to both IFAs and EFAs. More specifically, the signatories have chosen a range of respectively 18 and 25 different titles for these agreements. The only difference found is related to the spread use of the word 'European' in EFAs, while the terms 'global' and 'worldwide' are much more common in IFAs. This distinction, however, can be easily explained by the different scope of application of these agreements. Besides this, the signatories of both IFAs and EFAs do seem to identify a connection between the title of the agreement and the issues. The only exception can be found in EFAs dealing with restructuring and anticipation of change, which for the most part contain the word 'Agreement' in the title.

[B] Signatory Parties on the Employees' Side

Concerning the signatory parties of IFAs and EFAs examined, it can be observed that on the employees' side, both IFAs and EFAs have been mainly (co-)signed by EWCs. However, next to the significant involvement of national trade unions in both agreements, GUFs are the second actors in the conclusion of IFAs and EIFs in the conclusion of EFAs. As with the title of the agreements, this distinction is also linked to the scope of application of these agreements.

366. See footnote n. 361.
367. Text available at <http://ec.europa.eu/employment_social/empl_portal/transnational_agreements/Suez_Anticipation_EN.pdf> accessed on 14 July 2014.

[C] Sectors

As to the sectors, both IFAs and EFAs have been signed mainly by MNEs operating in the automotive (and food and drink especially for the first IFAs) sector and headquartered in France and Germany. The main reason behind this situation can be explained, at least for the agreements signed in the last couple of years, by the fact that the automotive sector has been dramatically involved in the recent economic crisis and this situation might have led MNEs and trade unions to look for alternative ways to regulate the labour relations within an enterprise.

Despite this similarity as to the automotive sector, IFAs and EFAs differ in one aspect. Whereas many IFAs have been concluded by MNEs active in the food and drink sector and in the utilities industry, many EFAs have been signed by MNEs involved in the banking and finance/insurance sectors.

[D] Content

The content of the agreement is one of the main aspects where IFAs and EFAs differ. However, one has to note that in the last years many EFAs have dealt with fundamental social rights and CSR, even though IFAs still address this topic more frequently and almost exclusively. In fact, 36 out of the 62 IFAs analysed cover fundamental social rights and CSR. The second most addressed issue is health and safety, with only 8 agreements concluded.

Moreover, compared to IFAs, the signatory parties of EFAs have addressed a broader range of topics and they seem more inclined to sign agreements on restructuring, social consequences stemming from mergers, transfer of undertaking, acquisitions, anticipation and management of changes and social dialogue.

[E] Addressees

By comparing IFAs and EFAs on this issue, one can observe that EFAs pay less attention to subsidiaries, suppliers, contractors and subcontractors compared to IFAs. This situation might be explained by the fact that the conclusion of EFAs is a much more recent phenomenon in comparison with the IFAs. Signatory parties of these texts might still be reluctant to consider the subsidiaries of a MNE and its business partners as subject to the standards set forth in the agreements.

[F] Duration, Renewal, Termination and Revision

There is a significant similarity between IFAs and EFAs when it comes to duration, renewal, termination and revision of the agreement: less than half of the texts address these issues. However, even if the signatories have not paid much attention to these aspects, a minor difference between IFAs and EFAs can be found in relation to the possibility to revise the agreement.

[G] Follow-Up Procedures

The establishment of follow-up mechanisms is a significant feature for ensuring the effectiveness of IFAs and EFAs. To that end, the signatory parties have focused their attention to the dissemination and implementation of the agreements as well as the development of procedures to monitor the effective implementation of the agreement and to resolve disputes that arise between the signatory parties.

From the analysis carried out on the texts of 62 IFAs and 60 EFAs, it emerges that there are many similarities between these texts with the exception of the importance attached to the mechanisms of dispute resolution. In fact, while more than half of the IFAs signed contain a reference to this follow-up instrument, just 15 out of 60 EFAs define how a conflict on the interpretation and/or application of the agreement should be resolved. The reason behind this choice might be explained by the fact that the EFAs are a much more recent phenomenon than IFAs and hence still need to be developed.

CHAPTER 3

Legal Issues concerning International Framework Agreements and European Framework Agreements at Company Level

§3.01 INTRODUCTION

This Chapter is devoted to the analysis of three legal issues concerning IFAs and EFAs: first, the legal status; second, the legal effects; third and last, the relationship between these transnational texts and other norms.

First, attention will be paid to the legal status of these agreements and more particularly to the possibility of considering them as (national) collective agreements. A comparative analysis of IFAs and EFAs will be carried out with the aim of identifying similarities and differences between these forms of corporate regulation as to their legal status.

In addition, this chapter will deal with the legal effects of IFAs and EFAs. Specifically, the prospect of including these agreements within the concept of hard law or soft law will be analysed. Are IFAs and EFAs legally binding instruments? Are they enforceable? Answering these questions will be the leading thread of this part.

Last, this chapter will examine the relationship between IFAs/EFAs and other norms, in particular national laws and national collective agreements. Which provision takes precedence? What happens in case of more favourable provisions? These questions will be addressed and answered in section §3.04 of this chapter.

§3.02 LEGAL STATUS

One of the most important, but still very problematic, legal issues concerning TCAs regards their legal status. Despite the noteworthy growth of these agreements in the last fifteen years, a question has emerged as to their legal status, namely if TCAs can be considered collective agreements.[368]

Legal literature has pointed out consistently that "TCAs cannot be termed as 'collective agreements'"[369] and further that "they may not be considered the same as collective agreements as they are defined in national labour".[370] This is because of a series of reasons identified by the European Commission already back in 2008:

- the party representing the employees (European Works Council, European or international union organisations) is not recognised as such or does not fulfil the conditions of representativeness;
- the negotiation of the transnational text does not follow the rules established for the negotiation of company agreements;
- the form and content of the transnational text do not follow the rules established for the negotiation of company agreements;
- the transnational text addresses issues that cannot be the subject of a company agreement;
- the transnational text is not registered as a collective agreement.[371]

Nevertheless, scholars have left open the possibility to consider TCAs as national collective agreements only to the extent that certain conditions are met. More specifically, as Sobczak explains in relation to IFAs (but this statement can be extended to TCAs in general), "[w]hen a national trade union signs the IFA, it changes it into a national collective agreement in the country in which the holding company has its headquarters, provided that the national rules are followed. Nevertheless, it is unlikely that such an agreement will be regarded as a collective agreement in other countries because national rules differ greatly. Principles of international private law also have to be taken into account".[372]

In addition, some scholars have examined this issue from another perspective, namely they analysed whether TCAs meet the criteria established by the ILO to define a collective agreement. More specifically, Papadakis bases his research on the definition of collective agreement set forth in paragraph 2.1 of Recommendation No 91 (1995). Pursuant to this provision, "collective agreements means all agreements in

368. This section is limited at identifying whether TCAs can be considered collective agreements. It does not intend to examine whether TCAs can be considered unilateral commitments, contracts or advertising. See Commission, 'Mapping of transnational texts negotiated at corporate level' (n. 114) 21. See also Commission, 'The role of transnational company agreements in the contexts of increasing transnational integrations' (n. 105) 8.
369. Schömann, 'Transnational Company Agreements: Towards an Internationalisation of Industrial Relations' (n. 3) 206. See also Van Hoek and Hendrickx (n. 279) 7.
370. Sobczak, 'Legal Dimensions of International Framework Agreements in the Field of Corporate Social Responsibility' (n. 86) 125-126.
371. Commission, 'Mapping of transnational texts negotiated at corporate level' (n. 114) 20.
372. Sobczak, 'Legal Dimensions of International Framework Agreements in the Field of Corporate Social Responsibility' (n. 86) 121. See also Schömann, 'Transnational Collective Bargaining: In Search of a Legal Framework' (n. 283) 222. Schömann, 'The Impact of Transnational Company Agreements on Social Dialogue and Industrial Relations' in Konstantinos Papadakis, *Shaping Global Industrial Relations – The Impact of International Framework Agreements* (Palgrave Macmillan 2012) 34. Commission, 'The role of transnational company agreements in the contexts of increasing transnational integrations' (n. 105) 8.

writing regarding working conditions and terms of employment concluded between an employer, a group of employers or one or more employers' organisations, on the one hand, and one or more representative workers' organisations, or, in the absence of such organisations, the representatives of the workers duly elected and authorised by them in accordance with national laws and regulations, on the other".[373] The scholar uses this definition pointing out that IFAs are akin to collective agreements but in some aspects; in fact, while at the first sight they are agreements jointly negotiated by two parties (MNEs and workers' representatives) as required by the provision at issue, there are still many asymmetries with the definition in Article 2.1 of Recommendation No 91. More specifically, the representativeness of the parties who engage into negotiations of IFAs is still up for discussion and, in addition, these agreements at company level deal with working conditions and terms of employment in a different way compared to traditional national collective labour agreements.[374]

Jagodzinski seems to reach a different conclusion relying not only on ILO Recommendation No. 91 but on all ILO Conventions and Recommendation that deal with collective bargaining and freedom of association. By the analysis of these ILO sources, he argues that TCAs "meet the criteria of collective bargaining defined by various acts of the International Labour Organisation".[375]

Next to the legal status, the involvement of national trade unions as (co-)signatories of these agreements has an important impact also on the legal effects of these texts. In fact, as next section will show, one way through which TCAs can be regarded as legally binding instruments is via the involvement of trade unions.[376]

The next two sub-sections will carry out a comparative analysis of the legal status of the IFAs and EFAs listed in Tables 2.1 and 2.2 of Chapter 2 and examine whether it is possible to identify a common pattern to these agreements. More specifically, the sub-sections will focus on identifying if there are any IFAs and EFAs that can be regarded as collective agreements under national law through the involvement of national trade unions. Particular attention will be paid to the national trade unions organizations that have (co-)signed the agreement in accordance with the national requirements.

373. ILO Recommendation R91: Collective Agreement Recommendation, (Recommendation concerning Collective Agreements) (34th Conference Session Geneva 29 June 1951). See also Jagodzinki, 'Involving European Works Councils in Transnational Negotiations – a Positive Functional Advance in their Operation or Trespassing?'(n. 253) 320.

374. Konstantinos Papadakis and Giuseppe Casale and Katerina Tsotroudi, 'International Framework Agreementsas Elements of a Cross-Border Industrial Relations Framework' in Konstantinos Papadakis (ed.), *Cross-Border Social Dialogue and Agreements: An Emerging Global Industrial Relations Framework?*(International Institute for Labour Studies 2008) 71ff.

375. Jagodzinski, 'European Works Councils and Transnational Company Agreements – Balancing on the Thin Line between Effective Consultation and Overstepping Competences' (n. 98) 162-164.

376. Telljohannet al., 'European and International Framework Agreements: New Tools of Transnational Industrial Relations' (n. 119) 510.

[A] International Framework Agreements and Their Legal Status

Not even half of the IFAs concluded by MNEs with more than 80,000 employees have been (co-) signed by national trade unions, which have been involved in the conclusion of these agreements in only 19 agreements (18 IFAs as co-signatory and 1 IFA as signatory). Even though this number is still limited, the increase involvement of national trade unions especially as of 2007 may be regarded as a sign of how the signatory parties have started considering these texts at national level and, more specifically, how the evolution of TCAs is taking shape.

MNEs headquartered in France have concluded nearly half of the agreements at issue (9 out of 19), followed by Germany, Luxembourg, United Kingdom, Sweden, Italy and Spain.

However, what is more relevant as to the legal status of the IFAs at issue is that 6 out of the 19 agreements contain a provision concerning filing the agreement to the relevant competent authorities in accordance with national law, a procedure that usually has to be followed for national collective agreements. More specifically, 5 of these agreements were concluded by companies headquartered in France and 1 in Sweden.

Hence, for example, the GDF SUEZ's 'Group agreement on fundamental principles regarding health and safety' (2010) reads:

> Article 3.3.: Effectiveness and duration of the Agreement
> The Agreement will become effective on the day following its filing at the Paris DDTE (Departmental Directorate of Labour and Employment) and the registry of the Paris "Conseil de Prud'hommes" (Industrial Court). The agreement is entered into for an unlimited period.
> Article 3.4.: Filing of the Agreement
> In accordance with the provisions of the Labour Code, the Agreement shall be filed at the Paris Departmental Directorate for Labour and Employment ("DDTE") and the registry of the Paris Industrial Court ("Conseil de Prud'hommes").[377]

Similarly and even more detailed, the Suez's 'Group Agreement on Employees Ownership Scheme' (2007) sets forth:

> ARTICLE 8 EFFECTIVE DATE AND DURATION OF THE AGREEMENT
> The Agreement will come into effect from the day following its registration at the Paris DDTE and at the registry of the Paris Conseil de Prud'hommes (Employment Inspectorate).
> ARTICLE 9 REGISTRATION OF THE AGREEMENT AND OTHER FORMALITIES, IF ANY
> In accordance with the provisions of Article L. 132-10 of the Employment Code, the agreement shall be registered at the Paris Direction départementale du travail et de l'emploi (Departmental Employment Management) and at the registry of the Paris Conseil de Prud'hommes (Employment Inspectorate). Should the case arise, it will

377. See footnote n. 341.

> be the Associated Companies' responsibility to ensure that any other formalities are completed and complied with, in accordance with the local law applicable.[378]

The Securitas 'Agreement between Securitas AB (publ) and Union Network International and Swedish Transport Workers' Union on the development of good working relations in the Securitas group' (2006) does not explicitly refer to the registration of the agreement. Nevertheless, it states that "the Agreement shall be construed and it is governed according to the law of Sweden".[379]

If registration (especially in regard to the French agreements) is the only procedure that the law prescribes for national collective agreements, then these IFAs can be regarded as collective agreements under national law. In particular, in relation to the two IFAs concluded by Suez in 2007, Van Hoek and Hendrickxargue that "the TCA is recognized within the national system as a collective agreement and is given the status and legal effects consequent with that. One of the results under French law is that the collective agreement is legally binding with regard to all employees of the employer who is a party to the agreement (directly or indirectly)."[380]

Despite the significant result reached following the national procedures in relation to collective bargaining, a question remains. In fact, with the exception of the GDF Suez's 'Group agreement on fundamental principles regarding health and safety', all the remaining IFAs have been concluded only by the trade unions organizations active in the MNE's country of origin. As explained, these IFAs have been 'reproduced' in French/Swedish national collective agreements. What is then the status of these IFAs in the countries where the MNEs operates but national trade unions have not (co-) signed the agreement?[381] This interesting and important issue requires further research.

Next to the IFAs that contains an explicit reference to the filing of the agreement, 2 of the 9 IFAs concluded by MNEs headquartered in France contain a vague formulation concerning the registration procedures. For example, the PSA Peugeot 'Agreement on the extension of the strategic equal committee' (2008) provides that:

> This agreement, which has an international scope, will be subject to official information to the government and administrative bodies of each country concerned, following the national regulations and customs in force.[382]

A similar text can be found in the PSA Peugeot' International Framework Agreement on PSA Peugeot Citroën's Social Responsibility' (2006-2010), according to which "[t]he

378. See footnote n. 341. A similar provision concerning the filing of the agreement with the relevant national authorities can be found also in the following IFAs: France Telecom's 'Agreement of France Telecom's WorldWide Works Council' (2010); Suez's 'Agreement on Commitment to promoting equality and diversity within the Group' (2007); France Telecom's 'Worldwide Agreement on Fundamental Labour Rights within the France Telecom Group' (2006).
379. See footnote n. 348.
380. Van Hoek and Hendrickx (n. 279) 7 and 33.
381. For an in-depth analysis of this issue see Van Hoek and Hendrickx (n. 279) 32 ff.
382. Text available at <http://ec.europa.eu/employment_social/empl_portal/transnational_agreements/PSA_GlobalCommittee_EN.pdf> accessed 10 August 2014.

governmental and administrative bodies of each country have been officially informed about this international framework agreement."[383]

The main feature of the two IFAs signed by PSA Peugeot is that the trade unions of the country of origin of the MNEs have not been the only signatories of the agreement but other national trade unions organizations have also (co-)signed the IFAs.

Interesting is also the IFAs concluded by GDF Suez ('Global Agreement on Fundamental Rights, Social Dialogue and Sustainable Development' – 2010). This agreement contains a provision on the registration of the agreement with the relevant French authorities, but it has not been signed or at least co-signed by national trade unions, only by GUFs. In this case, it is debatable whether one could still consider this IFA as transposed into a national collective agreement following the prescribed national procedures.

[B] European Framework Agreements and Their Legal Status

Amongst the EFAs listed in Table 2.2 in Chapter 2, 15 EFAs have been signed or co-signed by national trade unions. This is less than one quarter of the EFAs concluded by MNEs with more than 80,000 employees. In view of this number it can be argued that local unions have played a less relevant role in the conclusion of European agreements compared to global agreements. It is nevertheless worth verifying whether some (or all) of these texts follow the same pattern as described in the previous sub-section, namely whether they can be regarded as collective agreements under national law.

Just like IFAs, the majority of EFAs signed by national trade unions has involved MNEs headquartered in France, more specifically 8 texts out of 15. The remaining EFAs have been concluded by companies with headquarter in the Netherlands (EADS), Italy (ENI) and Germany.

Despite the (co-) signature of national trade unions, only 6 of the 15 texts contain an explicit reference to the procedure of registration of the agreement with the national authorities and/or the applicable law.[384] Similarly to what said for IFAs, these agreements may be considered national collective agreements if registration of the agreement is the only national formal requirement that has to be met.

383. See footnote n. 321.

384. Besides the EFAs mentioned in the text: 1) Suez 'Group agreement – Suez Group's Social Dynamics – section on "Employment and Expertise Plan"' (2007); 2) Axa 'Agreement on the AXA Group European Works Council' (2009); 3) EADS 'Agreement on the European Works Council of EADS N.V. and its derived committees concluded between European Aeronautic Defence and Space Company EADS N.V. and its employees' representatives' (2005); 4) Allianz's 'Agreement concerning the participation of employees in Allianz SE' (2006). The last three EFAs intend to set up a EWCand establish employees' participation in a SocietasEuropaea.

More specifically, the GDF SUEZ 'GDF Suez Group European agreement on professional equality between men and women' (2012) stipulates:

> ARTICLE 18 – Filing the agreement and any other formalities
> This agreement will be filed in accordance with the provisions in articles L. 2231-6 and D. 2231-4 et seq. of the French Labour Code, in the territorial unit of Paris (DIRECCTE – Ile-de-France). A copy will also be filed with the labour tribunal in Paris, whose jurisdiction the GDF SUEZ head offices fall within.[385]

In addition to that, the GDF SUEZ's 'European group agreement relating to the employment and expertise plan' (2010) reads:

> Article 8.3.: Date of effectiveness and duration of the Agreement
> The agreement shall become effective on the day after it is filed at the Paris Departmental Directorate for Labour and Employment ("DDTE") and the registry of the Paris Industrial Court ("Conseil de Prud'hommes"). The agreement is entered into for an unlimited period.
> Article 8.4.: Filing of the Agreement
> In accordance with the provisions of Article L. 132-10 of the Labour Code, the Agreement shall be filed with the Paris Departmental Directorate for Labour and Employment ("DDTE") and the registry of the Paris Industrial Court("Conseil de Prud'hommes").[386]

A common feature of these two EFAs just described is that they have been co-signed by a Special Negotiating Group composed of national trade unions from all over Europe. This raise the question described in the previous sub-section about the status of collective agreements in these countries, besides France.[387]

Besides the 15 agreements (co-)signed by national trade unions, it is worth mentioning that there are also 5 EFAs that have not been (co-)signed by these actors but contain a provision on the deposition of the agreement with the relevant competent authorities (including the European Commission in the agreements concluded by Total) and, in one of these texts,on the law applicable. All the agreements have been concluded by MNEs headquartered in France, namely Air France/KLM, Total and Schneider Electric.[388] For example, the Air France / KLM 'Social Rights and Ethics Charter' reads:

385. See footnote n. 337.
386. See footnote n. 329.
387. Other two EFAs have been concluded by a Special Negotiating Body composed of national trade unions: EADS' 'Agreement on the European Works Council of EADS N.V. and its derived committees concluded between European Aeronautic Defence and Space Company EADS N.V. and its employees' representatives' (2005); Allianz's 'Agreement concerning the participation of employees in Allianz SE' (2006). However, these two agreements are different from the others because they are meant to set up a EWC and employees' participation in a SocietasEuropaea.
388. Next to the EFAs mentioned in the text: Total's 'European agreement on assistance in creation purchase or development of small and medium sized businesses' (2007); Total's 'European agreement – social platform Total Group' (2004); Schneider Electric's 'European Agreement on the Anticipation of Change' (2007).

> This Charter will be registered with the competent authorities as stipulated by French Law, applicable to the present text.[389]

The Total 'European agreement on equal opportunity Total Group' (2005) sets forth:

> Article 10 – Publicity
> The present agreement will be filed with the Departmental Work and Employment Service to which the TOTAL Head office reports, as well as with the Clerk of the Nanterre Prud'hommes Council and with the European Commission in Brussels (EMPLOYMENT, SOCIALAFFAIRS AND EQUAL OPPORTUNITY DG).[390]

To conclude, the comparative analysis of IFAs and EFAs listed in Tables 2.1 and 2.2 of Chapter 2 has shown that the involvement of national trade unions in the conclusion of these texts is gradually increasing but it still a marginal phenomenon. Moreover, some IFAs and EFAs explicitly refer to the procedures of registration of the agreement under national law, hence changing the status of these transnational texts to national agreements (if registration procedures are the only formal procedure to be met according to national law). This is particularly common in transnational agreements concluded by French MNEs, which, as seen in the previous Chapters, have been the precursors and can still be considered the main 'developers' of this new form of social dialogue at company level.

§3.03 LEGAL EFFECTS: HARD LAW OR SOFT LAW?

One of the most debatable issues concerning TCAs regards the legal effects stemming from the conclusion of these agreements. In other words, do these agreements have legally binding force and as such can workers enforce the rights set forth in the textsbefore a court?

Legal doctrine is consistent in recognizing that TCAs cannot be included within the concept of hard law but rather they are regarded as instruments of soft law, hence not legally binding and not enforceable before a court.[391] Soft law has been defined as follows:

> Rules of conduct, which in principle, have no legally binding force but which nevertheless may have practical effects.[392]

389. See footnote n. 335.
390. Text available at <http://ec.europa.eu/employment_social/empl_portal/transnational_agreements/Total_equalopportunity-EN.pdf> accessed 24 July 2014.
391. Sobczak, 'Legal Dimensions of International Framework Agreements in the Field of Corporate Social Responsibility' (n. 86) 125; See also Carley (n. 131) 9. Sobczak, 'Ensuring the effective implementation of transnational company agreements' (n. 98) 139. See also Papadakis and Casale and Tsotroudi, 'International Framework Agreementsas Elements of a Cross-Border Industrial Relations Framework' (n. 374) 77.
392. Francis Synder, 'Soft Law and Institutional Practice in the European Community' in Stephen Martin (ed.), *The Construction of Europe: Essays in Honour of Emile Noël* (Kluwer Academic Publishers 1994) 198.

> Rules of conduct that are laid down in instruments which have not been attributed legally binding force as such, but nevertheless may have certain (indirect) legal effect, and that are aimed at and may produce practical effects.[393]

TCAs fall within these definitions. They are not legally binding instruments and the parties cannot rely on them before a national court in case of violations of their provisions.[394] However, the fact that these agreements are considered not legally binding does not imply that they do not have legal effects.[395] In fact, even though TCAs fall within the category of soft law, one cannot disregard that, as Sobczak argues referring to Lascoumes and Serverin, lack of legal enforceability does not mean that the agreements at issue are not effective.[396] This is why is important to look at the procedures established by the signatory parties to implement and monitor the correct implementation of the agreement.[397] As Sobczak asserts, "the difference between hard and soft law should not be overstated. They are not totally different in nature; rather, there are variations in effectiveness within both categories. (...) In order to ensure the effective implementation of a labour standard, it is therefore less important to achieve legally binding provisions than to set up appropriate internal monitoring processes and to provide local stakeholders with knowledge and understanding of the standard".[398]

Furthermore, even if IFAs and EFAs are not considered legally binding instruments, they may still have a morally binding effect similar to other soft law instruments (for instance, the OECD Guidelines and the ILO Tripartite Declaration), which 'translate the *mores* of the international community'.[399] This can be argued especially for IFAs and EFAs that contain a commitment to respect the rights set forth in the eight fundamental ILO Conventions, which can be said to contain 'rules society at large accepts and promotes'.[400]

In addition, even if TCAs can be classified as soft law instruments, there are two situations in which TCAs may become legally binding agreements in the absence of a legal framework conferring them legally binding effects. The first situation occurs when national trade unions (co-) sign the agreement following national procedures or when the agreement is implemented through national legislation (e.g., via national

393. Linda Senden, *Soft Law in European Community Law*(Hart Publishing 2004) 104.
394. As an exception, some IFAs/EFAs make an explicit reference to the national court that is competent in case of violation of a provision set forth in the agreement. These cases will be mentioned further in this chapter.
395. Sobczak, 'Ensuring the effective implementation of transnational company agreements' (n. 98) 141.
396. *Ibid.*, 142. See also Schömann, 'Transnational Collective Bargaining: In Search of a Legal Framework' (n. 283) 225-226.
397. Chapter 2 of this book provides a comprehensive analysis of the follow-up procedures set up by the signatory parties of a selected texts of IFAs and EFAs.
398. Sobczak, 'Ensuring the effective implementation of transnational company agreements' (n. 98) 143.
399. RogerBlanpain, 'Multinational Enterprises and Codes of Conduct: The OECD Guidelines for MNEs in Perspective', in Roger Blanpain (ed.), *Comparative Labour Law and Industrial Relations in Industrialized Market Economies* (Xth ed., Kluwer Law International2010), 211-212.
400. Blanpain and Colucci, *The Globalization of Labour Standards: The Soft Law Track* (n. 9) 122.

initiatives).[401] In the second situation, the signatory parties decide explicitly to provide these agreements with legally binding force.

These situations have drawbacks though. In the first scenario, 'the full effectiveness of transnational agreements is therefore attained by denying the very transnational nature of the agreement in question'.[402] In the third scenario, sub-section §3.03[B] of this chapter will show that seldom the signatory parties explicitly state that TCAs are legally binding instruments and it is questionable whether this agreement can be enforced before national courts if they have not been transposed into national collective agreements.

The following sub-sections will carry out a comparative analysis of the IFAs and EFAs listed in Tables 2.1 and 2.2 of Chapter 2 in relation to the two abovementionedsituations.

[A] Binding Effects through the Involvement of National Trade Unions or National Implementation

One way to provide TCAs with legally binding effects is via the (co-) signature of the agreement by a national trade unions or the reproduction of the agreement into a national collective agreement. Reference is made to the previous section on the legal status of TCAs for the enumeration of agreements that have been (co-)signed by national trade unions following the national legislation and practice of the country at issue.

In addition to that, the texts of some IFAs and EFAs set forth that the agreement acquires legally binding effects via national implementation. It is interesting to analyse these agreements because some of them have not been (co-signed) by national trade unions and/or their text does not require the registration with the competent national authorities. Nevertheless, they lay down that the agreement has to be implemented at national level following national legislation. The following sub-sections will analyse IFAs and EFAs that have become legally binding through national implementation.

[1] International Framework Agreements

Only 1 of the IFAs listed in Table 2.1 of Chapter 2 contain an explicit reference to national implementation following national legislation and practice.

More specifically, the ArcelorMittal 'Agreement on minimum requirements for Plant level Joint H&S Committee' (2008) sets forth:

> The actual implementation of the agreement on health and safety committees has to be reached between the management and employee representatives/trade

401. Telljohannet al., 'European and International Framework Agreements: New Tools of Transnational Industrial Relations' (n. 119) 510. European Commission, 'Implementation and Dispute Settlement in Transnational Company Agreements' (Issues paper), Brussels, 12 November 2009, EMPL F2 EP, 3.
402. Lo Faro, 'Bargaining in the shadow of 'optional frameworks'? The rise of transnational collective agreements and EU law' (n. 241) 159.

> unions at site level, and should be done following local and/or national traditions and legislation.[403]

In two IFAs, the signatory parties affirm that the national economic, social, regulatory context has to be taken into account in the implementation of the agreement. Hence, the Danone 'Convention on Diversity' (2007) reads:

> The social counterparts in the Group's companies are invited to negotiate actual applicational procedures for these commitments that take account of specific situations in the company/site concerned as well as economic and social contexts in the country and local employment areas.[404]

In addition to that, the EDF 'Agreement on EDF Group Corporate Social Responsibility' (2005-2009) stipulates:

> In each Group company concerned, dialogue between the management and the employee representatives shall enable consultation on the initiatives to be taken and the conditions for the implementation of this Agreement. These initiatives shall take into account the local economic, cultural, professional or regulatory characteristics and set out conditions for enforcement within a policy of ongoing improvement.[405]

[2] European Framework Agreements at Company Level

Similarly to IFAs, only a few of the EFAs listed in Table 2.2 of Chapter 2 (6) have foreseen the possibility to provide legally binding effects through the implementation of the agreement at national level following national legislation and practices. In particular, three EFAs concluded between General Motors Europe and the EWC set forth:

> Implementation of this framework shall occur on the national level.
> According to European legislation and National laws Management and Employee Representatives will ensure that the agreed provisions will become legally binding for individual employees as well as negotiating partners.[406]

In addition to that, Alstom 'Agreement on the Anticipation of Change or Development in Alstom' (2011) reads:

---

403. Text available at <http://ec.europa.eu/employment_social/empl_portal/transnational_agreements/ArcelorMittal_plantjointOSHcommittees_EN.pdf> accessed 24 August 2014.
404. Text available at <http://ec.europa.eu/employment_social/empl_portal/transnational_agreements/Danone_Diversity_EN.pdf > accessed 24 August 2014.
405. Footnote n. 339. On this IFA see also Commission, 'Mapping of transnational texts negotiated at corporate level' (n. 114) 21.
406. See GM's Restructuring Framework (2004), GM's 'European framework, dated 5 March 2001 at 20:30 ("The following framework agreement is in relation of GM's current restructuring initiatives")' (2001) and GM's Framework "regarding 'Project Olympia' initiatives"' (2001). Two EFAs, one concluded by GM (Europe) ('Framework – 2000) and one by Ford (Europe) (Agreement governing the separation of the Ford Visteon organization – 2000) mention only that the EFAs has to be implemented at national level.

> 6.1 Local Application
> The social partners of each country within the EWF scope will apply this Agreement at the appropriate level, ensuring that is effectively implemented at local level in line with local regulations.[407]

Similarly, Axa Assistance 'European agreement on anticipating changes within Axa Assistance' (2011) stipulates:

> Its effective implementation is based on the coordination between European and local entities. The social partners of Axa Assistance of each country included in the scope of the European Committee of Axa Group will apply this Agreement in appropriately with ensuring its effective implementation at the local level, in accordance with local regulation.[408]

Finally, the ABB's 'European Appendix to ABB social policy' reads:

> In accordance with European and national laws and applicable conventions, the Country Management and the employee representatives/trade unions shall assure that any contractual arrangement amongst themselves resulting from implementation of this agreement will be binding for all the interested/parties affected.[409]

To conclude, only in a few cases IFAs and EFAs have been provided with legally binding effects through national implementation following national legislation. Thus, it can be noted that the acknowledgement and attribution of legal force to IFAs and EFAs remain the exception, while, as a general rule, these agreements are soft law instruments.

[B] The Willingness of the Signatory Parties[410]

Section §3.03 has clarified that both IFAs and EFAs do not have legally binding effects. However, the willingness of the signatory parties as to the legal effects of the agreements concluded should not be disregarded.[411] Parties may indeed 'have the intention to be bound in good faith by these agreements'.[412] More specifically, sometimes the signatory parties have shown their willingness to be bound by the outcome of these negotiations by explicitly asserting that the agreements are legally

407. Text available at <http://ec.europa.eu/employment_social/empl_portal/transnational_agreements/Alstom_Anticipation_EN.pdf> accessed 20 July 2014.
408. Text available at <http://ec.europa.eu/employment_social/empl_portal/transnational_agreements/Axa_assistance_anticipation_FR.pdf> accessed 20 July 2014.
409. Text available at <http://ec.europa.eu/employment_social/empl_portal/transnational_agreements/ABB_EuropeanAppendix_EN.pdf> accessed 4 June 2014.
410. In a number of IFAs and EFAs, the signatory parties have specified that only the agreement written in a specific language is binding/authoritative/will prevail in case of disputes. These agreements have not been considered in this section.
411. Commission, 'Mapping of transnational texts negotiated at corporate level' (n. 114) 20.
412. Papadakis and Casale and Tsotroudi, 'International Framework Agreementsas Elements of a Cross-Border Industrial Relations Framework' (n. 374) 77.

binding on management and/or employees.[413] The following sub-sections will examine whether a common trend has been followed with respect to IFAs and EFAs on this point.

[1] International Framework Agreements

As to the IFAs analysed, only in four agreements have the signatory parties explicitly asserted the legally binding status of the agreement. One example is the Volkswagen 'Charter on Labour Relations within the Volkswagen Group' (2009).[414] This IFA sets forth:

> The Charter provides a binding framework within which to further develop existing labour relations in a responsible manner and in a spirit of co-operative conflict management
> The Volkswagen Group shall ensure that the Group companies in each respective country implement this Agreement by means of binding regulations.[415]

However, the same IFA specifies:

> (2) Legal effect
> This Charter shall provide no grounds whatsoever for any claims by local or third parties.[416]

In addition to that, 5 IFAs contain a reference to applicable national legislation (in 3 IFAs in case of revision of the text)[417] and in 1 of the 5 IFAs the signatory parties agreed that a national court is competent from any dispute arisen from the agreement. One can then argue that the agreement is enforceable and hence legally binding. More specifically, the latter agreement (the Arcelor 'Worldwide Agreement on the Principles of Arcelor's Corporate Social responsibility'- 2005) reads:

> Article 10: Validity of the Agreement
> This agreement is governed by Luxembourg law. Consequently, any disputes will fall within the exclusive competence of the Luxembourg courts.[418]

413. Commission, 'Mapping of transnational texts negotiated at corporate level' (n. 114) 20.
414. The other three IFAs are: DaimlerChrysler 'Occupational Health and Safety Principles of DaimlerChrysler' (2006); Lukoil 'Agreement between International Federation of Chemical, Energy, Mine and General Workers' Unions, Russian Oil and Gas Workers Union And Open Joint Stock Company "Oil Company LUKOIL"' (2004) (this agreement speaks about obligations); DaimlerChrysler 'Social Responsibility Principles of DaimlerChrysler' (2002).
415. See footnote n.306.
416. *Ibid.*
417. GDF Suez 'Group agreement on fundamental principles regarding health and safety' (2010); France Telecom 'Agreement of France Telecom's Worldwide Works Council (2010); Suez 'Agreement on Commitment to promoting equality and diversity within the Group' (2007); Suez 'Group Agreement on Employees Ownership Scheme' (2007); Worldwide Agreement on the Principles of Arcelor's Corporate Social responsibility (2005).
418. See footnote n. 310.

In all the remaining IFAs, the signatory parties do not provide the agreement with legally binding effects, and in 8 IFAs they have specified that no claims based on the IFA can be made by third parties.[419]

[2] European Framework Agreements at Company Level

Concerning EFAs, the situation is not different. Only in 4 EFAs the signatory parties have explicitly laid down that the agreement is legally binding.[420] More specifically, these agreements will become legally binding via the implementation at local level (for an in-depth analysis of this topic see section §3.03[A][2]).[421]

In addition to that, similarly to IFAs, 5 EFAs contain a reference to national law[422] and 1 to EU law.[423] Moreover, oneEFAs ('Philip Morris's Agreement by the EU Assembly for the workforce of Philip Morris tobacco companies in the European regions of Philip Morris on the protection of personal data processed by ITSC Europe S.A.R.L.') specifies not only the applicable law but it sets forth that a national court is competent from any dispute arisen from the agreement.

All remaining EFAs do not contain a similar provision and the text of 1 EFAs specifies that no claims can arise from the agreement at issue (ArcelorMittal 'Managing & Anticipating change at ArcelorMittal (V10)).

To conclude, the above-mentioned analysis can straightforwardly lead to the conclusion that the signatory parties of both IFAs and EFAs do not usually consider these agreements as legally binding. Only in a few cases the signatory parties have specified the opposite.

---

419. Itaú-Unibanco S.A. undertakes, in accordance with the laws of each country, to disclose information relating to this Framework Agreement in its Intranet environment (2012); Volkswagen 'Charter on Temporary Work' (2012); Siemens 'International Framework Agreement between Siemens AG, the Central Works Council of Siemens AG, the IG Metall and the IndustriALL Global Union (2012); Sodexo 'International Framework Agreement' (2011); Volskwagen 'Charter on Labour Relations within the Volkswagen Group' (2009); G4S 'A global Agreement – Ethical Employment Partnership' (2008); BMW 'Joint Declaration on Human Rights and on Working Conditions in the BMW Group' (2005); Volskwagen 'Declaration on Social Rights and Industrial Relationships at Volkswagen (2002).
420. In two EFAs concluded by EADS in 2011, the signatory parties have specified that the agreement is mandatory. However, these agreement have not been included in the list because the intention of parties to consider the agreement legally binding cannot be clearly retrieved from the text.
421. ABB 'European Appendix to ABB social policy' (2009); GME 'Restructuring Framework' (2004); GME 'European framework, dated 5 March 2001 at 20:30 ("The following framework agreement is in relation of GM's current restructuring initiatives")' (2001); GME 'Framework "regarding 'Project Olympia' initiatives"' (2001).
422. GDF Suez 'GDF Suez Group European agreement on professional equality between men and women' (2012); GDF Suez 'European Group Agreement relating to the employment and expertise plan' (2010); Veolia Environment 'Veolia Environment European Works Council Agreement' (2010); Suez 'Group Agreement – Suez Group's Social Dynamics – section on "Employment and Expertise Plan"' (2007); EADS 'Agreement on the European Works Council of EADS N.V. and its derived committees concluded between European Aeronautic Defence and Space Company EADS N.V. and its employees' representatives' (2005). It is important to emphasize that the latter agreement concerns the establishment of a EWC.
423. Axa 'Agreement on the Axa Group European Works Council' (2009).

§3.04 RELATIONSHIP BETWEEN INTERNATIONAL FRAMEWORK AGREEMENTS/EUROPEAN FRAMEWORK AGREEMENTS AT COMPANY LEVEL AND OTHER NORMS

The relationship between IFAs/EFAs and other norms is the third legal issue that will be further examined in this chapter. In the following subsections, particular attention will be paid to the connection between these agreements and national laws and/or national/company collective agreements and local legal requirements,among others.[424] It is interesting to verify how the signatories of IFAs and EFAs perceive the hierarchy among these norms because this might have implications at national level. An IFA or EFA that establishes the supremacy of its provisions over national laws and/or national/company collective agreements would indeed give rise to several concerns about conflict of norms.

[A] International Framework Agreements

Not even half of the IFAs listed in Table 2.1 of Chapter 2 contain a specific provision related to the relationship between the transnational text and other norms, such as national legislation, local laws, collective agreements at different levels. In fact, just in 30 cases out of 62, the signatories have specified such relationship. Despite the still limited attention paid to this issue, it is important to note that the parties have followed four different patters to define this relationship:[425]

(1) In some IFAs the signatory parties have committed themselves to respect, comply, take into consideration local, national standards, collective agreements. By way of example, the Banco do Brasil 'Global Framework Agreement for the Americas Union Network International (UNI) and Banco do Brasil' (2011-2013) sets forth:

> Article 16
> The Parties commit themselves to comply with the collective agreements in each country and with the commitments that come out as a result of this framework agreement.
> (...)
> Article 19
> The Parties will respect the national legislation about employment in each country.[426]

(2) In many IFAs, the signatory parties have clearly specified that the more favourable provisions take precedence, whether they are included in the IFAs or in the national laws, collective agreements, company practice.

424. For instance, company regulations, custom at the workplace.
425. It is important to take into account that some IFAs contain (a) provision(s) that follow one or more patter(s).
426. See footnote n. 117.

The EDF 'Agreement on EDF Group Corporate Social Responsibility' (2005-2009) reads:

> EDF Group companies hereby undertake to comply strictly with national and local laws as well as other collective agreements, and more particularly where such laws provide for more extensive requirements than the provisions of this Agreement.[427]

The Danone 'Convention on Diversity' (2007) states:

> The commitments of the present convention do not challenge more favourable arrangements existing in GroupeDanone companies or resulting from legislation.[428]

The Sodexo 'International Framework Agreement' (2011) sets forth:

> 6. Implementation
> 6.1. To the extent that the parties reach any agreements that impose obligations on one or the other that may go beyond local legislative requirements or existing agreements, those obligations will be implemented in phases so that the parties can work together to ensure the success of the agreement and minimize any potential adverse impact on either party.[429]

The Volkswagen 'Charter on Temporary Work' (2012) reads:

> If compliance with country-specific standards for temporary work represents a worsening in comparison to this Charter or other principles of the Volkswagen Group, then those regulations which are more favourable to the temporary external personnel always take effect. If national wage or company regulations or laws are favourable to the temporary external personnel, then the regulations will not be affected by this Charter.[430]

(3) Sometimes, the signatory parties have stated that provisions in the agreement are not intended to take the place of, replace, affect national laws, collective agreements, company labour practices, among others. No reference is made to whether the other norms are more or less favourable compared to the transnational text. For example, the G4S 'A global Agreement: Ethical Employment Partnership' (2008) reads:

> Nothing in this agreement shall in any way undermine existing labour relations practices or agreements relating to union rights or facilities already freely established by any trade union operating within the G4S group.[431]
> The Lukoil 'Agreement between International Federation of Chemical, Energy, Mine and General Workers' Unions, Russian Oil and Gas Workers

427. See footnote n. 339.
428. See footnote n.404.
429. Text available at <http://ec.europa.eu/employment_social/empl_portal/transnational_agreements/Sodexo_EN.pdf> accessed 24 July 2014.
430. Text available at <http://ec.europa.eu/employment_social/empl_portal/transnational_agreements/VW_Temporarywork_EN.pdf > accessed 24 July 2014.
431. See footnote n. 356.

> Union And Open Joint Stock Company "Oil Company LUKOIL"' (2004) stipulates:
> It is not intended that this agreement replace or substitute the results of collective bargaining and valid tariff agreements, or interfere with local industrial relations practices related to information exchange, problem solving and negotiations, rather it is intended to supplement these processes.[432]

(4) Some IFAs refer to national laws, for instance when the content of the agreement cover issues such as wages, working time. More specifically, instead of regulating in detail these areas, the signatory parties make reference to the laws/collective agreements that are applicable in the countries in which the MNEs has its activities. The BMW' 'Joint Declaration on Human Rights and on Working Conditions in the BMW Group' (2005) can be considered as an example of this fourth pattern. According to the text of this agreement:

> 1.5. Remuneration
> Remuneration in the BMW Group complies with current minimum rates of pay as guaranteed by law with no differentiation on the basis of gender. The BMW Group observes the minimum standards currently in place in the respective branches at national level and follows current trends on the respective labour markets.
> 1.6. Working time
> The BMW Group will comply with the respective national rules and agreements on working time and on paid leave.[433]

This analysis can lead to the conclusion that the signatory parties of the IFA listed in Table 2.1 of Chapter 2 have been quite reluctant in inserting in the agreement provisions related to the relationship of the text at issue with other norms and industrial relations practice.

[B] European Framework Agreements at Company Level

Just like for IFAs, the signatories of the EFAs listed in Table 2.2 of Chapter 2 have not introduced a provision concerning the relationship between the agreement and other norms in all the texts. More than half of the EFAsanalysed (40 out of 63) specify how this relationship is regulated. Six different patterns can be identified when parties have decided to delineate this relationship:[434]

(1) The majority of EFAs contain a non-regression clause, according to which the agreement is applicable unless existing (and, sometimes, also future) national

432. See footnote n. 338.
433. See footnote n. 320.
434. It is important to take into account that some EFAs contain (a) provision(s) that follow one or more patter(s).

legislation, collective agreements, etc., provide for more favourable conditions.[435]

Hence, the GDF's 'European agreement on the corporate social responsibility of the Gaz de France group' (2008) reads:

> The Gaz de France Group's companies undertake to enforce both national and local legislation strictly, as well as any collective conventions and agreements that concern them. In the event that these conventions and legislative provisions are more favourable than this current agreement, the former shall have precedence over the latter.[436]

The Alstom and Schneider Electric 'European Agreement' (2010) stipulates:

> The present agreement cannot be used in lieu of more favourable national legislations and/or conventions agreed at company level, at local, national or regional level.[437]

(2) Two agreements concluded by Allianz state that "the agreement is valid unless the issue concerned is regulated by peremptory norms of national law in the EU or the contracting States of the EEA or of Switzerland".[438]

(3) Similar to IFAs, some signatory parties have included a provision pursuant to which they commit themselves to comply, apply, take into account, draft the agreement pursuant to national and/or EU legislation. For example, the Air France/KLM's 'Social Rights and Ethics Charter' (2013) sets forth:

> All the provisions of this Charter are drafted in compliance with the provisions and laws of each country as well as with individual and collective labour agreements.[439]

Moreover, the ArcelorMittal 'Managing & Anticipating change at ArcelorMittal (V10)' (2009) reads:

> (...) the signatory partners intend to comply with all existing legislation and collective agreements at national and company level and with social dialogue structures and traditions.[440]

435. One EFAs concluded between Ford of Europe and the EWC (Ford of Europe and the Ford European Works Council (FEWC) Agreed upon Social Rights and Social Responsibility Principles – 2003) specifies only that national laws, local laws, collective agreements take precedence in certain situations.

436. See footnote n. 328.

437. Text available at <http://ec.europa.eu/employment_social/empl_portal/transnational_agreements/Alstom%20Schneider_SocialCommittments_EN.pdf> accessed 4 June 2014.

438. Allianz 'Agreement on guidelines concerning Lifelong Learning' (2012) and 'Agreement on Guidelines Concerning Work Related Stress' (2011).

439. See footnote n. 335.

440. See footnote n. 361.

(4) Some EFAs refer to national laws, collective agreements, etc., to set the standards addressed in the agreement. For instance, the ABB 'European Appendix to ABB Social policy' (2009) reads:

> 4. Pensions and benefits
> ABB provides a pension scheme or retirement pay, and other benefits, for its employees that are at least in accordance with the given national laws, collective agreements or other relevant regulations and standards customary in this industry.[441]

(5) In a few EFAs the signatory parties explicitly provide that the conclusion of the agreement does not affect the application of relevant legislation/agreements. For instance, the DiamlerChrysler 'Framework agreement for information and consultation with employees and employee representatives in the local European operations of DaimlerChrysler AG' (2006) stipulates:

> Existing national regulations and agreements with labour unions and employee representatives remain unaffected.[442]

(6) Finally, two EFAs concluded by General Electric Plastics (Europe) contain a clear rule in case of conflict between the content of the transnational agreement and the applicable local and/or European law. According to the 'GEPE Agreement on use of electronic communication systems' (2002) and the Agreement on Pre-employment screening ('background checks') (2004):

> As this agreement is supposed to be used for all European sites of the company, all local legislation will be taken into account. In case any part of this agreement is in conflict with any applicable local and/or European legislation, the latter prevails. In order to comply with local law country guidelines have been put together.[443]

§3.05 CONCLUSION

The analysis of the legal status and the legal effects of IFAs and EFAs and their relationship with other norms has led to interesting – albeit perhaps not so surprising – results.

As to the legal status of IFAs and EFAs, it can be observed that these agreements rarely can be regarded as collective agreements under national law. Even if some, but not so many, IFAs and EFAs have been concluded by national trade unions, this fact is

441. See footnote n. 409.
442. Text available at <http://ec.europa.eu/employment_social/empl_portal/transnational_agreements/DaimlerChrysler_informationandconsultation_EN.pdf> accessed 4 June 2014.
443. Texts available at <http://ec.europa.eu/employment_social/empl_portal/transnational_agreements/Gepe_pre-employmentscreaning_EN.pdf> and <http://ec.europa.eu/employment_social/empl_portal/transnational_agreements/Gepe_ElectronicCommunication_EN.pdf> accessed 4 June 2014.

not sufficient to classify the text as a national agreement. In fact, other requirements (e.g., registration formalities) still need to be fulfilled.

Concerning the attribution of legally binding effects to these agreements, it is argued that both IFAs and EFAs fall within the category of soft law and not hard law. These agreements are not enforceable before a court. However, even if TCAs do not produce legal obligations, one cannot disregard that signatory parties have often set up internal mechanisms to implement and monitor the correct implementation of the agreement. These procedures may involve annual meetings in which the application of the agreement is evaluated and in which, in some texts, the agreement may be revised. Despite the lack of legally binding effects, the presence of these mechanisms can ensure the effective implementation of the agreement.

In addition to that, from the analysis conducted on the texts of IFAs and EFAs it has emerged that in two situations TCAs may acquire legally binding effects. The signatory parties have not made often use of these possibilities, which, nevertheless, represent an important step due to the absence of a European and international legal framework that provide TCAs with legally binding effects.

Finally, with respect to the relationship between IFAs and EFAs and other norms, this chapter has shown a very significant feature of these agreements, namely that the signatory parties are sometimes very clear as to the hierarchy between IFAs and EFAs and other norms. National laws, local laws and national collective agreements indeed take precedence if more favourable.

Conclusions

Globalization has been the driving force behind the changes of the labour market over the last years. The internationalization of MNEs' activities has given rise to numerous concerns as to the respect of working and employment conditions in the host countries. More specifically, the decentralized process of production has reduced and undermined the powers of trade unions to represent and defend the rights of MNEs' workers. Hence, one has witnessed the development of new modes of corporate governance, such as IFAs and EFAs. These agreements have been considered as the "stepping stone towards the development of a global IR [industrial relations] framework"[444] and aim at giving a response to the adverse effects on working conditions stemming from the market economy led by MNEs, whose economic interests usually do not match with those of the workers.[445]

This book examined in-depth the texts of the IFAs and EFAs concluded by MNEs with more than 80,000 in 2013 with the aim of identifying the differences and similarities between these two categories of agreements and, based on that, clarify if this distinction can still be in place.

Primarily, the study of the texts of IFAs and EFAs has led to the conclusion that it is difficult to draw a clear distinction between these agreements. Schömann supports this conclusion by arguing that "[i]n general, IFAs differ in scope and content from framework agreements with a European dimension, whereby this distinction is slowly disappearing".[446] In addition, also the European Commission states that "a clear distinction of transnational texts, according to their scope and character, between European and global texts is not always possible as there is a continuum between both types and also both categories have had a quite comparable evolution".[447]

Arguably, in many aspects under examination in this book the signatory parties do not seem to make a clear-cut distinction between IFAs and EFAs. For instance, the title most used for both IFAs and EFAs is 'Agreement' and only approximately a third

444. Vos (n. 12) 52.
445. Papadakis, 'Introduction' (n. 2) 4-5.
446. Schömann, 'Transnational Company Agreements: Towards an Internationalisation of Industrial Relations' (n. 3) 202.
447. Commission, 'Mapping of Transnational Texts Negotiated at Corporate Level' (n. 114) 4.

of IFAs and a third of EFAs have a title that reflects the distinction between these two categories.

In addition, also the content is not a significant criterion to differentiate these agreements. The analysis conducted on the texts of IFAs and EFAs has pointed out that fundamental social rights and CSR are the issues that EFAs cover the most after restructuring. Similarly, the signatory parties of IFAs address mostly fundamental social rights and CSR (next to anticipation of change).

Likewise, as to signatory parties of IFAs and EFAs on employees' side, EWCs are the pivotal actors in the conclusions of both types of agreement. GUFs and EIFs only come after national trade unions. Thus, the 'traditional' distinction between IFAs and EFAs based on the employees' side signature seems disappearing.[448] The same can be argued in relation to the sectors in which MNEs are active. Signatory parties have paid most attention to the conclusion of both IFAs and EFAs in the automotive sector.

A similar conclusion can be reached if the other features examined in this book are taken into consideration, with the exception of the addressees. More specifically, only a few differences can be found concerning the aspects related to the duration and follow-up procedures. For instance, the signatory parties of EFAs have paid more attention to the aspect of the revision of the agreement while the signatories of IFAs have regulated more often how a dispute on the interpretation and/or application of the agreement ought to be solved.

The absence of a clear distinction between IFAs and EFAs is also visible when the legal status, legal effects and relationship between the transnational agreements and other norms are taken into consideration. As to the legal status, the comparative analysis has shown that the involvement of national trade unions in the conclusion of both types of text is gradually increasing but it still a marginal phenomenon. Moreover, some IFAs and EFAs explicitly refer to the procedures of registration of the agreement under national level, hence changing the status of these transnational texts to national collective agreements (if registration procedures are the only formal procedure to be met according to national law). This is particularly common in transnational agreements concluded by French MNEs, which, as seen in this book, have been the precursors and can still be considered the main 'developers' of this new form of social dialogue at company level. Furthermore, concerning the legal effects signatory parties of IFAs and EFAs follow the same patterns: only a few transnational agreements have become legally binding instruments via the involvement of national trade unions, the implementation at national level and the willingness of the signatory parties. More specifically, only approximately 10% of the agreements have legally binding effects.

To conclude, more than 250 TCAs have been signed so far, involving more than 160 MNEs and 10 million workers. More than half of them are IFAs, making EFAs the minority. This phenomenon is developing faster over the years, although the path towards regulating the working relations via these agreements is still rather limited. In fact, approximately 82,000 MNEs are active in the labour market and the workforce

448. Telljohann et al., 'European and International Framework Agreements: New Tools of Transnational Industrial Relations' (n. 119) 508.

consists of about 77 million of workers.[449] In light of these numbers, one can observe that this emerging form of corporate regulation is still not the main feature of the current system of industrial relations. Moreover, many issues are still debatable (e.g. legal status and legal effects) and some aspects of these agreements need to be improved, starting with the follow-up procedures and, in particular, the dispute settlement mechanisms that should ensure that the violation of any provision of the agreements is punished and that decisions are enforced.

449. This data refer to 2008. See UNCTAD, 'World Investment Report 2009' (n. 13).

Annexes

Table 1 IFAs concluded between 1988 and May 2014

Company	*Country of Origin*	*Title of the Agreement*	*Year of Signature*	*Number of Employees*	*Signatories on the Employees' Side*
GDF Suez	France	Global Health and Safety Agreement of the GDF Suez Group	2014	147,200 (2013)[450]	PSI, BWI, IndustriALL
Itaú-Unibanco S.A.	Brazil	Framework Agreement between Banco Itaú-Unibanco S.A. and Union Network International for the Americas	2014	Approximately 96,000 (2013)[451]	UNI for the Americas
Solvay	Belgium	Global Corporate Social Responsibility Agreement between Solvay and IndustriALL Global Union	2013	29,400 (2013)[452]	IndustriALL
Norske Skog	Norway	Agreement between Fellesforbundet/IndustriAll Global Union and Norske Skogindustrier ASA on the development of good working relations in Norske Skogindustrier's worldwide operations	2013	3,274 (2013)[453]	IndustriALL

450. Information available at <http://library.gdfsuez.com/uhttp:/library.gdfsuez.com/uid_5644c3ca-3ea9-4085-bb8f-e24430fefecf/html/en/page50.html> accessed 10 April 2014.
451. Information available at <http://www.itau.com/about-itau/> accessed 10 April 2014.
452. Information available at <http://interactivedocument.labrador-company.com/Labrador/EN/Solvay/2013AnnualReport/> accessed 14 April 2014.
453. Information available at <http://www.norskeskog.com/Investors/Reports.aspx> accessed 10 April 2014.

Company	*Country of Origin*	*Title of the Agreement*	*Year of Signature*	*Number of Employees*	*Signatories on the Employees' Side*
Metro	Germany	Joint Statement of Metro Group & UNI Global Union	2013	269,493 (2013)[454]	UNI Global Union
ENEL	Italy	Global framework agreement on social dialogue guidelines	2013	71,394 (2013)[455]	IndustriALL, PSI
Melia	Spain	Global Agreement IUF-UITA / Melia Hotels International S.A.	2013	18.370 (2013)[456]	IUF UITA
Loomis AB	Sweden	Global agreement between Loomis AB (publ) and UNI Global Union and Swedish Transport worker's union	2013	19,442 (19448) (2013)[457]	UNI Global Union
Renault	France	Global framework agreement on social, societal and environmental responsibility between the Renault Group, the Renault Group Works' Council and IndustriALL Global Union	2013	121,807 (2013)[458]	Renault Group Works Council (Global Works Council), IndustriALL
Telenor	Norway	Global Agreement between Telenor ASA and UNI Global Union	2013	34,000 (2013)[459]	UNI Global Union
Volks-wagen	Germany	Charter on Temporary Work	2012	572,800 (2013)[460]	Volkswagen European Group Works Council, Volkswagen Group Global Works Council, IndustriALL

454. Information available at <http://reports.metrogroup.de/2013/ar/downtobusiness/metrogroupinfigures.html> accessed 10 April 2014.
455. Information available at <http://www.enel.com/en-GB/doc/report2013/Annual_Report_2013.pdf> accessed 10 April 2014.
456. Information available at <http://www.meliahotelsinternational.com/sites/default/files/informes-financieros/mhi_inf_financiero_13_es_04jun_0.pdf> accessed 10 April 2014.
457. Information available at < http://www.loomis.com/PageFiles/7016/LoomisYearEndReport-JanuaryDecember2013.pdf.
458. Information available at <http://group.renault.com/en/our-company/renault-at-a-glance-2/renault-at-a-glance/> accessed 10 April 2014.
459. Information available at <http://www.telenor.com/wp-content/uploads/2014/04/Telenor-Group-Annual-Report-2013.pdf> accessed 10 April 2014.
460. Information available at <http://www.volkswagenag.com/content/vwcorp/content/en/the_group.html> accessed 10 April 2014.

Company	*Country of Origin*	*Title of the Agreement*	*Year of Signature*	*Number of Employees*	*Signatories on the Employees' Side*
Thyssen-Krupp AG	Germany	Global agreement of an ideamanagement Health & Safety at ThyssenKrupp Elevator Operating Units	2012	156,856 (2013)[461]	EWC, IndustriALL, National trade unions
Man SE	Germany	Global framework agreement on Human Rights and Working Conditions	2012	53,509 (2013)[462]	IndustriALL
FCC Cons-trucción	Spain	Global framework agreement on employees rights	2012	79,568 (2013)[463]	BWI
Ford	USA	Global framework agreement	2012	181,000 (2013)[464]	IMF
Inditex	Spain	Global agreement on the involvement of unions to monitor the respect of worker's conditions at supplier	2012	128,313 (2013)[465]	ITGLWF
Ferrovial	Spain	Framework agreement between ferrovial, the building and wood workers' international, FECOMA and MCA	2012	66,088 (2013)[466]	BWI, National trade unions
OHL	Spain	Framework agreement between Obrascon Huarte Lain S.A., Building and Wood Workers' International, FECOMA and MCA	2012	23.795 (2013)[467]	BWI, National trade unions

461. Information available at <http://www.thyssenkrupp.com/financial-reports/12_13/download/en/ThyssenKrupp_2012_2013_AR.pdf> accessed 10 April 2014.
462. Information available at <http://www.corporate.man.eu/en/investor-relations/financial-reports-and-publications/factsheet/Factsheet.html> accessed 10 April 2014.
463. Information available at <http://www.fcc.es/fccweb/wcm/idc/groups/public/documents/document/mdaw/mdcz/~edisp/cscp089930.pdf> accessed 10 April 2014.
464. Information available at <http://corporate.ford.com/microsites/sustainability-report-2013-14/people-workplace-employees> accessed 13 April 2014.
465. Information available at <http://www.inditex.com/documents/10279/18789/Inditex_Group_Annual_Report_2013.pdf/88c623b8-b6b0-4d38-b45e-45822932ff72> accessed 10 April 2014.
466. Information available at <http://memoria2013.ferrovial.com/en/Social-dimension/People> accessed 10 April 2014.
467. Information available at <http://www.ohl.es/Plantillas/template11.aspx?IdA=121&IdF=245&IdL=183&idM=414&nvl=1&lan=en#a0> accessed 10 April 2014.

Company	*Country of Origin*	*Title of the Agreement*	*Year of Signature*	*Number of Employees*	*Signatories on the Employees' Side*
Saab	Sweden	International Framework Agreement between SAAB AB and employee representatives Organisations in Saab AB and IF Metall and Industri All Global Union	2012	14,140 (2013)[468]	IndustriALL National trade union
Eurosport	France	Global agreement on fundamental social rights	2012	750 (2012)[469]	UNI Global Union
Siemens	Germany	International Framework Agreement between Siemens AG, the Central Works Council of Siemens AG, the IG Metall and the IndustriALL Global Union	2012	362,000 (2013)[470]	Central Works Council, National trade unions, IndustriALL
Banco do Brasil	Brazil	Global Framework Agreement for the Americas Union Network International (UNI) and Banco do Brasil	2011 (renewed in 2013)	112,216 (2013)[471]	UNI for the Americas
Norske Hydro	Norway	Global Framework Agreement between Norsk Hydro ASA and IMF/ICEM Fellesforbundet and IndustriEnergi for the the development of good working relations in Norsk Hydro ASA operations worldwide	2011	12,564 (2013)[472]	IMF, ICEM

468. Information available at < http://www.saabgroup.com/en/About-Saab/Investor-relations/Annual-Report-2013/Saab-in-brief/ > accessed 10 April 2014.
469. Information available at <http://www.emlyonforever.com/s/groups/portraits-en/blog/arnaud_simon_esc_91_managing_director_of_eurosport_france/Y5Qfqri0_Jz5Piqm2rCGtw > accessed 10 April 2014.
470. Information available at <http://www.siemens.com/investor/en/company_overview.htm > accessed 10 April 2014.
471. Information available at <http://www45.bb.com.br/docs/ri/ra2013/eng/downloads/FinancialStatements4Q13.pdf > accessed 10 April 2014.
472. Information available at <http://www.hydro.com/upload/Annual_reporting/annual_2013/downloadcenter/Reports/01_annual_report_2013.pdf > accessed 10 April 2014.

Company	*Country of Origin*	*Title of the Agreement*	*Year of Signature*	*Number of Employees*	*Signatories on the Employees' Side*
Danone	France	Danone / IUF Agreement on health, safety, working conditions and stress	2011	104,642 (2013)[473]	IUF
Mizuno	Japan	Global Framework Agreement	2011	5,368 (2013)[474]	ITGLWF
Sodexo	France	International Framework Agreement	2011	428,000[475]	IUF
ZF Friedrichshafen	Germany	Global framework agreement on rights at work	2011	72,643 (2013)[476]	German Central Works Council, National trade unions
Petrobas	Brazil	Terms of Understanding of Good Labor Relations	2011	86,111 (2013)[477]	ICEM
Media Prima	Malaysia	Memorandum of Understanding between TV3 System Televisyen Malaysia Berhad and Uni Global Union - Malaysia Liaison Council	2010	4,605 (2009)[478]	UNI (Malaysia Liason Council)
GDF Suez	France	Group agreement on fundamental principles regarding health and safety	2010	147,200 (2013)	EPSU, Special Negotiating Group composed of national trade unions
Electrolux	Sweden	Agreement between AG Electrolux and employee representatives of IF metal, Unionen, IMF and the KFD[1] of the AB Electrolux Board of Directors	2010	60,783 (2013)[479]	IMF, National trade unions

473. Information available at <http://phx.corporate-ir.net/External.File?item=UGFyZW50SUQ9MjI2MzY1fENoaWxkSUQ9LTF8VHlwZT0z&t=1> accessed 10 April 2014.
474. Information available at <http://www.mizuno.com/corporate/> accessed 10 April 2014.
475. Information available at <http://www.sodexo.com/en/group/presentation.aspx> accessed 10 April 2014.
476. Information available at <http://www.zf.com/corporate/en/company/organization/facts_figures/annual_report/annual_report.html> accessed 10 April 2014.
477. Information available at <http://www.petrobras.com.br/en/about-us/profile/> accessed 11 April 2014.
478. Information on the database of the European Commission on TCAs.
479. Information available at <http://annualreports.electrolux.com/2013/en/Financialreporting/Employees.html> accessed 11 April 2014.

Company	*Country of Origin*	*Title of the Agreement*	*Year of Signature*	*Number of Employees*	*Signatories on the Employees' Side*
GDF Suez	France	Global Agreement on Fundamental Rights, Social Dialogue and Sustainable Development	2010	147,200 (2013)	BWI, ICEM, PSI
France Telecom (now Orange S.A.)	France	Agreement of France Telecom's Worldwide Works Council	2010	165,000 (2013)[480]	Special negotiating body (Members of EWC and UNI-France TELECOM Global Trade Union Alliance), UNI Global Union (advisor)
Telkom Indonesia	Indonesia	Global Framework Protocol between Telkom Indonesia and UNI Global Union	2010	25,011 (2013)[481]	UNI Global Union (AsiaPacific)
Antara	Indonesia	Labour Management Agreement on Code of Conduct between Antara, Antara Employees' Union and UNI Global Uni	2010	NA	UNI Global Union
Kimberly Clark	USA	Joint Statement between Kimberly-Clark and UNI/K-C Union Network	2010	57,000 (2013)[482]	UNI/K-C Network
Pflei-derer[483]	Germany	International Framework Agreement between Pfleiderer AG (hereinafter "Pfleiderer"), and IG Metall Germany, Building and Wood Workers International (BWI) and the European Works Council of Pfleiderer AG	2010	41,277[484]	BWI, EWC, National trade unions

480. Information available at <http://ar2013.orange.com/#Accueil> accessed 11 April 2014.
481. Information available at <http://www.telkom.co.id/assets/uploads/2013/05/AR_ENG_13.pdf> accessed 11 April 2014.
482. Information available at http://www.cms.kimberly-clark.com/umbracoimages/UmbracoFileMedia/2013%20Annual%20Report%20print-ready%20FINAL_20140220_umbracoFile.pdf> accessed 11 April 2014.
483. Since 2012 it is a subsidiary of Atlantik S.A – Luxembourg.
484. Information available in the database of the European Commission: <http://ec.europa.eu/social/main.jsp?catId=978&langId=en&agreementId=125> accessed 14 April 2014.

Company	*Country of Origin*	*Title of the Agreement*	*Year of Signature*	*Number of Employees*	*Signatories on the Employees' Side*
Shoprite Checkers	South Africa	Global Framework agreement	2010	111,338 (2013)[485]	UNI Global Union
Electrolux	Sweden	International Framework Agreement between AG Electrolux and employee representatives of IF metal, Unionen, IMF and the KFD[1] of the AB Electrolux Board of Directors	2010	60,783 (2013)	IMF, National trade unions
Tel Tele-comuni-cacoes LTDA	Brazil	UNI-TEL Telecomunicacoes LTDA Code of Conduct	2009	Approxi-mately 10,000[486]	UNI Global Union, UNI for the Americas
Elanders	Sweden	Global Framework Agreement on the respect and promotion of international labour standards and trade union rights	2009	1,898 (2013)[487]	UNI Global Union
Volks-wagen	Germany	Charter on Labour Relations within the Volkswagen Group	2009	572,800 (2013)	Volkswagen European Group Works Council, Volkswagen Group Global Works Council
Wilkhahn	Germany	International Framework Agreement on Social Responsibility and promotion of Employees' Rights	2009	More than 500[488]	BWI

485. Information available at <http://www.shopriteholdings.co.za/InvestorCentre/Documents/2013/Shoprite_2013_Integrated_Report.pdf> accessed 11 April 2014.
486. Information available at <http://www.teltelecom.com.br/en/Sobre/7/business_profile> accessed 11 April 2014.
487. Information available at <http://www.elanders.com/group/investor-relations/financial-overview/> accessed 11 April 2014.
488. Information available at <http://www.eurofound.europa.eu/areas/populationandsociety/cases/de006.htm> accessed 11 April 2014.

Company	*Country of Origin*	*Title of the Agreement*	*Year of Signature*	*Number of Employees*	*Signatories on the Employees' Side*
Inditex	Spain	Global agreement for implementation of fundamental labour rights and decent work	2009	128,313 (2013)	UNI Global Union
ENEL	Italy	CSR Protocol	2009	71,394	National trade unions
Ability Tecno-logias e Servicos S/A	Brazil	Code of conduct UNI – Ability Tecnologias e Servicos S/A	2008	1,897[489]	UNI Global Union, UNI for the Americas
Europcar	France	Europcar declaration on respect of social rights	2008	About 6,500 (2012)[490]	Instance of European personnel representation (EWC)
Arcelor-Mittal	Luxem-bourg	Agreement on minimum requirements for Plant level Joint H&S Committees	2008	232,000 (Dece-mber 2013)[491]	IMF, EMF, National trade unions
Adecco	Switzer-land	Memorandum of understanding between CIETT corporate members and Uni on temporary agency workers	2008	31,329 (2013)[492]	UNI Global Union
Arcelor-Mittal	Luxem-bourg	Terms of reference for a joint global OSH committee in ArcelorMittal	2008	232,000 (2013)	EMF, National trade unions IMF
ICONOM	Brazil	Codigo de conduta UNI – ICONOM	2008	NA	UNI Global Union, UNI for the Americas

489. Information available at <http://www.securities.com/Public/company-profile/BR/Ability_Tecnologia_e_Servicos_SA_en_2191610.html> accessed 11 April 2014.
490. Information available at <http://www.europcar.com/EBE/module/render/Facts-And-Figures> accessed 11 April 2014.
491. Information available at <http://corporate.arcelormittal.com/news-and-media/press-releases/2014/feb/07-02-2014> accessed 13 April 2014.
492. Information available at <http://annualreport2013.adecco.com/fileadmin/user_upload/redakteure/ar2013/pdf/Adecco_Group_AR2013.pdf> accessed 11 April 2014.

Company	*Country of Origin*	*Title of the Agreement*	*Year of Signature*	*Number of Employees*	*Signatories on the Employees' Side*
Kelly Services	USA	Memorandum of understanding between CIETT corporate members and Uni on temporary agency workers	2008	About 7,000[493]	UNI Global Union
Randstad	Nether-lands	Memorandum of understanding between CIETT corporate members and Uni on temporary agency workers	2008	28,030 (2013)[494]	UNI Global Union
Italce-menti	Italy	International Framework Agreement to promote and protect workers' rights	2008	18,500 (2013)[495]	BWI
Aker	Norway	Agreement on an International Framework Agreement for the development of good working relations in companies that are part of Aker	2008	27,299 (2013)[496]	IMF
Man-power	USA	Memorandum of understanding between CIETT corporate members and Uni on temporary agency workers	2008	30,000 (2010)[497]	UNI Global Union
Olympia Flexgroup	Germany	Memorandum of understanding between CIETT corporate members and Uni on temporary agency workers	2008	Over 8,000 (2009)[498]	UNI Global Union

493. Information available at <http://www.kellyservices.com/Global/About-Us/Company_Overview/> accessed 11 April 2014.
494. Information available at <http://www.randstadannualreport.com/financial-statements/notes-to-the-consolidated-financial-statements/other/number-of-employees-average> accessed 11 April 2014.
495. Information available at <http://www.italcementigroup.com/ENG/Italcementi+Group/> accessed 11 April 2014.
496. Information available at <http://www.akersolutions.com/Documents/Investors/Annual%20reports/AkerSolutions_AnnualReport_interactive_2013.pdf> accessed 11 April 2014.
497. Information available at <https://www.manpowergroup.com.au/about/about.aspx> accessed 11 April 2014.
498. Information available at <http://files.flexnieuws.nl/wp-uploads/Olympia_Q3_2009_5-nov-09.pdf> accessed 11 April 2014.

Company	*Country of Origin*	*Title of the Agreement*	*Year of Signature*	*Number of Employees*	*Signatories on the Employees' Side*
G4S	UK	A global Agreement: Ethical Employment Partnership	2008	618,260 (2013)[499]	UNI Global Union, National trade unions
PSA Peugeot	France	Agreement on the extension of the strategic equal committee	2008	200,682 (2013)[500]	National trade unions
Takashi-maya	Japan	Global Framework Agreement Labour-Management Agreement on Code of Conduct between Takashimaya Company Limited, Takashimaya Labour Union, JSD and UNI Global Union	2008	7,760 (2013)[501]	UNI Global Union, National trade unions
Danske Bank	Denmark	Global Framework Agreement on fundamental labour rights within Danske Bank Group	2008	19,122 (2013)[502]	UNI Global Union, UNI Finance National trade unions
Vallourec	France	Agreement on the principles of responsibilities	2008	24,000 (2013)[503]	IMF, EWC
USG People	Nether-lands	Memorandum of understanding between CIETT corporate members and Uni on temporary agency workers	2008	54,705[504]	UNI Global Union

499. Information available at <http://www.g4s.com/en/Who%20we%20are/Our%20people/Our%20employees/> accessed 11 April 2014.
500. Information available at <http://www.psa-peugeot-citroen.com/en/publications#> accessed 11 April 2014.
501. Information available at <http://www.takashimaya.co.jp/corp/ir/factbook/index2.html> accessed 11 April 2014.
502. Information available at <http://www.danskebank.com/en-uk/ir/Documents/2013/Q4/Annualreport-2013-parent-company.pdf> accessed 11 April 2014.
503. Information available at <http://www.vallourec.com/EN/GROUP/MEDIA/Publications/Lists/Publications/DRF_EN_BAT.PDF> accessed 11 April 2014.
504. Information available at <http://jaarverslag.usgpeople.com/en/overview-and-strategy/key-figures> accessed 11 April 2014.

Company	*Country of Origin*	*Title of the Agreement*	*Year of Signature*	*Number of Employees*	*Signatories on the Employees' Side*
Thyssen-Krupp AG	Germany	Principles of Social Responsibility in Labor Relations in the ThyssenKrupp Group	2007	156,856 (2013)	Group Works Councils, EWC
Dexia	Belgium	Evolution of the principles of social management of the Dexia Group: sale	2007	1,885 (2013)[505]	EWC
Siemens	Germany	Joint Statement between group management and Siemens Europe Committee concerning Compliance	2007	362,000 (2013)	Siemens Europe Committee (EWC)
Quebecor World Inc.[506]	Canada	Joint Statement on the respect and promotion of international labour standards	2007	25,000[507]	UNI Global Union
Danone	France	Convention on Diversity	2007	104,642 (2013)	IUF
Inditex	Spain	International Framework Agreement on the Implementation of International Labour Standards throughout the Inditex Supply Chain	2007	128,313 (2013)	ITGLWF
Brunel	Germany	Global Framework Agreement on Social resonsibility – A commitment to social responsibility without borders	2007	More than 13,000 (2013)[508]	IMF National trade unions
Umicore	Belgium	Sustainable Development Agreement	2007	14,056 (2013)[509]	IMF, ICEM, National trade unions

505. Information available at <http://www.dexia.com/EN/journalist/publications/annual_reports/Documents/RA_2013_GB.pdf> accessed 11 April 2014.
506. Acquired in 2010 by Quad/Graphics (USA).
507. Information available at <http://www.qg.com/news/quad_news_detail.asp?NewMessageID=38776> accessed 11 April 2014.
508. Information available at <http://www.brunel.net/about-us/corporate-profile.593440.lynkx> accessed 11 April 2014.
509. Information available at <http://www.umicore.com/en/aboutUs/keyFactsFigures/> accessed 11 April 2014.

Company	*Country of Origin*	*Title of the Agreement*	*Year of Signature*	*Number of Employees*	*Signatories on the Employees' Side*
WAZ	Germany	Framework Agreement between Westdeutsche Allgemeine Zeitung Mediengruppe (WAZ) and International Federation of Journalists/European Federation of Journalists (IFJ/EFJ on the defence and the promotion of press freedom, quality journalism and sound industry	2007	Approximately 15,000 (2012)[510]	IFJ, EFJ
Suez (now GDF Suez)[511]	France	Agreement on Commitment to promoting equality and diversity within the Group	2007	147,200 (2013)	ETUC, National trade unions, CEC, European Consultative Committee (EWC)
Volker-Wessels	Nether-lands	VolkerWessels: Signed between Royal Volker Wessels Stevin NV (VolkerWessels) and the Building and Wood Workers International (BWI) to promote and protect worker's rights	2007	14,500 (2013)[512]	BWI
Suez (now GDF Suez)	France	Group Agreement on Employees Ownership Scheme	2007	147,200 (2013)	ETUC, National trade unions, CEC, European Consultative Committee (EWC)

510. Information available at <http://www.adflow-systems.de/index.php/en/case-studies/170-westdeutsche-allgemeine-zeitung-waz-mediengruppe-2> accessed 11 April 2014.
511. GDF Suez was founded in 2008 via the merger of Gaz de France and Suez. The number of employees of GDF Suez has been used as a criterion to select this agreement.
512. Information available at <http://en.volkerwessels.com/dynamics/modules/SFIL0200/view.php?fil_Id=347239> accessed 11 April 2014.

Company	*Country of Origin*	*Title of the Agreement*	*Year of Signature*	*Number of Employees*	*Signatories on the Employees' Side*
France Telecom	France	Worldwide Agreement on Fundamental Labour Rights within the France Telecom Group	2006	165,000 (2013)	UNI Global Union, 'Alliance Syndicale Mondiale France Telecom', French employee representatives represented by national trade unions
PSA Peugeot	France	International Framework Agreement on PSA Peugeot Citroën's Social Responsibility	2006 (revised in 2010)	200,682 (2013)	IMF, EMF, EWC, National trade unions
Nampak	South Africa	Global Agreement on the Respect and Promotion of International Labour Standards between Nampak LTD. And Union Network International	2006	12,291 (2013)[513]	UNI Global Union
National Australia Group	Australia	Global Agreement – The National Australia Group and Global Union Engagement Strategy	2006	Over 42,000 (2013)[514]	UNI Global Union, National trade unions
Euradius	Nether-lands	Global Agreement	2006	700 (2012)[515]	UNI Global Union National trade unions
Daimler-Chrysler	Germany	Occupational Health and Safety Principles of DaimlerChrysler	2006	274,616 (2013)[516]	IMF

513. Information available at <http://www.nampak.com/DynamicData/AnnualReport/Current/Nampak%20IAR%202013.pdf> accessed 11 April 2014.
514. Information available at <http://www.nab.com.au/content/dam/nab/about-us/shareholder-centre/annual-reports/pdf-reports/annual-financial-report-2013.pdf> accessed 11 April 2014.
515. Information on the database of the European Commission on TCAs.
516. Information available at <http://www.daimler.com/Projects/c2c/channel/documents/2432177_Daimler_2013_Annual_Report.pdf> accessed 13April 2014.

Company	*Country of Origin*	*Title of the Agreement*	*Year of Signature*	*Number of Employees*	*Signatories on the Employees' Side*
Portugal Telecom	Portugal	Social Responsibility Code of Conduct	2006	12,729 (2013)[517]	UNI Global Union, National trade unions
Staedler	Germany	International Framework Agreement between STAEDTLER, IG Metall Germany and Building and Woodworkers' International (BWI)	2006	2,200 (2012)[518]	BWI, National trade unions
Securitas	Sweden	Agreement between Securitas AB (publ) and Union Network International and Swedish Transport Workers' Union on the development of good working relations in the Securitas group	2006	Nearly 310,000 (2013)[519]	UNI Global Union, National trade unions
Royal BAM	Nether-lands	Framework agreement signed between Royal BAM Group nv and Building and Woodworkers International (BWI) to promote and protect worker's rights	2006	23,502 (2013)[520]	BWI
EDF	France	Agreement on EDF Group Corporate Social Responsibility	2005 (renewed in 2009)	158,467 (2013)[521]	Group employee representative, representatives of national trade unions, ICEM, PSI, IFME

517. Information available at < http://www.telecom.pt/NR/rdonlyres/A4A58A50-2DD6-4254-855B-FC4908B3934F/1469941/140521RCCIngFINALbaixaresol.pdf> accessed 11 April 2014.
518. Information available at <http://www.staedtler.com/en/company/staedtler-today/company-profile/> accessed 11 April 2014.
519. Information available at <http://www.securitas.com/Global/Serbia/Annual%20report%202013/Annual_Report_2013.pdf> accessed 11 April 2014.
520. Information available at <http://www.bam.eu/investor-relations/key-figures> accessed 11 April 2014.
521. Information available at <http://about-us.edf.com/profile/key-figures-43669.html> accessed 11 April 2014.

Company	*Country of Origin*	*Title of the Agreement*	*Year of Signature*	*Number of Employees*	*Signatories on the Employees' Side*
Schwan Stabilo	Germany	International Framework Agreement between Schwanhäußer Industrie Holding GmbH & Co KG, 90562 Heroldsberg, Germany and IG Metall, Germany / International Federation of Building and Wood Workers (IFBWW)	2005	About 3,500[522]	IFBWW National trade unions
Rhodia[523]	France	Global Corporate Social Responsibility Agreement between Rhodia and ICEM	2005 (revised in 2008 and 2010)	29,400 (2013)	ICEM
EADS	Nether-lands	International Framework Agreement	2005	143,358 (2013)[524]	EWC, IMF, EMF
UPU	Switzer-land	Memorandum of Understanding	2005	5.5 million (2012)[525]	UNI Global Union
Danone	France	Fundamental Social Principles	2005	104,642 (2013)	IUF
Lafarge	France	Global Agreement on Corporate Social Responsibility and International Industrial Relations	2005 (amended in 2013)	64,000 (2013)	BWI, IndustriALL
Danone	France	Convention on the setting up of social indicators at group level	2005	104,642 (2013)	IUF
Coca Cola	USA	Joint Coca-Cola and IUF Statement	2005	130,600 (2013)[526]	IUF

522. Information available in the database of the European Commission: < http://ec.europa.eu/social/main.jsp?catId=978&langId=en&agreementId=149 > accessed 11 April 2014.
523. Acquired by Solvay Group in 2011. The number of employees refers to Solvay.
524. Information available at <http://uk.reuters.com/article/2013/07/31/idUSnHUGdd5t+70+ONE20130731> accessed 13April 2014.
525. Information available at <http://news.upu.int/fileadmin/user_upload/PDF/Reports/annual_report_2012.pdf> accessed 11 April 2014.
526. Information available at <http://www.sec.gov/Archives/edgar/data/21344/0000021344140000008/a2013123110-k.htm> accessed 11 April 2014.

Company	*Country of Origin*	*Title of the Agreement*	*Year of Signature*	*Number of Employees*	*Signatories on the Employees' Side*
Veidekke	Norway	Global Framework Agreement between Fellesforbundet, Norsk Arbeidsmandsforbund/IFBWW and Veidekke ASA on the development of good working relations in Veidekke ASA operations worldwide	2005	6,300 (2013)[527]	IFBWW, National trade unions
BMW	Germany	Joint Declaration on Human Rights and on Working Conditions in the BMW Group	2005	110,351 (2013)[528]	EWC, IMF
Arcelor[529]	Luxem-bourg	Worldwide Agreement on the Principles of Arcelor's Corporate Social responsibility	2005	232,000 (2013)	EMF, IMF
GeoPost	Germany	Framework agreement on the principles of GeoPost international management & Development Holding GmB regarding social policy and employment in its sector	2005	20,000[530]	UNI, National trade unions
Falck	Denmark	Falck Agreement of 21 March 2005 between Falck A/S of Copenhagen. Denmark and UNI (Union Network International) establishing a Social Dialogue through a Worldwide Works Council	2005	32,009 (2013)[531]	UNI Global Union

527. Information available at <http://hugin.info/172/R/1776653/606185.pdf> accessed 11 April 2014.
528. Information available at <http://www.bmwgroup.com/bmwgroup_prod/e/0_0_www_bmw-group_com/investor_relations/finanzberichte/geschaeftsberichte/2013/_pdf/report2013.pdf> accessed 11 April 2014.
529. Arcelor merged with Mittal Steel to form ArcelorMittal since 2006. The number of employees of ArcelorMittal has been used as a criterion to select this agreement.
530. Information available at <http://www.geopostgroup.com/jahia/Jahia/geopost/profile/hu-man-resources> accessed 11 April 2014.
531. Information available at <http://www.falck.com/SiteCollectionDocuments/Annual%20re-ports/Falck_annual_report_2013.pdf> accessed 11 April 2014.

Company	*Country of Origin*	*Title of the Agreement*	*Year of Signature*	*Number of Employees*	*Signatories on the Employees' Side*
SCA	Sweden	Framework Agreement – Agreement between SCA and IndustriAll Global union/Pappers / SCA EWC	2004 (2013)	34,004 (2013)[532]	IndustriALL, EWC, National trade unions
Bosch	Germany	Basic Principles of Social Responsibility at Bosch	2004	281,381 (2013)[533]	IMF, European Committee (EWC)
Club Médi-terranée	France	Agreement on the respect of fundamental rights at work and transnational mobility	2004 (amended in 2009)	12,865 (2013)[534]	IUF
CSA Czech Airlines	Czech Republic	Code of conduct on CSR	2004	5,500[535]	NA
Lukoil	Russia	Agreement between International Federation of Chemical, Energy, Mine and General Workers' Unions, Russian Oil and Gas Workers Union And Open Joint Stock Company "Oil Company LUKOIL"	2004	150,000 (2011)[536]	ICEM, National trade unions
H&M	Sweden	Agreement between H & M hennes & Mauritz AB (H &M) and Union Network International (UNI) on Cooperation in order to secure and promote fundamental worker's rights at H&M's workplaces worldwide	2004	Over 116,000 (2013)[537]	UNI Global Union

532. Information available at <http://www.sca.com/Documents/en/Annual_Reports/SCA-Annual-Report-2013.pdf?epslanguage=en> accessed 11 April 2014.
533. Information available at <http://www.bosch.com/en/com/bosch_group/bosch_figures/bosch-figures.php> accessed 11 April 2014.
534. Information available at <http://www.clubmed-corporate.com/wp-content/uploads/2014/02/VCONSO-ENG-VDEF.pdf> accessed 14 April 2014.
535. Information in the database of the European Commission on TCAs.
536. Information in the database of the European Commission.
537. Information available at <http://about.hm.com/content/dam/hm/about/documents/en/Annual%20Report/Annual-Report-2013_en.pdf> accessed 11 April 2014.

Company	*Country of Origin*	*Title of the Agreement*	*Year of Signature*	*Number of Employees*	*Signatories on the Employees' Side*
Impregilo	Italy	Framework Agreement	2004	31,000 (2013)[538]	IFBWW National trade unions
Renault	France	Renault Group employees' fundamental rights declaration	2004	121,807 (2013)	IMF, Renault Group Works Council, National trade unions
Röchling	Germany	Principles of Social Responsibility Codes of Conduct Gebr. Röchling KG	2004	7,500[539]	IMF, EWC, EMF
Prym	Germany	Declaration of the Social rights and Industrial relations within the Prym Group	2004	About 3,500 (2013)[540]	IMF, EWC
ISS	Denmark	Uni – ISS Global Agreement	2003 (replaced in 2008)	533,544 (2013)[541]	UNI Global Union
GEA	Germany	Codes of Conduct of GEA AG	2003	18,000 (2013)[542]	IMF, EWF, EWC
SKF	Sweden	SKF Code of Conduct	2003	48,401 (2013)[543]	IMF, EMF
RAG[544]	Germany	Agreement between RAG and IG BCE/ICEM on Cooperative Labor	2003	About 33,000 (2013)[545]	ICEM, National trade unions

538. Information available at <http://www.salini-impregilo.com/static/upload/imp/impregilo-annual-20131231/impregilo-annual-20131231.pdf> accessed 11 April 2014.
539. Information available at <http://www.roechling.com/en/roechling-group/about-the-group.html> accessed 11 April 2014.
540. Information available at <http://www.prym.com/prym/proc/docs/0H04001Jz.html?nav=0H04001dZ> accessed 11 April 2014.
541. Information available at <http://www.annualreport.issworld.com/2013/> accessed 11 April 2014.
542. Information available at <http://www.gea.com/imperia/pb/1%20GEA%20Group/Medien/Factsheet%20GEA%20Group/GEA_FACTSHEET_EN.pdf> accessed 11 April 2014.
543. Information available at <http://www.skf.com/group/investors/skf-fact-sheet> accessed 11 April 2014.
544. Evonik Industries was created in 2007 as a successor of RAG. The number of employees refers to Evonik Industries.
545. Information available at <http://corporate.evonik.com/en/company/pages/default.aspx> accessed 11 April 2014.

Company	*Country of Origin*	*Title of the Agreement*	*Year of Signature*	*Number of Employees*	*Signatories on the Employees' Side*
		Relationships and the Protection of Good Working Conditions within the Worldwide Business Activity of the RAG Group			
Rhein-metall	Germany	Social Responsibility Guidelines Code of Conduct of Rheinmetall AG	2003	21,081 (2013)[546]	IMF, EMF, EWC
ENI	Italy	Agreement on transnational industrial relations and corporate social responsibility	2002 (updated in 2004 and 2009)	82,289[547]	ICEM, National trade unions
Leoni	Germany	Declaration of Social Rights and Industrial Relationshsips at Leoni	2002	53, 163 (2013)[548]	IMF, EWC
Daimler-Chrysler	Germany	Social Responsibility Principles of DaimlerChrysler	2002	274,616 (2013)	Company's World Employee committee (on behalf of IMF)
Norske Skog	Norway	Agreement between Fellesforbundet/ICEM and Norske Skogindustrier ASA on the Development of Good Working Relations in Norske Skogindustrier's Worldwide Operations	2002	3,274 (2013)	ICEM, National trade unions
Volks-wagen	Germany	Declaration on Social Rights and Industrial Relationships at Volkswagen	2002	572,800 (2013)	Group global works council, IMF
Suez (now GDF Suez)	France	Charter Health and Safety at Work	2002	147,200 (2013)	European Consultative Committee (EWC)

546. Information available at <http://www.rheinmetall.com/en/rheinmetall_ag/group/facts_and_figures/facts-and-figures.php> accessed 11 April 2014.
547. Information available at <http://www.eni.com/en_IT/attachments/publications/reports/reports-2013/Annual-Report-2013.pdf> accessed 14 April 2014.
548. Information available at <https://d3gx8i893xzz0e.cloudfront.net/fileadmin/corporate/investors/events/2014/2013_group_management_report.pdf?1398351625> accessed 11 April 2014.

Company	*Country of Origin*	*Title of the Agreement*	*Year of Signature*	*Number of Employees*	*Signatories on the Employees' Side*
Ballast Nedam	Nether-lands	Framework agreement between Ballast Nedam and IFBWW	2002	About 425 (2013)	IFBWW National trade unions
Anglo-gold[549]	South Africa	Global agreement on the promotion and implementation of good human and industrial relations in anglogold operations worldwide	2002	66,434 (2013)[550]	ICEM, National trade unions
Fonterra	New Zealand	Agreement between Fonterra, the IUF and the New Zealand Dairy Workers Union	2002	17,500 (2013)[551]	IUF, National trade unions
Endesa[552]	Spain	ICEM Global Agreement with Endesa	2002	22.995 (2013)[553] ENEL: 71,394 (2013)	ICEM
Triumph	Switzer-land	Triumph International's Code of Conduct	2001	13,900 (2013)[554]	EWC, European regional organisation of the ITGLF
Tele-fonica	Spain	UNI-Telefonica Code of conduct	2001	More than 126,000 (2013)[555]	UNI Global Union, National trade unions

549. It merged in 2004 with Ashanti Goldfields Corporation. The number of employees refers to Ashanti Goldfields Corporation.
550. Information available at <http://www.aga-reports.com/13/os> accessed 11 April 2014.
551. Information available at <http://www.rspo.org/file/acop/fonterra-co-operative-group-ltd/M-GHG-Emissions-Report.pdf> accessed 11 April 2014.
552. Endesa is a subisdiary of ENEL.
553. Information available at <http://www.endesa.com/en/aboutEndesa/keyFfigures> accessed 11 April 2014.
554. Information available at <http://phx.corporate-ir.net/phoenix.zhtml?c=61870&p=irol-reportsannual> accessed 11 April 2014.
555. Information available at <http://annualreport2013.telefonica.com/sites/default/files/documentos/TELEF_Informe%20Integrado%20ENG%20%2803_07%29.pdf> accessed 11 April 2014.

Company	*Country of Origin*	*Title of the Agreement*	*Year of Signature*	*Number of Employees*	*Signatories on the Employees' Side*
Skanska	Sweden	Agreement between Skanska and IFBWW	2001	57,105 (2013)[556]	IFBWW
OTE	Greece	Global agreement	2001	22,667 (2013)[557]	UNI Global Union, National trade unions
IKEA	Sweden	Framework agreement between IKEA and the IFBWW	2001	135,000 (2013)[558]	IFBWW
Merloni (know now as Indesit)	Italy	Statement of Agreement	2001	16,000 (2013)[559]	IMF, National trade unions
Chiquita	USA	Agreement on Freedom of Association, Minimum labour Standards and Employment in Latin American Banana Operations	2001	20,000 (2013)[560]	IMF, General director ILO
Faber Castell	Germany	AGREEMENT between A.W. Faber-Castell Unternehmensverwaltung GmbH & Co, 90546 Stein and Industriegewerkschaft Metall/Bau- und Holzarbeiter Internationale, BHI	2000 (amended in 2008)	About 7,000[561]	IFBWW, National trade unions

556. Information available at <http://www.group.skanska.com/cdn-1cf50054c5df1fc/Global/Investors/Reports/2013/Annual-Report-2013.pdf> accessed 11 April 2014.
557. Information available at <https://www.ote.gr/documents/10280/30244/ANNUAL_REPORT_2013_ENGLISH.pdf/7c824279-de82-41ed-b904-84fb5990772d> accessed 11 April 2014.
558. Information available at <http://www.ikea.com/ms/en_US/pdf/yearly_summary/ikea-group-yearly-summary-fy13.pdf> accessed 11 April 2014.
559. Information available at <http://annualreport13.indesitcompany.com/index_en.html> accessed 11 April 2014.
560. Information available at <http://investors.chiquita.com/phoenix.zhtml?c=119836&p=irol-reportsannual> accessed 11 April 2014.
561. Information available at <http://www.faber-castell.co.uk/company/facts-and-figures> accessed 11 April 2014.

Company	*Country of Origin*	*Title of the Agreement*	*Year of Signature*	*Number of Employees*	*Signatories on the Employees' Side*
Hochtief	Germany	Framework agreement between Hochtief and IFBWW	2000	80,912 (2013)[562]	IFBWW, National trade unions, Company General Works' Council
Carrefour	France	Global Agreement Carrefour – UNI Union Network International	2000	364,795 (2013)[563]	UNI Global Union
Freud-enberg	Germany	Cooperation, Responsibility and Social Dialogue in the Freudenberg Group	2000	39,897 (2013)[564]	ICEM, National trade unions
Suez-Lyonnaise des Eaux[565]	France	International social charter	1998	147,200 (2013)	European Instance of Dialogue (EWC)
Statoil-Hydro	Norway	The exchange of information and the development of good working practice within Statoil worldwide operations	1998 (renewed in 2001, 2008 and 2010)	More than 23,400 (2013)[566]	ICEM
Danone	France	Convention applicable in the event of changes in business activities affecting employment or working conditions	1997 (updated in 2005)	104,642 (2013)	IUF

562. Information available at <http://www.hochtief.com/hochtief_en/174.jhtml> accessed 11 April 2014.
563. Information available at <http://www.carrefour.com/content/key-figures> accessed 11 April 2014.
564. Information available at <http://www.freudenberg.com/en/Company/Pages/Facts-and-Figures.aspx> accessed 11 April 2014.
565. This company was merged in 1997 to form Suez, which in turn was merged to form GDF Suez. The number of employees of GDF Suez has been used as a criterion to select this agreement.
566. Information available at <http://www.statoil.com/no/InvestorCentre/AnnualReport/AnnualReport2013/Documents/DownloadCentreFiles/01_KeyDownloads/AnnualReport20-F.pdf> accessed 11 April 2014.

Company	*Country of Origin*	*Title of the Agreement*	*Year of Signature*	*Number of Employees*	*Signatories on the Employees' Side*
Vivendi (Veolia Générale des Eaux)[567]	France	Charter of fundamental social rights	1996	202,800 (2013)[568]	European Social Dialogue Body (management and employee representatives) (EWC)
Accor	France	Agreement between the IUF and the Accor Group on Trade Union Rights	1995	172,841 (2013)[569]	IUF
Danone	France	Convention on trade union rights	1994 (updated in 2005)	104,642 (2013)	IUF
Danone	France	Convention on skills training	1992 (updated in 2005)	104,642 (2013)	IUF
Danone	France	Convention on economic and social data in Group Danone companies	1989 (updated in 2005)	104,642 (2013)	IUF
Danone	France	Convention for the promotion of equality of men and women in the workplace	1989 (updated in 2005)	104,642 (2013)	IUF
Danone	France	Common viewpoint IUF/BSN	1988	104,642 (2013)	IUF

567. The number of employees of Veolia Environment has been used as a criterion to select this agreement. Veolia Environment (previously known as Vivendi Environment) is one of the company resulting from the spin-off of Vivendi.
568. Information available at <http://www.veolia.com/en/veolia-group/profile/csr-performance/HR-performance> accessed 12 April 2014.
569. Information available at <http://www.accor.com/fileadmin/user_upload/Contenus_Accor/Finance/Documentation/2014/UK/2013_registration_document.pdf> accessed 11 April 2014.

Table 2 EFAs concluded between 1996 and May 2014

Company	*Country of Origin*	*Title of the Agreement*	*Year of Signature*	*Number of Employees*	*Signatories on the Employees' Side*
Pernod Ricard	France	Pernod Ricard European agreement on CSR	2014	Approximately 18,000 (2012)[570]	EFFAT
Michelin	France	European framework agreement on social responsibility and sustainable development	2014	105,700 (2013)[571]	EWC
Safran	France	European framework agreement for professional integration of young people	2013	66,300 (2013)[572]	IndustriALL
Lafarge	France	Declaration "well-being at work". Appendix to the Health, Safety & Security declaration of June 1st 2011	2013	64,000 (2013)[573]	EWC, EFBWW
Groupama	France	Joint declaration relative to quality of life at work	2013	16,009 (2013)[574]	EWC
Air France/ KLM	France	Framework agreement regarding the Air France KLM and Martinair Cargo organisation in Europe	2013	95,961 (2013)[575]	EWC
Air France/ KLM	France	Framework agreement regarding the Outstations in Europe	2013	95,961 (2013)	EWC

570. Information available at <http://pernod-ricard.com/files/fichiers/Commun/Documents/RA 2012_13_VGB_MiseEnLigne_28102013.pdf> accessed 10 April 2014.
571. Information available at <http://www.michelin.com/eng/finance/key-figures-indicators/ consolidated-data> accessed 10 April 2014.
572. Information available at <http://www.safran-group.com/IMG/pdf/Leaflet_Safran_EN-May-2014.pdf> accessed 10 April 2014.
573. Information available at <http://www.lafarge.com/07092014-finance_publication-shareholders_guide_2014-en.pdf#page=1&zoom=auto,-107,260> accessed 10 April 2014.
574. Information available at < http://en.groupama-sa.com/finance/groupama-s-a-at-a-glance/ key-figures/key-figures-@/article.jspz?id=2792> accessed 10 April 2014.
575. Information available at <http://corporate.airfrance.com/en/the-company/key-figures/work force/> accessed 10 April 2014.

Company	*Country of Origin*	*Title of the Agreement*	*Year of Signature*	*Number of Employees*	*Signatories on the Employees' Side*
Air France/ KLM	France	Social Rights and Ethics Charter	2013	95,961 (2013)	EWC
Rhein-metall	France	Framework agreement on the management of health Rheinmetall Group	2012	21,081 (2013)	EWC
Allianz SE	Germany	Agreement on guidelines concerning Lifelong Learning	2012	171,340 (2013)[576]	SE Works Council
Veolia Environ-ment	France	Letter of commitment from the General Human Resources Management and the members of the Bureau of Veolia environment's European Works Council	2012	202,800 (2013)	EWC, Health and Safety Prevention Committee
Valeo	France	Agreement on Social Responsibility	2012	74,800 (2013)[577]	EWC
Alstom	France	European agreement on social commitments during the transition period of the Joint-venture between Alstom and Shanghai Electric on Boilers	2012	93,000 (2013)[578]	EMF
GDF Suez	France	European agreement on professional equality between men and women	2012	147,200 (2013)	Special Negotiating Group, IndustriALL, CEC, EPSU

576. Information available at < http://www.itec-sde.eu/en/search_results?search = % > accessed 12 April 2014.
577. Information available at <http://www.valeo.com/en/our-commitments/ethics/> accessed 12 April 2014.
578. Information available at <http://www.alstom.com/Hungary/about-us/> accessed 12 April 2014.

Company	*Country of Origin*	*Title of the Agreement*	*Year of Signature*	*Number of Employees*	*Signatories on the Employees' Side*
BNP Paribas	France	European social charter employment management	2012	185,000 (2013)[579]	EWC, FECEC, UNI-Europa
AXA Assistance	France	European agreement on anticipating changes within Axa Assistance	2011	Approxi-mately 6,800[580] AXA Group: 157,000	UNI-Europa Finance, National trade unions
AXA Group	France	European agreement on anticipating changes within Axa Assistance	2011	157,000 (2013)[581]	UNI-Europa Finance, National trade unions
Lafarge	France	Joint declaration concerning Health, Safety and Hygiene	2011	64,000 (2013)	EWC, EFBWW
Allianz SE	Germany	Agreement on Guidelines Concerning Work Related Stress	2011	171,340 (2013)	SE Works Council
Areva	France	Group Memorandum of Agreement on Professions and Competences Forecast and Management with the Areva Group in Europe	2011	45,340 (2013)[582]	EMF
Alstom	France	Agreement on the anticipation of change or development in Alstom	2011	93,000 (2013)	EMF
EADS	France	Group agreement on the harmonisation of the variable remuneration of Senior	2011	143,358 (2013)	EWC, European Negotiating Group

579. Information available at <http://annualreport.bnpparibas.com/2013/ra/BNPParibas_2013_Annual_Report.pdf> accessed 13 April 2014.
580. Information available at <http://www.axa-assistance.us/downloads/AXA_Assistance_press_release__2013_results.pdf > accessed 13 April 2014.
581. Information available at <http://annualreport.axa/group-results> accessed 13 April 2014.
582. Information available at <http://areva.com/EN/group-3870/groupekey-figures2013-key-figures.html> accessed 13 April 2014.

Company	*Country of Origin*	*Title of the Agreement*	*Year of Signature*	*Number of Employees*	*Signatories on the Employees' Side*
		Managers within the EADS Group			(composed of representatives of national trade unions)
EADS	Nether-lands	Group Agreement for the Implementation of a Success-Sharing Plan within the EADS-NV Group	2011 (this text replaces the text of 2009)	143,358 (2013)	EWC, National trade unions members of the European Negotiating Group
Air France/ KLM	France	Framework agreement regarding the Outstations in Europe	2011	95,961 (2013)	EWC
Santander	Spain	Joint declaration of the European Works Council (EWC) and the Central Management of Santander Group regarding the labour relations framework for the provision of financial services	2011	182,958 (2013)[583]	EWC
DBApparel	France	Anticipation task force	2010	7,500 (2013)[584]	EWC, ETUF-TCL
EADS	Nether-lands	Agreement relating to the procedure for labor negotiations at European level	2010	143,358 (2013)	Representatives of national trade unions
Etex	Belgium	Health, Safety and Environment on the workplace Charter	2010	17,442 (2013)[585]	EWC
Veolia Environ-ment	France	Veolia Environment European Works Council Agreement	2010 (it replaces the text of 2005)	202,800 (2013)	EWC Assisted by: CES and CEC

583. Information available at <http://www.santanderannualreport.com/2013/en/sustainability-report/main-figures> accessed 13 April 2014.
584. Information available at <http://www.dbapparel.com/people> accessed 13 April 2014.
585. Information available at <http://www.etexgroup.com/sites/etex/files/Etex_AR2013.pdf> accessed 13April 2014.

Company	*Country of Origin*	*Title of the Agreement*	*Year of Signature*	*Number of Employees*	*Signatories on the Employees' Side*
Thales	France	European Collective Agreement – A Transparent annual Activity Discussion for mutual Listening (TALK)	2010	65,000 (2013)[586]	Central Works Council (EWC)
PPR (now known as Kering since June 2013)	France	Framework of Commitments on Quality of life at Work and Prevention of Work-related Stress for Employees within the PPR Group in Europe	2010	35,000 (2013)[587]	EWC Select Committee
RWE	Germany	Agreement on the application of minimum standards for restructuring in the RWE Group between the European works council and RWE AG while acting on behalf of the companies represented in the European Works council	2010 (2007)[588]	66,341 (2013)[589]	EWC
Recticel	Belgium	Code of Conduct Temporary Workers	2010	11,590[590]	Select Committee (EWC)
Alstom	France	European Agreement on Social Commitments in the	2010	93,000 (2013)	EMF

586. Information available at <https://www.thalesgroup.com/en/worldwide/facts-and-figures-0> accessed 13April 2014.
587. Information available at <http://www.kering.com/en/group/about-kering> accessed 13 April 2014.
588. It is not clear from the agreement concluded in 2010 if it is a replacement, a revision or an update of the agreement concluded in 2007 (see Commission, 'Mapping of transnational texts negotiated at corporate level' (n 113) 35).
589. Information available at <http://www.rwe.com/web/cms/mediablob/en/2320248/data/10122/5/rwe/about-rwe/RWE-Annual-Report-2013.pdf> accessed 13April 2014.
590. Information available at <http://www.rebiofoam.eu/project-partners-recticel.php> accessed 13 April 2014.

Company	Country of Origin	Title of the Agreement	Year of Signature	Number of Employees	Signatories on the Employees' Side
		framework of the take-over of Areva T&D			
Schneider Electric	France	European Agreement on Social Commitments in the framework of the take-over of Areva T&D	2010	More than 150,000 (2013)[591]	EMF
Air France/ KLM	France	Framework agreement on sales agencies in airports (ATOs) in Europe between, on the one hand, the management of CDL Europe/North Africa and, on the other, the European Group Council	2010	95,961 (2013)	European Group Council
Adam Opel AG[592]	Germany	Agreement on European restructuring ("Opel Plan for the Future")[593]	2010	GM: more than 212,000 (2013)[594] Opel: more than 35,000 in Europe (2013)[595]	EWC[596]

591. Information available at <http //www2.schneider-electric.com/sites/corporate/en/group/company-profile.page> accessed 13April 2014.
592. Adam Opel AG is a subsidiary of General Motors. The number of employees of the parent company has been taken into consideration as a selection criterion.
593. Further information on this EFA available in Da Costa and Rehfeldt, 'Transnational Restructuring Agreements: General Overview and Specific Evidence from the European Automobile Sector' (n. 89) 158-159; Pulignano et al., 'Local Actors and Transnational Structures – Explaining Trends in Multinational Company-Level Negotiations in Europe' (n. 240) 148. See also <http://media.opel.com/media/intl/en/opel/news.detail.html/content/Pages/news/intl/en/2010/OPEL/05_21_opel_plan_future.html> accessed 13 April 2014.
594. Information available at <http://www.gm.com/company/aboutGM/our_company.html> accessed 13April 2014> accessed 13 April 2014.
595. Information available at <http://media.gm.com/content/dam/Media/e-books/Facts-and-Figures-2013/FF2013.pdf> accessed 13 April 2014.
596. As the text of the agreement is not available in the database of the European Commission and cannot be retrieved in the website of the MNE, the information about the employees' side

Company	*Country of Origin*	*Title of the Agreement*	*Year of Signature*	*Number of Employees*	*Signatories on the Employees' Side*
Areva	France	Open dialogue through equal opportunities (ODEO) – 2010 Amendment of the Agreement on Equal Opportunities within the Areva Group in Europe	2010	45,340 (2013)	EMF
GDF Suez	France	European group agreement relating to the employment and expertise plan	2010	147,200 (2013)	EPSU, EMCEF, Special Negotiated Group (represented by national trade unions)
ABB	Switzer-land	European Appendix to ABB social policy	2009	147,700 (2013)[597]	Employees Council Europe (EWC)
Econocom	Belgium	European Framework Agreement	2009	8,300 (2013)[598]	European Works Council representatives: SETCA, FGTB, CGSLB (Belgium) and CGT, CFDT, CFTC, FO, CGC (France)
Thales	France	European agreement on 'Improving professional Development through Effective Anticipation' (IDEA)	2009	65,000 (2013)	EMF

signatories can be found in Da Costa and Rehfeldt, 'Transnational Restructuring Agreements: General Overview and Specific Evidence from the European Automobile Sector' (n. 89) 158.

597. Information available at <http://www400.abbext.com/annual-report-2013/servicepages/welcome.html> accessed 13 April 2014.

598. Information available at <http://www.econocom.com/sites/default/files/global_compact_2014_25022014-def.pdf> accessed 12 April 2014.

Company	*Country of Origin*	*Title of the Agreement*	*Year of Signature*	*Number of Employees*	*Signatories on the Employees' Side*
Axa Group	France	Agreement on the Axa Group European Works Council	2009	157,000 (2013)	UNI Europa National trade unions
General Motors Europe[599]	Switzer-land[600]	Working time reduction	2009	GME (defunct): 54,500 (2009) GM: more than 212,000 (2013)	EWC[601]
Arcelor-Mittal	Luxem-bourg	Managing & Anticipating change	2009	232,000 (2013)	EMF
Unicredit	Italy	Joint declaration on equal opportunities	2009	148,341 (2013)[602]	EWC
Santander	Spain	Declaration on Social Rights and Labour Relations in Santander Group	2009	182,958 (2013)	EWC
Unicredit	Italy	Joint declaration on "training, learning and professional development	2008	148,341 (2013)	EWC
BP	Germany	Agreement on "Business Service Centre (BSC)" Consultation	2008	83,900 (2013)[603]	EWC

599. General Motors Europe was a subsidiary of General Motors, a company headquartered in the United States of America. The number of employees of General Motors has been taken into consideration as a selection criterion.
600. Da Costa and Rehfeldt, 'Transnational Restructuring Agreements: General Overview and Specific Evidence from the European Automobile Sector' (n. 89) 153 (as of 2010 the European headquarter of General Motors Europe has been moved to Germany).
601. As the text of the agreement is not available in the database of the European Commission and cannot be retrieved in the website of the MNE, the information about the employees' side signatories can be found in Da Costa and Rehfeldt, 'Transnational Restructuring Agreements: General Overview and Specific Evidence from the European Automobile Sector' (n. 89) 158.
602. Information available at <https://www.unicreditgroup.eu/content/dam/unicreditgroup/documents/en/investors/financial-reports/2013/Consolidated_Interim_Report_as_at_September_30_2013.pdf> accessed 13April 2014.
603. Information available at <http://www.bp.com/en/global/corporate/about-bp/bp-at-a-glance.html> accessed 13April 2014.

Company	*Country of Origin*	*Title of the Agreement*	*Year of Signature*	*Number of Employees*	*Signatories on the Employees' Side*
Santander	Spain	Joint Declaration to be signed in the meeting on 21.05.2008 between the European Works Council and the representatives designated by group Santander's senior management	2008	182,958 (2013)	EWC
Solvay	Belgium	Charter on Sustainable Development and Corporate Social Responsibility	2008	29,400 (2013)	EWC
PPR	France	Commitment for the Employment of Disabled Persons in Europe	2008	35,000 (2013)	EWC
Suez (now GDF Suez)	France	Agreement on social guarantees for Suez Group employees	2008	147,200 (2013)	ETUC, CEC, National trade unions, European Consultative Committee
PPR	France	Charter on Senior Employment	2008	35,000 (2013)	EWC
Unicredit	Italy	Establishment of the Joint Commissions	2008	148,341 (2013)	EWC
GDF (now GDF Suez)	France	European agreement on the corporate social responsibility of the Gaz de France group	2008	147,200 (2013)	EMCEF, EPSU, EMF, National trade unions
Strawood Lodging	USA	Agreement regarding the transnational transfer of Starwood Employees	2007	181,400 (2013)[604]	European Employee Communication

604. Information available at <http://www.sec.gov/Archives/edgar/data/316206/000119312514065122/d645634d10k.htm> accessed 13April 2014.

Company	*Country of Origin*	*Title of the Agreement*	*Year of Signature*	*Number of Employees*	*Signatories on the Employees' Side*
					and Consultation Committee (SEECCC) Assisted by EFFAT
Total	France	European agreement on assistance in creation, purchase or development of small and medium sized businesses	2007 (amended in 2012)	Nearly 99,000 (2013)[605]	EMCEF, FECCIA, FECER, ETUC
Daimler-Chrysler	Germany	Framework Regulation with the European Works Council (EWC) on the Realignment of the Sales Organization in the European Union	2007	274,616 (2013)	EMF, EWC[606]
General Motors (Europe)	Switzer-land	Restructuring at Antwerp	2007	GME (defunct): 54,500 (2009) GM: more than 212,000 (2013)	EWC, EMF, National trade unions
General Motors (Europe)	Switzer-land	Allocation of next Astra	2007	GME (defunct): 54,500 (2009) GM: more than 212,000 (2013)	EWC, EMF[607]

605. Information available at <http://www.total.com/sites/default/files/atoms/file/total-at-a-glance-2013> accessed 13 April 2014.
606. As the text of the agreement is not available, this information can be found in Commission, 'Mapping of transnational texts negotiated at corporate level' (n. 114) 32.
607. Ibid.

Company	*Country of Origin*	*Title of the Agreement*	*Year of Signature*	*Number of Employees*	*Signatories on the Employees' Side*
Suez (now GDF Suez)[608]	France	Group agreement Employment and Expertise Plan (GPEC)	2007	147,200 (2013)	ETUC, CEC, European Consultative Committee (EWC), National trade unions
Schneider Electric**	France	European Agreement on the Anticipation of Change	2007	More than 150,000 (2013)	EMF
Kraft Foods[609]	USA	European Framework Agreement regarding Project One Europe to be Concluded Between Kraft Foods Europe Management and the Employee Representatives	2007	107,000 (2013)[610]	EFFAT, EWC
Daimler-Chrysler	Germany	Framework agreement for information and consultation with employees and employee representative in the local European operation of DaimlerChrysler AG	2006	274,616 (2013)	EWC, EMF
Areva	France	Group Memorandum of Agreement on Equal Opportunities within the Areva Group in Europe	2006	45,340 (2013)	EMF

608. GDF Suez was founded in 2008 via the merger of Gaz de France and Suez. The number of employees of GDF Suez has been used as a criterion to select this agreement.
609. Kraft Food Inc, was spun off in October 2012. Kraft Foods Inc. was renamed Mondelez International. Information available at < http://www.mondelezinternational.com/investors/stock-information/spin-off-information > accessed 14 April 2014. The number of employees of Mondelez International has been used as a criterion to select this agreement.
610. Information available at < Annual Report 2013, http://ir.mondelezinternational.com/secfiling.cfm?filingID = 1193125-14-79175&CIK = 1103982 > accessed 13April 2014.

Company	*Country of Origin*	*Title of the Agreement*	*Year of Signature*	*Number of Employees*	*Signatories on the Employees' Side*
Allianz SE	Germany	Agreement concerning the participation of employees in Allianz SE	2006	171,340 (2013)	Special Negotiating Body (composed of national trade unions)
Generali	Italy	European Social Charter of the Generali Group	2006	77,000 (2013)[611]	EWC
IF insurance[612]	Sweden	Nordic negotiation on working conditions	2006	NA	National unions (Nordic finance unions)
Total	France	European agreement on equal opportunity Total Group	2005	Nearly 99,000 (2013)	EMCEF, FECCIA, FECER
EADS	Netherlands	Agreement on the European Works Council of EADS N.V. and its derived committees concluded between European Aeronautic Defence and Space Company EADS N.V. and its employees' representatives	2005	143,358 (2013)	Special Negotiating Body (composed of national trade unions), EWC
Philip Morris (Kraft Jacobs)	Switzerland (USA)	Guidelines on information and consultation, employment	2005	More than 91,000 (2013)[613]	EWC[614]
Unilever	UK/	Agreed joint statement	2004	More than	EWC

611. Information available at <http://www.generali.com/Generali-Group/About-us/key-figures/> accessed 14 April 2014.
612. Fully owned subsidiary of Sampo. Information available at <http://www.if-insurance.com/web/industrial/about/pages/default.aspx?country=en> accessed 14 April 2014.
613. Information available at <http://www.pmi.com/eng/about_us/company_overview/pages/key_facts_and_financial_data.aspx> accessed 14 April 2014.
614. As the text of the agreement is not available, this information can be found in Commission, 'Mapping of transnational texts negotiated at corporate level' (n 113) 34.

Company	*Country of Origin*	*Title of the Agreement*	*Year of Signature*	*Number of Employees*	*Signatories on the Employees' Side*
	Nether-lands	UEWC and Unilever on protection of personal data		174,000 (2013)[615]	
General Electric Plastics (Europe)[616]	USA	Agreement on Pre-employment screenings ("background checks")	2004	GE: approximately 307,000 (2013)	EWC
Total	France	European agreement – social platform Total Group	2004	Nearly 99,000 (2013)	EMCEF, CEC/FECCIA, FECER
Deutsche Bank	Germany	Common Standpoint of the Deutsche Bank Group and the EWC	2004	98,254 (2013)[617]	EWC
Ford (Europe)[618]	Germany	IOS restructuring: maintenance of jobs, investments, employability	2004	FORD: 181,000 (globally) (2013) Ford Europe: approximately 48,000 (2013)	EWC[619]
General Motors (Europe)	Switzer-land	Restructuring Framework	2004	GME (defunct): 54,500 (2009) GM: more than 212,000 (2013)	European Employee Forum (EWC)

615. Information available at <http://www.unilever.com/aboutus/introductiontounilever/unileverataglance/> accessed 14 April 2014.
616. General Electric's Plastic Division was acquired by Sabic, a company headquartered in Saudi Arabia, in 2008.
617. Information available at <https://annualreport.deutsche-bank.com/2013/ar/management-report/employees.html> accessed 14 April 2014.
618. Ford Europe is a subsidiary of Ford Motor Company. The number of employees of the parent company has been taken into consideration.
619. As the text of the agreement is not available in the database of the European Commission and cannot be retrieved in the website of the MNE, the information about the employees' side signatories can be found in Pulignano et al., 'Local Actors and Transnational Structures – Explaining Trends in Multinational Company-Level Negotiations in Europe' (n. 240) 146.

Company	*Country of Origin*	*Title of the Agreement*	*Year of Signature*	*Number of Employees*	*Signatories on the Employees' Side*
Porr	Austria	Agreement on data protection in the Porr group and the EWC	2003	10,823 (2013)[620]	EWC
Solvay	Belgium	Guidelines on Social Policy in Joint Ventures	2003	29,400 (2013)	EWC
General Electric Plastics (Europe)	USA	Amendment to the GEPE EBR Agreement on the introduction of regulations (including methodology and practice) during negotiations between the GEPE Central Management ("CM") and the GEPE EWC ("EWC")	2003	GE: approximately 307,000 (globally) (2013)	EWC
Ford (Europe)	Germany	Ford of Europe and the Ford European Works Council (EWC) Agreed upon Social Rights and Social Responsibility Principles	2003	FORD: 181,000 (globally) Ford Europe: approximately 48,000	EWC
Lafarge	France	Joint Declaration concerning health and safety	2003	64,000 (2013)	EWC
Dexia	Belgium	The Charter of the principles of social management at the Dexia group	2002	1,892 (2013)	EWC
Solvay	Belgium	European Charter – Health and safety for the staff	2002	29,400 (2013)	EWC
Lhoist	Belgium	Charter on subcontracting	2002	5,500 (2012)[621]	NA

620. Information available at <http://www.porr.at/uploads/media/PORR-HJB2013-eng.pdf> accessed 14 April 2014.
621. Information in the database of the European Commission on TCAs.

Company	*Country of Origin*	*Title of the Agreement*	*Year of Signature*	*Number of Employees*	*Signatories on the Employees' Side*
General Electric Plastics (Europe)	USA (now acquired by Sabic, head-quartered in Saudi Arabia)	GEPE Agreement on use of electronic communication systems	2002	GE: approxi-mately 307,000 (globally) (2013)[622]	EWC
General Motors (Europe)	Switzer-land	General Motors Europe and the European Employee Forum agree on Principles of Social Responsibility	2002	GME (defunct): 54,500 (2009) GM: more than 212,000 (2013)	EMF, European Employee Forum (EWC)
Philip Morris (Kraft Jacobs)	Switzer-land (USA)	Processing key HR data (part of EWC agreement)	2002	More than 91,000	EWC[623]
ENI	Italy	Agreement Report	2002	82,289 (2013)	EMCEF, National trade unions (representing EWC)
Etex	Belgium	Social Charter	2002	17,442 (2013)	EWC
Diageo	UK	Appendix to the EWC on best practice guidelines on redeployment, redundancy and outplacement	2002	28,410 (2013)[624]	Diageo Europe Forum (EWC)

622. Information available at <http://www.ge.com/ar2013/pdf/GE_AR13.pdf> accessed 14 April 2014.
623. As the text of the agreement is not available, this information can be found in Commission, 'Mapping of transnational texts negotiated at corporate level' (n. 114) 34.
624. Information available at <https://www.unglobalcompact.org/system/attachments/34861/original/2013%20Sustainability%20&%20Responsibility%20Report%20-%20Diageo%20plc.pdf?1379623058> accessed 14 April 2014.

Company	*Country of Origin*	*Title of the Agreement*	*Year of Signature*	*Number of Employees*	*Signatories on the Employees' Side*
Kraft Foods (text not available)	USA	Framework understanding concerning the protection and processing of employment related personal data of employees of Kraft Foods International in EU/EEA Countries	2002	107,000 (2013)	NA
Club Méditerranée	France	Joint declaration on sub-contracting	2001	12,865 (2013)	European Social Dialogue Committee of the Club Méditerranée Group (EWC)
Danone	France	Joint opinion on the applicable social standards for all the undertakings concerned by the restructuring program of the Biscuits Pole in Europe presented on 29 March 2001	2001	104,642 (2013)	IUF
Bouygues	France	European Social Charter of the Bouygues Group	2001	More than 128,000 (2013)[625]	CEC, ETUC, European Council for Dialogue(EWC), Group Council for France
Unilever	UK/ Netherlands	Responsible Restructuring	2001	More than 174,000 (2013)	EWC

625. Information available at <http://www.bouygues.com/wp-content/uploads/2014/04/DDR_2013_Activite_RSE_RFA_16_04_14_VA.pdf> accessed 14 April 2014.

Company	*Country of Origin*	*Title of the Agreement*	*Year of Signature*	*Number of Employees*	*Signatories on the Employees' Side*
Marazzi	Italy	Declaration of intent – Joint Initiatives on Health and Safety	2001	More than 6,000[626]	EWC National trade unions
General Motors (Europe)	Switzer-land	European framework, dated 5 March 2001 at 20:30 ("The following framework agreement is in relation of GM's current restructuring initiatives")	2001	GME (defunct): 54,500 (2009) GM: more than 212,000 (2013)	EWC
Philip Morris (Kraft Jacobs)	Switzer-land (USA)	Agreement on the use of data recorded by sales forces	2001	More than 91,000 (2013)	EWC
Sara Lee (defunct 2012)	USA	Agreement on cooperation and CSR	2001	9,100 (2013)[627]	NA (text not available)
Philip Morris (Kraft Jacobs)	Switzer-land (USA)	Agreement by the EU Assembly for the workforce of Philip Morris tobacco companies in the european regions of Philip Morris on the protection of personal data processed by ITSC Europe S.A.R.L.	2001	More than 91,000 (2013)	President of the EU Assembly for the employees of Philip Morris' tobacco companies (EWC)
General Motors (Europe)	Switzer-land	Framework "regarding "Project Olympia" initiatives"	2001	GME (defunct): 54,500 (2009) GM: more than 212,000 (2013)	EWC

626. Information available at <http://www.marazziarchitectural.com/company> accessed 14 April 2014.
627. Information available at <http://www.annualreportowl.com/Sara%20Lee/2013/Annual%20 Report?p=8> accessed 14 April 2014.

Company	*Country of Origin*	*Title of the Agreement*	*Year of Signature*	*Number of Employees*	*Signatories on the Employees' Side*
General Motors (Europe)	Switzer-land	Framework	2000	GME (defunct): 54,500 (2009) GM: more than 212,000 (2013) (2013)	EWC, EMF
Ford (Europe)	Germany	Joint Venture CFT: maintenance of Ford contracts, investments	2000	FORD: 181,000 (globally) (2013) Ford Europe: approximately 48,000 (2013)	EWC[628]
Ford	Germany	Agreement governing the separation of the Ford Visteon organisation	2000 (renegotiated in 2003)	FORD: 181,000 (globally) (2013) Ford Europe: approximately 48,000 (2013)	EWC, Visteon employees representatives
Solvay	Belgium	Group's Practices for Subcontracting	1999	29,400 (2013)	EWC[629]
Hartmann Group	Germany	A Charter signed between the management of the PAUL HARTMANN AG and the European Works Council of the Hartmann-Group	1999	10,257 (2013)[630]	EWC

628. As the text of the agreement is not available, this information can be found in Commission, 'Mapping of transnational texts negotiated at corporate level' (n. 114) 31.
629. Information available in Commission, 'Mapping of transnational texts negotiated at corporate level' (n. 114) 36. The text of the EFA does not specify the signatory party on the employee's side.
630. Information available at <http://www.hartmann.info/EN/company.php> accessed 14 April 2014.

Company	*Country of Origin*	*Title of the Agreement*	*Year of Signature*	*Number of Employees*	*Signatories on the Employees' Side*
Vivendi (Veolia Générale des Eaux)	France	Charter on the safety at the workplace in the Group	1999	202,800 (2013)	European Social Dialogue Body (EWC)
Philip Morris (Kraft Jacobs)	Switzer-land (USA)	Principles on the introduction of euro	1999	More than 91,000 (2013)[631]	EWC
Philip Morris (Kraft Jacobs)	Switzer-land (USA)	Code of conduct smoking at the workplace	1998	More than 91,000 (2013)	EWC
ENI	Italy	Agreement	1996 (updated in 2004)	82,289 (2013)	EMCEF National trade unions

Table 3 Subsidiaries and Business Partners in IFAs concluded between 1988 and May 2014 [632]

Company	*Title of the Agreement*	*Addresses*
GDF Suez	Global Health and Safety Agreement of the GDF Suez Group	SUBSIDIARIES It is therefore applicable to all GDF Suez sites and operations, and globally consolidated subsidiaries within the GDF Suez Consolidation Group. BUSINESS PARTNERS The signatories of this agreement therefore resolve to define and implement some fundamental principles regarding health and safety at work within the GDF Suez companies, and, to the fullest extent possible, GDF Supply chain and sphere of influence.[633] To the fullest extent possible it is also applicable to sites and operations within the GDF Suez's sphere of influence, without any geographical restrictions.

631. Information available at <http://www.pmi.com/eng/about_us/company_overview/pages/key_facts_and_financial_data.aspx> accessed 14 April 2014.
632. This table contains extracts from the text of IFAs or a summary of it.
633. This agreement refers to the concept of sphere of influence of the OECD Guidelines for Multinational Corporations and UN Guiding Principles on Business and Human Rights.

Company	*Title of the Agreement*	*Addresses*
Itaú Unibanco S.A.	Framework Agreement between Banco Itaú-Unibanco S.A. and Union Network International for the Americas	SUBSIDIARIES Not defined. BUSINESS PARTNERS Not defined.
Metro	Joint Statement of Metro Group & UNI Global Union	SUBSIDIARIES The Agreement is applicable to Metro Group BUSINESS PARTNERS Not defined
Renault	"Global framework agreement on social, societal and environmental responsibility between the Renault Group, the Renault Group Works' Council and IndustriALL Global Union"	SUBSIDIARIES This agreement (...) is applicable to the entire Renault Group, i.e. to any company in which Renault s.a.s holds, directly and indirectly, over half of the share capital. When a new company enters into the scope described here above, the signatories shall together examine the terms of its adhesion to the present agreement, including any related action plan, with the exception of the fundamental social rights stipulated in chapter 1 of this agreement, which shall apply with immediate effect. BUSINESS PARTNERS Respect for fundamental rights is a determining criterion in the selection of suppliers and Subcontractors. The Renault Group undertakes to communicate this agreement to its suppliers and sub-contractors. It asks them to commit to applying the fundamental social rights stipulated in chapter 1 of this agreement within their own company. If necessary, corrective action plans may be set up with the Renault Group's support. Once identified, any failure not corrected may lead to various measures, including the Renault Group terminating its relationship with the company concerned. Such a commitment does not entail the Renault Group to step in to assume the legal responsibility of said suppliers and subcontractors.

Company	*Title of the Agreement*	*Addresses*
Volkswagen	Charter on Temporary Work	SUBSIDIARIES It is valid for the companies that are represented in the Volkswagen European Group Works Council and the Volkswagen Group Global Works Council. BUSINESS PARTNERS e) Selection of temporary employment agencies Loan contracts are finalised only with suppliers, who recognise the 'Volkswagen Group requirements regarding sustainability in its relationships with business partners'. If a country has a wage agreement for temporary work or regulates through the legal mini-mum wage, Volkswagen pledges to coordinate only with companies which maintain minimum standards.
ThyssenKrupp AG	Global agreement of an ideamanagement Health & Safety at ThyssenKrupp Elevator Operating Units	SUBSIDIARIES The agreement is applicable to the Group. BUSINESS PARTNERS Not defined
Ford	Global framework agreement	SUBSIDIARIES Not defined BUSINESS PARTNERS Ford will encourage business partners to adopt and enforce similar policies to those contained in these Principles, as the basis for establishing mutuable and durable business relationships. The company will seek to identify and utilize business partners who aspire in the conduct of their business to standards that are consistent with this document and will provide the network an opportunity to raise issue sfor discussion and resolution. The Company conducts assessements of selected existing and persepctive Tier 1 suppliers in multiple countries.
Inditex	Global agreement on the involvement of unions to monitor the respect of worker's conditions at supplier	This agreement is about the role of trade unions in the implementation of the IFA between Inditex and ITGLWF within the supply chain.

Company	*Title of the Agreement*	*Addresses*
Siemens	International Framework Agreement between Siemens AG, the Central Works Council of Siemens AG, the IG Metall and the IndustriALL Global Union	SUBSIDIARIES Not defined BUSINESS PARTNERS Moreover we require our suppliers to abide by our own high standards, and insist on uncompromising compliance with the law. The principles of this agreement are reflected in the Siemens Code of Conduct for Suppliers. Thus Siemens also actively endeavors to have these principles incorporated into the business policy of its suppliers. Siemens regards the application of these principles to supplier and contractor companies as a positive prerequisite for mutual business relationships.
Banco do Brasil	Global Framework Agreement for the Americas Union Network International (UNI) and Banco do Brasil	SUBSIDIARIES Not defined BUSINESS PARTNERS BANCO DO BRASIL recognises that the respect for the practices agreed in this framework agreement represents a step forward in its labour relations, committing itself to recommend these same practices to the suppliers and subcontractors with whom the company has contractual relationships.
Danone	Danone / IUF Agreement on health, safety, working conditions and stress	SUBSIDIARIES The agreement is applicable to "Group companies". BUSINESS PARTNERS Danone shall circulate this Agreement, in accordance with best practice, to its suppliers and subcontractors.
Sodexo	International Framework Agreement	SUBSIDIARIES Sodexo" refers to Sodexo SA and its controlled subsidiaries. BUSINESS PARTNERS Not defined
Petrobas	Terms of Understanding of Good Labor Relations	SUBSIDIARIES Not defined BUSINESS PARTNERS 3. Coverage In connection with contracting companies abroad, Petrobras commits itself to striving

Company	*Title of the Agreement*	*Addresses*
		toward getting these companies to comply with what is laid down in this present instrument.
GDF Suez	Group agreement on fundamental principles regarding health and safety	SUBSIDIARIES This agreement applies to European subsidiaries that are fully consolidated within the GDF SUEZ Group's scope of consolidation and those in which the Group has dominant influence. Outside of Europe, for subsidiaries fully consolidated within the GDF SUEZ scope of consolidation and those in which the Group has dominant influence, this agreement will also be applied as a unilateral decision. Moreover, administrators in companies for which GDF SUEZ does not have operational control must also promote the initiatives stated in this agreement. BUSINESS PARTNERS Not defined
GDF Suez	Global Agreement on Fundamental Rights, Social Dialogue and Sustainable Development	SUBSIDIARIES This agreement applies to all present and future GDF SUEZ companies [fully consolidated within the GDF SUEZ Group's scope of consolidation and those in which the Group has dominant influence], employees, subcontractors and suppliers. BUSINESS PARTNERS GDF SUEZ undertakes to circulate information on the agreement in the relevant languages using the most appropriate methods throughout all its sites and with its business partners in order to ensure that the agreement is understood and to encourage compliance with it
France Telecom	Agreement of France Telecom's Worldwide Works Council	SUBSIDIARIES This agreement applies to: – France Telecom SA, a controlling company as per the Law of 12 November 1996 – All the companies simultaneously meeting the following 3 conditions: • Whose capital is at least 10% owned by France Telecom SA and the permanent nature and extent of the relationship with these companies establish that they belong to the Group

Company	*Title of the Agreement*	*Addresses*
		• France Telecom SA exercises actual control, as demonstrated by consolidation in its account • Having at least 1 employee. BUSINESS PARTNERS Not defined
Shoprite Checkers	Global Framework agreement	SUBSIDIARIES The principles set out in this global agreement will apply to all Shoprite Checkers operations and its subsidiaries where Shoprite Checkers formally recognises UNI Global Union alliance members. BUSINESS PARTNERS Shoprite Checkers will strive, in dealings with suppliers, to engage with those suppliers which share its commitments to the principles of good governance.
Volkswagen	Charter on Labour Relations within the Volkswagen Group	SUBSIDIARIES This Charter shall apply for all companies and sites represented on the Volkswagen Group's European Group Works Council and Group Global Works Council. BUSINESS PARTNERS Not defined
Inditex	Global agreement for implementation of fundamental labour rights and decent work	SUBSIDIARIES This Agreement shall apply throughout Inditex SA and its subsidiaries, irrespective of the country in which they operate. BUSINESS PARTNERS Inditex and UNI will thus establish a cooperation framework which will contribute to the effective implementation of fundamental labour rights and decent work in the Group's commercial and distribution network, for the purposes of which they agree to sign the present global framework agreement (...). The undertaking shall not knowingly use for its commercial network the services of third parties who violates the principles of this Global Agreement.

Company	*Title of the Agreement*	*Addresses*
ArcelorMittal	Agreement on minimum requirements for Plant level Joint H&S Committees	Not defined
ArcelorMittal	Terms of reference for a joint global OSH committee in Arcelor Mittal	Not defined
G4S	A global Agreement: Ethical Employment Partnership	SUBSIDIARIES This agreement will apply to companies over which G4S has direct control as owner or in which it has a controlling interest. Where the Company does not have a controlling interest or cannot exercise effective control for reasons of local legislation it will use its influence in order to seek to secure compliance with the standards set out in this agreement. BUSINESS PARTNERS The company will also endeavour to work with business partners who conduct their business in a way that is compatible with the terms of this agreement.
PSA Peugeot	Agreement on the extension of the strategic equal committee	Not defined
ThyssenKrupp AG	Principles of Social Responsibility in Labor Relations in the ThyssenKrupp Group	SUBSIDIARIES These agreed principles shall be valid worldwide for all subsidiaries. Through their publication on the internet/intranet, ThyssenKrupp shall ensure that this Agreement is brought to the knowledge of employees and can be implemented in the subsidiaries. BUSINESS PARTNERS ThyssenKrupp makes sure that these principles are made known to customers and suppliers via publication in internet. ThyssenKrupp shall thereby encourage its customers and suppliers to consider corresponding principles in their own corporate policies with a view inter alia to promoting mutual relations.

Company	*Title of the Agreement*	*Addresses*
Siemens	Joint Statement between group management and Siemens Europe Committee concerning Compliance	Not defined
Danone	Convention on Diversity	SUBSIDIARIES "the implementing of systems to favour diversity is a way of progressing towards equal opportunities for all Groupe employees and for all those who apply for jobs in the Groupe" BUSINESS PARTNERS Groupe DANONE will circulate this convention as a good practice to its suppliers and subcontractors.
Inditex	International Framework Agreement on the Implementation of International Labour Standards throughout the Inditex Supply Chain	SUBSIDIARIES Not defined BUSINESS PARTNERS " The Inditex Group (hereinafter, Inditex) is committed to ensuring that: (...) All Inditex's External Manufacturers and Suppliers (production centres that are not the property of Inditex) fully adhere to these commitments and undertake to ensure that both themselves and all of their subcontractors meet the standards covered by this Code of Conduct for External Manufacturers and Suppliers (hereinafter, the Code)"
Suez	Agreement on Commitment to promoting equality and diversity within the Group	SUBSIDIARIES SUEZ S.A., whose registered office is located at 16, rue de la Ville l'Evêque, Paris (75008), and its subsidiary companies meeting the conditions defined in Clause 2-1 of the Agreement, jointly represented by Mr. Gérard Mestrallet in his capacity as Chief Executive Officer of Suez S.A. 2.1 – Those Concerned This statement is addressed to all Group employees; they are all liable to be involved in a discriminatory situation at some point in their careers.

Company	*Title of the Agreement*	*Addresses*
		BUSINESS PARTNERS The principle of equal opportunity must be extended to all our relations with our shareholders, partners and subcontractors.
Suez	Group Agreement on Employees Ownership Scheme	SUBSIDIARIES For each of the years considered (2007, 2008 and 2009), the scope of the agreement includes all companies which meet the conditions defined in (i) and (ii) below (the "Associated Companies") as at 31 March of the year considered. (i) To be fully integrated in the consolidated structure of the Suez Group or, failing this, to meet the conditions so as to be included in it, in accordance with the provisions of Community Regulation No. 1606/2002 of 19 July 2002 (or any other provision that is issued to replace or amend it) concerning the application of international accounting standards and the laws relating to its application; and (ii) To have the registered office in the country of one of the European Union Member States or of EFTA. BUSINESS PARTNERS Not defined
France Telecom	Worldwide Agreement on Fundamental Labour Rights within the France Telecom Group	SUBSIDIARIES The present agreement applies to companies directly controlled by the France Telecom Group, i.e. companies in which France Telecom Group holds the majority of the capital or a majority of voting rights or in which it appoints more than half the members of the administrative, management or monitoring bodies. BUSINESS PARTNERS The France Telecom Group will inform its suppliers and subcontractors of the existence of this agreement. Effectively demonstrating the adoption of these principles is a favourable foundation for long-term partnerships.

Company	*Title of the Agreement*	*Addresses*
		In line with the France Telecom Group Code of Ethics and its support for the Global Compact, the directors and employees ensure compliance with the principles of fairness, integrity and objectivity in their relations with customers and suppliers. They undertake not to seek gifts or advantages and not to accept any such gifts or advantages if they are of significant economic value. They abstain from any illegal action and from any participation in acts of corruption.
PSA Peugeot	International Framework Agreement on PSA Peugeot Citroën's Social Responsibility	SUBSIDIARIES This international framework agreement applies directly to all of the consolidated automobile division (research and development, manufacturing, sales and support functions), as well as the financing and transport and logistics divisions, for the present and future subsidiaries over which the Group exercises a dominant influence either through a majority financial holding or where this is limited to 50 %, through its responsibility in the social management of this subsidiary. BUSINESS PARTNERS Without replacing its suppliers', sub-contractors', industrial partners' and distribution networks' legal responsibility, PSA PEUGEOT CITROËN undertakes to communicate this agreement to these companies and request that they apply the previously mentioned ILO international conventions. PSA PEUGEOT CITROËN requests from its suppliers a similar commitment in respect of their own suppliers and sub-contractors. As part of calls for proposals, PSA PEUGEOT CITROËN undertakes to ensure that the respect of human rights as set out in chapter 2 is a determining criterion in the selection of the suppliers that will join the panel. Any failing relating to the respect of human rights shall lead to corrective action plans after a warning from PSA PEUGEOT CITROËN. Non-respect of these rights shall lead to sanctions, which may, ultimately, lead to withdrawal from the panel.

Company	*Title of the Agreement*	*Addresses*
DaimlerChrysler	Occupational Health and Safety Principles of DaimlerChrysler	Not defined
Securitas	Agreement between Securitas AB (publ) and Union Network International and Swedish Transport Workers' Union on the development of good working relations in the Securitas group	SUBSIDIARIES The agreement refers to the "Securitas Group". BUSINESS PARTNERS Securitas insists that the principles in this Code of Conduct are respected and applied throughout the organisation and, within Securitas' sphere of influence, by all those with whom Securitas does business.
EDF	Agreement on EDF Group Corporate Social Responsibility	SUBSIDIARIES The EDF Group CSR Agreement is intended to be a common foundation for the companies in which EDF exercises direct control. Given the formalised conditions for follow-up that it henceforth implies, this Agreement shall apply to EDF SA as well as the companies included in the attached Annexe 1, starting from the date of its entry into force. After this date, this Agreement shall be intended to be applied to companies of over 50 employees over which EDF SA holds direct control (i.e. companies in which EDF owns a majority shareholding, or enjoys a majority of voting rights linked to the stock issued) as well as the companies of over 50 employees in which EDF SA directly or indirectly holds at least 45% of the capital. The effective application of this Agreement to the companies mentioned in the previous paragraph is contingent on the express adherence of said companies to this Agreement, as evidenced by the conclusion of an Adherence Agreement in accordance with the model enclosed in Annexe 2. As these are companies with over 50 employees, of which EDF SA directly or indirectly holds between 45% and 50% of the capital, the validity of the adherence agreement is furthermore contingent on its signature by the representative of the EDF SA Management.

Company	Title of the Agreement	Addresses
		The conclusion of an Adherence Agreement is possible at any time during the period of validity of this Agreement and is deemed acceptance of these provisions. The entry into force of the Adherence Agreement also implies acceptance of this adherence by EDF SA and all the companies already covered by the Agreement. In the event that a company no longer fulfils the criteria defined above, this Agreement shall then cease immediately to be applicable. The companies included in the list in Annexe 1, as well as those that will have effectively adhered to this Agreement will hereinafter be designated as "the Companies of the Group", "EDF Group" or "the Group". In those companies where EDF SA exercises significant influence without exercising any direct control, as well as in the companies with fewer than 50 employees in which EDF SA exercises direct control, the signatory parties undertake to promote this Agreement in an effort to encourage the adoption and application of its provisions. EDF Group companies hereby undertake to comply strictly with national and local laws as well as other collective agreements, and more particularly where such laws provide for more extensive requirements than the provisions of this Agreement. BUSINESS PARTNERS EDF Group reaffirms its adherence to the Ten Principles of the United Nations Global Compact of July 2000 (10th principle adopted in June 2004). It undertakes, with the signatory parties, to promote them to its suppliers. Article 8 Relations with our subcontractors in the area of legal compliance, health and safety, ethical behaviour with customers and respect for the environment 1- The companies of EDF Group systematically ensure that the sub-contracting companies they call upon provide quality work and labour in full compliance with applicable laws and international standards (for example regarding

Company	*Title of the Agreement*	*Addresses*
		the ban on child labour). They strive to enable the subcontracting companies and their employees to intervene on their behalf in working and health and safety conditions at the best level of the companies of the sector and the country in question. The Group's requirements shall be applied in particular to: - Legal compliance - Employee health and safety - Ethical behaviour towards customers, and particularly respect for people and integrity - Respect for the environment 2- The companies of the Group shall implement with regards to their subcontractors the appropriate selection and assessment procedures meeting these requirements. 3- These requirements shall be conveyed to the subcontractors. Any serious failure, not remedied following notification, to comply with legislation, the rules concerning employee health and safety, the principles governing relations with customers and the regulations in force with regard to the environment, shall result in the termination of our relations with the subcontracting company, in accordance with contractual obligations. 4- Regarding more specifically the safety of employees of the sub-contracting companies, reporting will be requested for workplace accidents occurring in the framework of jobs entrusted to them.
EADS	International Framework Agreement	SUBSIDIARIES The provisions of this framework agreement define EADS standards to be applied wherever the Group operates, insofar as more favourable conditions do not exist already. BUSINESS PARTNERS Fostering a mutually beneficial relationship with its suppliers, EADS aims to integrate them into its ethical approach to business. Compliance with EADS standards serves as a criterion for selecting suppliers.

Company	*Title of the Agreement*	*Addresses*
		EADS therefore expects all its suppliers to recognise and apply the principles of this framework agreement and encourages them to introduce and implement equivalent principles in their own companies. "EADS asks its suppliers and subcontractors to cooperate as best as they can in the application of the principles of this agreement and to remedy the situation in the case of possible infringement.
Danone	Fundamental Social Principles	SUBSIDIARIES The conventions establish minimum standards throughout Groupe DANONE operations. (Foreword "Danone IUF Conventions" booklet) BUSINESS PARTNERS Groupe DANONE is committed to gaining compliance with the fundamental social rights defined in this text, not only by management teams at its sites, but also by companies in which the Group has a minority shareholding, as well as its main suppliers and subcontractors. (Foreword "Danone IUF Conventions" booklet)
Danone	Convention on the setting up of social indicators at group level	SUBSIDIARIES The conventions establish minimum standards throughout Groupe DANONE operations. (Foreword "Danone IUF Conventions" booklet) BUSINESS PARTNERS Groupe DANONE is committed to gaining compliance with the fundamental social rights defined in this text, not only by management teams at its sites, but also by companies in which the Group has a minority shareholding, as well as its main suppliers and subcontractors. (Foreword "Danone IUF Conventions" booklet)
Coca Cola	Joint Coca-Cola and IUF Statement	Not defined
BMW	Joint Declaration on Human Rights and on Working Conditions in the BMW Group	SUBSIDIARIES No specific mention to subsidiaries but the agreement is applicable to BMW Group.

Company	*Title of the Agreement*	*Addresses*
		BUSINESS PARTNERS The BMW Group's business partners and suppliers will be encouraged to introduce comparable principles in their corporate structures and to apply them in the context of their own corporate policy. The BMW Group expects its business partners and suppliers to use these principles as a basis in their mutual dealings and regards them as a suitable criterion for lasting business relationships.
Arcelor	Worldwide Agreement on the Principles of Arcelor's Corporate Social responsibility	SUBSIDIARIES This agreement applies to the entities over which the Group exercises a dominant influence, be it through direct ownership, financial participation or governance rules. When an entity leaves the perimeter of the Group as defined above, this agreement ceases to apply to it. Conversely, when an entity enters its perimeter, the signatory parties undertake to carry out all necessary steps to integrate this company within the effective implementation of the agreement. Group subsidiaries over which ARCELOR exercises a dominant influence ensure that the provisions of this agreement are implemented, while taking local factors (rules and practices) into consideration. In the subsidiaries where the ARCELOR Group has a significant presence, but does not exercise a dominant influence, the signatory parties undertake to jointly put to use all of the resources at their disposal in order to promote the principles stated in this agreement. BUSINESS PARTNERS In accordance with Article 8 of this agreement, companies in which the ARCELOR Group has a significant presence, albeit without exercising a dominant influence there, along with contractors and suppliers also fall within the scope of this agreement.

Company	*Title of the Agreement*	*Addresses*
		ARCELOR supports and encourages its contractors and suppliers to take this agreement into consideration in their own company policy. This agreement is indeed considered a foundation favourable to mutual and sustainable relations. In the event that an enterprise working at ARCELOR's sites does not take part in programmes for effective improvement of occupational Health & Safety, ARCELOR will draw all the consequences in the context of their business relations, which could result in the termination of contractual relations.
Bosch	Basic Principles of Social Responsibility at Bosch	SUBSIDIARIES Our aim is to implement these principles throughout the Bosch Group. These principles will be incorporated into the "Management System Manual for Quality, Environment, Safety, and Security in the Bosch Group". Responsibility for their implementation lies with the senior management of the respective divisions, regional subsidiaries and company locations. BUSINESS PARTNERS Bosch will not work with any suppliers who have demonstrably failed to comply with basic ILO labor standards.
Lukoil	Agreement between International Federation of Chemical, Energy, Mine and General Workers' Unions, Russian Oil and Gas Workers Union And Open Joint Stock Company "Oil Company LUKOIL"	SUBSIDIARIES The Agreement covers all activities and operations where LUKOIL has direct control. Where LUKOIL does not have overall control it will exercise its best efforts in order to secure compliance with the standards and principles set out in the Agreement. BUSINESS PARTNERS LUKOIL will notify its contractors, licensees and major suppliers of the existence of the Agreement and encourage them to comply with the standards and principles contained within it.

Company	*Title of the Agreement*	*Addresses*
		Annual meeting 5.1. LUKOIL and ICEM will meet annually to review practice and experience of the agreed principles as part of the follow-up to this Agreement. The purpose shall be to discuss the issues covered by the Agreement with a view to agreeing joint actions that will further develop good working practices. In addition to general industrial issues and health, safety and environmental matters, the following topics may be addressed: 5.1.1. General corporate policy on employment, occupational health, safety and environmental issues and challenges affecting those within the LUKOIL Group and, as appropriate, between LUKOIL and its related companies, including suppliers and subcontractors;
H&M	Agreement between H & M hennes & Mauritz AB (H &M) and Union Network International (UNI) on Cooperation in order to secure and promote fundamental worker's rights at H&M's workplaces worldwide	SUBSIDIARIES Not explicitly defined (only reference to 'All H & M's workplaces worldwide'). BUSINESS PARTNERS Not defined
Renault	Renault Group employees' fundamental rights declaration	SUBSIDIARIES No direct reference but the IFA is applicable to the Renault Group. BUSINESS PARTNERS One of the selection criteria for suppliers is to have a policy of occupational risks prevention that complies with the principles set out by Renault. As provided by ILO convention No. 138 on the minimum working age, Renault agrees not to employ people younger than the mandatory school-leaving age in the relevant country or, in any event, below the age of fifteen. Suppliers and service providers must comply with this policy in order to work with Renault.

Company	*Title of the Agreement*	*Addresses*
		Renault informs its own suppliers of the contents of this declaration and the Global Compact and urges them to consider adhering to it. It encourages them to introduce and implement equivalent principles in their own companies. The actual adoption of these principles is a basis for long-term relations.
ISS	Uni - ISS Global Agreement	SUBSIDIARIES "Union" refers to UNI Global Union and its affiliated unions and "ISS" refers to ISS A/S and its subsidiaries. BUSINESS PARTNERS Not defined
ENI	Agreement on transnational industrial relations and corporate social responsibility	SUBSIDIARIES No explicit reference to subsidiaries but the IFA speaks about Group's principles. BUSINESS PARTNERS With particular reference to issues concerning the protection of social, economic and cultural rights, Eni recognises the right to employment, to join a trade union, rejection of forced labour and child labour, rejection of all forms of discrimination, safeguarding of dignity, health and safety in the working environment, respect of natural biodiversities and protection of the environment, as well as the fight against corruption. Eni also declares that it intend to take steps to apply these principles in its own activities and those performed jointly with its Business Partners. In particular Eni shall ensure: (...) Compliance with laws, regulations and the human rights referred to in international regulations and conventions in relations with suppliers, contractors and subcontractors, contractor workers, agents or consultants; any serious violations, also concerning health and safety of employees, regulations on protection of the environment or human rights, which are not eliminated, will lead to termination of the relationship with the company concerned in compliance with contractual obligations.

Company	*Title of the Agreement*	*Addresses*
DaimlerChrysler	Social Responsibility Principles of DaimlerChrysler	SUBSIDIARIES No direct reference but the IFA reads that: "The following principles, that are orientated at the conventions of the International Labor Organization, have been implemented by DaimlerChrysler worldwide". BUSINESS PARTNERS DaimlerChrysler supports and encourages its suppliers to introduce and implement equivalent principles in their own companies. DaimlerChrysler expects its suppliers to incorporate these principles as a basis for relations with DaimlerChrysler. DaimlerChrysler regards the above as a favorable basis for enduring business relations.
Volkswagen	Declaration on Social Rights and Industrial Relationships at Volkswagen	SUBSIDIARIES No direct reference but the IFA reads that "Volkswagen AG, the Group Global Works Council of Volkswagen AG and the International Metalworkers' Federation agree on the following goals for the countries and regions represented in the Group Global Works Council. BUSINESS PARTNERS Volkswagen supports and expressly encourages its contractors to take this declaration into account in their own respective corporate policy. It views this as an advantageous basis for mutual relationships.
Suez	Charter Health and Safety at Work	SUBSIDIARIES The Charter applies to each individual in each of the Group's companies worldwide. It must be sent to, explained to and implemented by everyone. BUSINESS PARTNERS Protection of both physical and mental integrity and health Being a responsible Group, SUEZ carries out its activities while ensuring the physical and psychological health and integrity of its employees. This concerns not only the men and women working for the Group, but also our customers, partners, subcontractors and more generally all those affected by our activities.

Company	*Title of the Agreement*	*Addresses*
		D. Taking action and measuring its effectiveness The managers run this operation on a daily basis. Their credibility depends on their exemplary behavior. Managers will implement the actions decided upon and follow the principles stated below: (…) Ensure that the health & safety criteria stated in the Charter and the code of conduct are adopted when selecting, informing and coordinating unit subcontractors.
Telefonica	UNI-Telefonica Code of conduct	SUBSIDIARIES No explicit reference to subsidiaries but the IFA reads that: "Telefónica S.A. will provide information concerning this agreement to all companies of the Group." BUSINESS PARTNERS The company will tell the companies that would like to provide contracts and services the need to adhere to these principles.
IKEA	Framework agreement between IKEA and the IFBWW	SUBSIDIARIES The text mentions "IKEA Group". BUSINESS PARTNERS IKEA wants to influence and support their suppliers to achieve the requirements stated in "The IKEA Way on Purchasing Home Furnishing Products". A contract based on "The IKEA Way on Purchasing Home Furnishing Products" has been introduced world-wide and is being implemented in relation to all suppliers of IKEA products. IKEA has established a compliance organisation with the task to support and monitor the compliance work. Both IKEA and IFBWW appreciate the value of a continued co-operation and henceforth see it beneficial to have a joint group that will meet twice per year, one meeting being organised by IKEA and the other by IFBWW. IKEA will inform IFBWW of the progress of the implementation of "The IKEA Way on Purchasing Home Furnishing Products" for advice and comments from the group. Should the IFBWW become aware of any contravention of "The IKEA Way on Purchasing Home Furnishing Products",

Company	*Title of the Agreement*	*Addresses*
		IFBWW will report this to the group which will review the matter and propose appropriate measures. Furthermore, the parties will at such meetings exchange general information and experiences within the field of subjects covered by the "The IKEA Way on Purchasing Home Furnishing Products".
Hochtief	Framework agreement between Hochtief and IFBWW	SUBSIDIARIES No explicit reference to subsidiaries but the IFA reads: "HOCHTIEF, one of the world's biggest construction groups, today signs an agreement committing it to observe – in its building activities anywhere in the world – the social standards of the International Labour Organization (ILO). The agreement imposes the same obligation on all HOCHTIEF's subcontractors". BUSINESS PARTNERS HOCHTIEF, one of the world's biggest construction groups, today signs an agreement committing it to observe – in its building activities anywhere in the world – the social standards of the International Labour Organization (ILO). The agreement imposes the same obligation on all HOCHTIEF's subcontractors. "HOCHTIEF is the first international construction company to conclude an agreement of this kind with the international labour union movement. It lays down that in future, HOCHTIEF and its contractual partners will comply with what is called a social charter that imposes certain minimum standards in the world of work. These include freedom of employment, ban on child labour, freedom of association and collective bargaining, adequate wages, working time and working conditions.
Carrefour	Global Agreement Carrefour – UNI Union Network International	SUBSIDIARIES No direct reference but the IFA reads that: "Respect for union rights and recognition of fundamental rights are part of the corporate culture of the Carrefour Group."

Company	*Title of the Agreement*	*Addresses*
		BUSINESS PARTNERS Carrefour has also condemned child labor in order to prevent slavery and forced labor, and it intends to ensure that the principles established by the ILO are respected by its suppliers.
Suez-Lyonnaise des Eaux	International social charter	SUBSIDIARIES No direct reference but the IFA reads that: This international social charter shall be distributed amongst all employees of the Group's companies in the same way as the SUEZ ethics charter." BUSINESS PARTNERS Not defined
Danone	Convention applicable in the event of changes in business activities affecting employment or working conditions	SUBSIDIARIES The conventions establish minimum standards throughout Groupe DANONE operations. (Foreword "Danone IUF Conventions" booklet) BUSINESS PARTNERS Groupe DANONE is committed to gaining compliance with the fundamental social rights defined in this text, not only by management teams at its sites, but also by companies in which the Group has a minority shareholding, as well as its main suppliers and subcontractors. (Foreword "Danone IUF Conventions" booklet)
Vivendi (Veolia Générale des Eaux)	Charter of fundamental social rights	SUBSIDIARIES Not explicit reference but the text speaks about "Group". BUSINESS PARTNERS Not defined
Accor	Agreement between the IUF and the Accor Group on Trade Union Rights	SUBSIDIARIES In this spirit, the Accor Group and the IUF shall undertake to (...) 2. encourage the management of subsidiaries and entities to allow union representatives to carry out their mandates and to have access to the same opportunities for training, pay increases and advancement as all other equally qualified employees. BUSINESS PARTNERS Not defined

Company	*Title of the Agreement*	*Addresses*
Danone	Convention on trade union rights	SUBSIDIARIES In this spirit, Groupe DANONE and the IUF are committed to 1. check throughout all Groupe DANONE subsidiaries the correct application of ILO conventions 87, 98 and 135 which concern respectively. The conventions establish minimum standards throughout Groupe DANONE operations. (Foreword "Danone IUF Conventions" booklet) BUSINESS PARTNERS Groupe DANONE is committed to gaining compliance with the fundamental social rights defined in this text, not only by management teams at its sites, but also by companies in which the Group has a minority shareholding, as well as its main suppliers and subcontractors. (Foreword "Danone IUF Conventions" booklet)
Danone	Convention on skills training	SUBSIDIARIES The conventions establish minimum standards throughout Groupe DANONE operations. (Foreword "Danone IUF Conventions" booklet) BUSINESS PARTNERS Groupe DANONE is committed to gaining compliance with the fundamental social rights defined in this text, not only by management teams at its sites, but also by companies in which the Group has a minority shareholding, as well as its main suppliers and subcontractors. (Foreword "Danone IUF Conventions" booklet)
Danone	Convention on economic and social data in Group Danone companies	SUBSIDIARIES The conventions establish minimum standards throughout Groupe DANONE operations. (Foreword "Danone IUF Conventions" booklet) BUSINESS PARTNERS Groupe DANONE is committed to gaining compliance with the fundamental social rights defined in this text, not only by management teams at its sites, but also by companies in which the Group has a minority shareholding,

Company	*Title of the Agreement*	*Addresses*
		as well as its main suppliers and subcontractors. (Foreword "Danone IUF Conventions" booklet)
Danone	Convention for the promotion of equality of men and women in the workplace	SUBSIDIARIES The conventions establish minimum standards throughout Groupe DANONE operations. (Foreword "Danone IUF Conventions" booklet) BUSINESS PARTNERS Groupe DANONE is committed to gaining compliance with the fundamental social rights defined in this text, not only by management teams at its sites, but also by companies in which the Group has a minority shareholding, as well as its main suppliers and subcontractors. (Foreword "Danone IUF Conventions" booklet)
Danone	Common viewpoint IUF/BSN	SUBSIDIARIES Following the work achieved by the IUF's affiliates and the management of the BSN Group during several meetings, the two parties agree that it is necessary to develop various co-ordinated initiatives to promote in BSN establishments, taking into account national legislation and collective agreements,: (...) 2. A policy aiming to achieve the same level and the same quality of information, both in the economic and the social fields, in all locations of BSN subsidiaries. To achieve this objective, the social partners concerned will seek, both through national legislation as well as collective agreement, to reduce the differences observed in terms of the information between one country and another or between one location and another; BUSINESS PARTNERS Not defined

Table 4 Subsidiaries and Business Partners in EFAs concluded between 1996 and May 2014 [634]

Company	*Title of the Agreement*	*Addresses*
Michelin	European framework agreement on social responsibility and sustainable development	Text not available
Air France/KLM	Framework agreement regarding the Air France KLM and Martinair Cargo organisation in Europe	SUBSIDIARIES Not defined. BUSINESS PARTNERS Not defined.
Air France/KLM	Framework agreement regarding the Outstation and commercial organisations in Europe	SUBSIDIARIES Not defined. BUSINESS PARTNERS Not defined.
Air France/KLM	Social Rights and Ethics Charter	SUBSIDIARIES The present Charter applies to AIR FRANCE and KLM and all their subsidiaries and sub subsidiaries in which they exercise dominant influence, as defined by French Law, and which have signed the Charter and are based in Europe (according to the "Protocol for European Works Council in the AIR FRANCE KLM Group"). A list has been drawn up in Appendix 2, which will be updated every year conformed to the Protocol for the EWC and communicated to the Select Committee members of the European Works Council AIR FRANCE KLM. When a change in shareholding or shareholders leads to the withdrawal of a company from the scope of this agreement, the Charter no longer automatically applies. On the other hand, when a new company enters this scope, its management shall be requested to sign the Charter."

634. This table contains extracts from the text of EFAs or a summary of it.

Company	*Title of the Agreement*	*Addresses*
		BUSINESS PARTNER Companies of the AIR FRANCE KLM Group (see Appendix 2) will be particularly attentive to ensuring that these principles and fundamental social rights are respected by all subcontractors with whom they maintain relations anywhere in the world, in the respect of the Procurement principles defined in the Sustainable Development Charter, described in Appendix 3. The contact person at the Procurement Division will attentively monitor the situation, particularly in case of specific problems. APPENDIX 1 AIR FRANCE KLM CORPORATE SOCIAL RESPONSIBILITY STATEMENT We undertake to enforce Human rights, to oppose all forms of child and force labour, to apply the law and to request our suppliers and subcontractors to comply with these principles. (...) We request our suppliers and subcontractors to implement measures aimed at reducing the environmental impact of their activities. (...) We expect our suppliers and employees as well as all others who are committed to building a responsible air transport industry, to endorse the above commitments." APPENDIX 3 SUSTAINABLE DEVELOPMENT CHARTER Both Chairmen of AIR FRANCE and KLM have made a commitment to support and promote the principles of the "UN Global Compact" which fall within the sphere of influence of the AIR FRANCE KLM Group, and to incorporate them in the Group's strategy and day-to-day operations with its partners.

Company	*Title of the Agreement*	*Addresses*
		This document formalizing AIR FRANCE and KLM's commitment to ethics and sustainable development has prompted the Procurement Organization to remind their providers of goods and services (hereafter referred to as "Suppliers" or individually as the "Supplier") of the principles that each undertakes to defend and respect when entering into a contract with AIR FRANCE and KLM. By entering into a contract with AIR FRANCE and/or KLM, the Supplier commits to respect specifically the principles of the following areas: (...).
Allianz SE	Agreement on guidelines concerning Lifelong Learning	SUBSIDIARIES This Agreement applies to Allianz SE and its subsidiaries (...) with registered offices in the Member States of the EU, the contracting States of the EEA, and Switzerland ("Allianz Group"). BUSINESS PARTNERS Not defined.
Veolia Environment	Letter of commitment from the General Human Resources Management and the members of the Bureau of Veolia environnement's European Works Council	SUBSIDIARIES La présente letter d'engagement s'applique dans l'ensemble des entités du périmétre du Comité de Groupe Européen de VEOLIA ENVIRONMENT ainsi que toutes ses filiales ou sous filiales à l'intérieur de l'Union Européenne ainsi que dans les Etats membres de l'Espace Economique Européen. BUSINESS PARTNERS Not defined.
Alstom	European agreement on social commitments during the transition period of the Joint-venture between Alstom and Shanghai Electric on Boilers	SUBSIDIARIES Not defined. BUSINESS PARTNERS Not defined.

Company	Title of the Agreement	Addresses
GDF Suez	GDF Suez Group European agreement on professional equality between men and women	SUBSIDIARIES This agreement applies to GDF SUEZ and its subsidiaries which are globally integrated in the GDF SUEZ consolidation scope in Europe, or which are more than 50% owned, subject to compliance with the criterion of dominant influence in the EU and EFTA (European Free Trade Association). It will also be distributed to subsidiaries within European Union candidate countries which will have to comply with these clauses when they join the European Union. However, if one of the company's trade union organisations requests it, a meeting must be organised with the company's Board in order to discuss any voluntary application of this agreement within the companies concerned. BUSINESS PARTNERS With an active role in the lives of its employees, customers and its suppliers, GDF SUEZ must be firmly and visibly committed to equal opportunities, and apply this principle in practical terms, as a key factor for attracting customers and building loyalty for all these involved parties. ARTICLE 13 In compliance with the global agreement on fundamental rights, social dialogue and sustainable development, the company is committed to ensuring that its suppliers and subcontractors comply with the principles of equality between women and men.
BNP Paribas	European social charter – employment management agreement	SUBSIDIARIES The present agreement applies to all BNP Paribas-controlled branches and fully-integrated subsidiaries within the geographical remit of the European Works Council. BUSINESS PARTNERS Not defined.

Company	*Title of the Agreement*	*Addresses*
AXA Assistance	European agreement on anticipating changes within AXA Assistance	SUBSIDIARIES Le present accord s'applique aus entreprises d'AXA Assistance implantees en Europe et entrant dans le champ d'application de l'accord sur le Comite Europeen Groupe. BUSINESS PARTNERS Not defined.
AXA Group	European agreement on anticipating changes	SUBSIDIARIES Le present accord s'applique aus entreprises du Groupe AXA implantées en Europe et tombant dans le champ d'application de l'accord du 29 juin 2009 sur le CEG. BUSINESS PARTNERS Not defined.
Allianz SE	Agreement on Guidelines Concerning Work Related Stress	SUBSIDIARIES This Agreement applies to Allianz SE and its subsidiaries (...) with registered offices in the Member States of the EU, the contracting States of the EEA, and Switzerland ("Allianz Group"). BUSINESS PARTNERS Not defined.
Alstom	Agreement on the anticipation of change or developments in Alstom	SUBSIDIARIES The agreement covers all ALSTOM staff within the countries covered by the EWC scope of application and all the countries where the EMF has affiliated organizations. ALSTOM will regularly update the list of all the companies and establishments concerned appended to this agreement. BUSINESS PARTNERS Not defined.
EADS	Group agreement on the harmonisation of the variable remuneration of Senior Managers within the EADS Group	SUBSIDIARIES The agreement applies and is mandatory in all four Divisions of the Group to all companies with more than 10 Senior Managers, of which EADS holds more than half the capital and which are located in one of the four following countries:

Company	Title of the Agreement	Addresses
		Germany, Spain, France and the United Kingdom. Other companies majority-owned by EADS, but employing 10 or less Senior Managers or which are located outside the four countries mentioned above, may apply the provisions of this Agreement by decision of the Division to which they belong or by EADS for companies which are directly part of the Group. BUSINESS PARTNERS Not defined.
EADS	Agreement for the Implementation of a Success-Sharing Plan within the EADS-NV Group	SUBSIDIARIES "TITLE 1: Scope of application Article 1: Founding countries This agreement is mandatory for all companies with 1,000 or more employees in which EADS holds more than 50% of the capital and which are located in one of the following four founding countries: France, Germany, Spain and the United Kingdom. Companies controlled by EADS (more than 50% of capital) and located in one of the above countries but with fewer than 1,000 employees can apply the provisions of this Group agreement based on a decision at divisional level. With the agreement of the Division, the company in question can decide that its economic situation does not enable it to apply the provisions of the Group success-sharing agreement and will then enter into alternative negotiations with a view to concluding a profit-sharing agreement adapted to its own situation. In this situation, the social partners of the said company can take the initiative of requesting the local Management to launch such negotiations.

Company	*Title of the Agreement*	*Addresses*
		Article 2: Non-founding countries With reference to companies controlled by EADS and located in a non-founding country, in Europe or elsewhere, EADS or the Division on the one hand and the company concerned on the other hand will jointly decide if the Group success-sharing agreement can be applied directly. If this approach is considered, it must be implemented in accordance with national legislation and, if necessary, a specific agreement must be signed with social partners in the company concerned. Should this approach not be possible due to the economic or social context of the country in question, in accordance with EADS or the Division, the company concerned may take the initiative of proposing negotiations with local social partners with a view to defining an employee profit-sharing scheme adapted to the national environment. Local social partners may also take the initiative of proposing a specific negotiation according to the national legislation. BUSINESS PARTNERS Not defined.
Air France/KLM	Framework agreement regarding the Outstations in Europe	SUBSIDIARIES Not defined. BUSINESS PARTNERS Not defined.
Santander	Joint Declaration of the European Works Council (EWC) and the Central Management of Santander Group regarding the labour relations framework for the provisions of financial services	SUBSIDIARIES No explicit reference, but the EFA speaks about the Group. BUSINESS PARTNERS Not defined.

Company	*Title of the Agreement*	*Addresses*
EADS	Agreement relating to the procedure for labor negotiations at European level	SUBSIDIARIES No explicit reference, but the EFA speaks about the EADS Group and its Divisions. BUSINESS PARTNERS Not defined.
Veolia Environment	Veolia Environment European Works Council agreement	SUBSIDIARIES ARTICLE 2. SCOPE "The Veolia Environnement European Works Council encompasses Veolia Environnement S.A. and all its subsidiaries or sub-subsidiaries within the European Union and in Member States of the European Economic Area in which it has a controlling interest, in accordance with the provisions of Article L.2343-2 of the French Labour Code. The list of companies concerned as of 31 December 2009 is shown in Appendix 1. It is an integral part of this Agreement and will be updated every 4 (four) years at the end of the year. This scope may be extended to include other countries under the conditions set out in ARTICLE 3. BUSINESS PARTNERS Not defined.
Alstom	European Agreement	SUBSIDIARIES Not defined. BUSINESS PARTNERS Not defined.
Schneider Electric	European Agreement	SUBSIDIARIES Not defined. BUSINESS PARTNERS Not defined.
Air France	Framework agreement on sales agencies in airports (ATOs) in Europe between, on the one hand, the management of CDL Europe/North Africa and, on the other, the European Group Council	SUBSIDIARIES Not defined. BUSINESS PARTNERS Not defined.

Company	*Title of the Agreement*	*Addresses*
Adam Opel AG	Agreement on European restructuring ("Opel Plan for the Future")	Text not available
GDF Suez	European group agreement relating to the employment and expertise plan	SUBSIDIARIES *Article 1.1.: Scope of Application* This agreement applies to GDF SUEZ and its subsidiaries which are globally integrated in the GDF SUEZ consolidation scope in Europe, or which are more than 50% owned, subject to compliance with the criterion of dominant influence. BUSINESS PARTNERS Not defined.
ABB	European Appendix to ABB social policy	SUBSIDIARIES The following also applies specifically to ABB companies and employees coverred by the ECE [Employees Council Europe]. BUSINESS PARTNERS Not defined.
Axa	Agreement on the AXA Group European Works Council	SUBSIDIARIES This agreement applies to Group companies located in EU Member States or countries belonging to the European Economic Area, regardless of their legal form, operating in the Insurance, Assistance or Banking divisions or the financial or Real Estate sectors, and which have financial or legal ties to AXA S.A. – "Financial ties" means that AXA SA directly or indirectly owns a majority of the shares or interest in the entity. - "Legal ties" means that the entity is bound to AXA SA under an agreement or contract, in particular an Economic Interest Grouping (GIE) agreement, or has financial ties to AXA SA. A list of the countries that fall within the scope of this definition is attached as Schedule 2 to this agreement; the Schedule also includes a list of Group employees in the country on December 31, 2008.

Company	*Title of the Agreement*	*Addresses*
		BUSINESS PARTNERS Not defined.
General Motors Europe	Working time reduction	Text not available
ArcelorMittal	Managing & Anticipating change at ArcelorMittal (V10)	SUBSIDIARIES This Agreement applies to all workers employed in ArcelorMittal group companies in the European countries listed in the appendix # 1 to this Agreement. Any change in this list will be subject to an amendment between the signatories of this Agreement. BUSINESS PARTNERS Not defined.
Unicredit	Joint declaration on "equal opportunities and non-discrimination"	SUBSIDIARIES No explicit reference but the EFA reads that: "This Joint Declaration intends to define common Group guidelines and definitions on Diversity, Equal Opportunities and Non-Discrimination, aimed at directing the Group's corporate culture." BUSINESS PARTNERS Not defined.
Santander	Declaration on Social Rights and Labour Relations in Santander Group	SUBSIDIARIES No explicit reference, but the EFAs speaks about the Group. BUSINESS PARTNERS Not defined
Unicredit	Joint declaration on "training, learning and professional development"	SUBSIDIARIES No explicit reference but the EFA reads that: "This Joint Declaration intends to define common Group guidelines on Training, Learning and Professional Development, aimed at orienting the whole Group's initiatives and activities. BUSINESS PARTNERS Not defined.

Company	*Title of the Agreement*	*Addresses*
BP	Agreement on "Business Service Centre (BSC)" Consultation	SUBSIDIARIES Not defined. BUSINESS PARTNERS Not defined.
Santander	Joint Declaration to be signed in the meeting on 21.05.2008 between the European Works Council and the representatives designated by grupo santander's senior management	SUBSIDIARIES No explicit reference but the EFA speaks about Grupo Santander. BUSINESS PARTNERS Not defined.
Suez (now GDF Suez)	Agreement on social guarantees for Suez Group employees	SUBSIDIARIES a) Area of application The current agreement applies to subsidiaries globally integrated within the scope of consolidation of the SUEZ Group in Europe without prejudging more favourable dispositions existing locally. BUSINESS PARTNERS Not defined.
Unicredit	Establishment of the Joint Commissions	SUBSIDIARIES Not defined BUSINESS PARTNERS Not defined.
GDF (now GDF Suez)	European agreement on the corporate social responsibility of the Gaz de France group	SUBSIDIARIES This agreement applies, on a European scale (The European Union, The European Economic Space, countries that have applied for Union membership), to the fully integrated and monitored entities, namely: - Companies in which Gaz de France holds, directly or indirectly, a fraction of the capital which gives it a majority of the voting rights in the meetings of these companies. - Companies over which Gaz de France, by virtue of voting rights, held either directly or indirectly, has the possibility of ensuring that its point of view takes precedence at general meetings.

Company	*Title of the Agreement*	*Addresses*
		- Companies in which Gaz de France is, directly or indirectly, either associated or a shareholder and thus has the power to appoint or abrogate the majority of the members constituting the administrative, managerial or regulatory bodies of this company. The list of entities concerned is communicated regularly to the signing parties Furthermore, in order to increase the awareness of all of its companies with respect to the CSR process, the Gaz de France Group shall bring this agreement to the knowledge of companies that do not fall within the scope of application. BUSINESS PARTNERS 4.4) Relations with suppliers and sub-contractors The Gaz de France Group's suppliers and sub-contractors will be informed of this agreement. Relations with suppliers and sub-contractors should not generally cause situations to arise in which the Group's ethical commitments and those described in this agreement are brought into question. All Gaz de France companies expect their suppliers and sub-contractors to observe the current international laws and agreements. Any disregard for Human Rights will be made the subject of corrective measures further to a warning issued by the Group's companies. Non-observance of these rights will lead to cessation of the commercial partnership. Within the general framework of its policy of "best bidder" the Gaz de France Group recognises and appreciates the efforts undertaken by various suppliers who voluntarily engage in a process of social responsibility adapted to their company, particularly the proportion of capital investment dedicated to safety at work.

Company	*Title of the Agreement*	*Addresses*
		The Gaz de France Group ensures that its suppliers' contractual time limits for settlement are respected. Gaz de France's companies contribute to local economical development by means of local partnerships. They ensure that small local companies and firms employing disabled workers or people being reintegrated into society are referenced by the Group's companies. Solidarity clauses may be introduced into sub-contracting contracts. Furthermore, Group companies are attentive to the situation of suppliers with which they do a significant amount of business in order to limit situations of dependency.
Strawood Lodging	Agreement regarding the transnational transfer of Starwood Employees	SUBSIDIARIES Starwood Hotels & Resorts Worldwide Inc. and its daughter companies and affiliated companies, in Europe ("Starwood"), excluding franchise, will endeavour to fill any positions internally in hotels within countries which are located in the SEECCC area." BUSINESS PARTNERS Not defined.
Total	European agreement on assistance in creation, purchase or development of small and medium sized businesses	SUBSIDIARIES The present agreement applies to all the legally autonomous entities of the Total Group mentioned in Article 1 of the agreement relating to the European Works Council of 29th June 2005. In order to enable the Group's subsidiaries to adhere under the best conditions possible to the objectives contained in the present agreement and to enable the employees to be made aware of the procedures provided for by the present agreement, the Group's General Management will implement a campaign for presenting these objectives and the provisions contained therein.

Company	*Title of the Agreement*	*Addresses*
		BUSINESS PARTNERS Not defined.
DaimlerChrysler	Framework Regulation with the European Works Council (EWC) on the Realignment of the Sales Organization in the European Union	SUBSIDIARIES Not defined. BUSINESS PARTNERS Not defined.
General Motors (Europe)	Restructuring at Antwerp	Text not available
General Motors (Europe)	Allocation of next Astra	Text not available
Suez (now GDF Suez)	Group agreement – Suez Group's Social Dynamics – section on "Employment and Expertise Plan"	SUBSIDIARIES Article 1.1. Scope This agreement applies to all the subsidiary companies fully integrated in the consolidated structure of the SUEZ Groupe in Europe. BUSINESS PARTNERS Not defined.
Schneider Electric[635]	European Agreement on the Anticipation of Change	SUBSIDIARIES 1.1. Geographical scope of application The present agreement applies to all the legally autonomous entities of Schneider Electric in Europe (scope of the European Committee as defined by Article 1 of the agreement in respect of the Schneider Electric European Committee signed on 21st January 1998 and modified on 20th January 2005). BUSINESS PARTNERS Not defined.
Kraft Foods	European Framework Agreement regarding Project One Europe to be Concluded Between Kraft Foods Europe Management and the Employee Representatives	SUBSIDIARIES Not defined. BUSINESS PARTNERS Not defined.

635. Schneider Electric is a group of companies.

Company	*Title of the Agreement*	*Addresses*
DaimlerChrysler	Framework agreement for information and consultation with employees and employee representatives in the local European operations of DaimlerChrysler AG	SUBSIDIARIES Not defined. BUSINESS PARTNERS Not defined.
Allianz SE	Agreement concerning the participation of employees in Allianz SE	SUBSIDIARIES The SE Works Council is a representation of employees of Allianz SE and its subsidiaries within the meaning of Section 2 paragraph 3 of the SE Participation Act – "SEBG" ("Subsidiaries") with registered offices in the Member States of the EU, the contracting states of the EEA, and Switzerland ("Allianz Group"), as far as these employees are employed ("Allianz Employees") within the concerned countries ("Concerned Countries"). BUSINESS PARTNERS Not defined.
Total	European agreement on equal opportunity Total Group	SUBSIDIARIES Article 1 – Scope of application This agreement applies to all legally autonomous entities of the Total Group mentioned in article 1 of the agreement concerning the Total European Works Council (EWC) dated 29 June 2005. BUSINESS PARTNERS Not defined.
EADS[636]	Agreement on the European Works Council of EADS N.V. and its derived committees concluded	SUBSIDIARIES 2. Scope Pursuant to the aforementioned Dutch Law and European Directives, the present Agreement is applicable to EADS N.V. and its companies located in the Member States of the European Economic Area.

636. EADS (now Airbus Group) was a group of companies.

Company	*Title of the Agreement*	*Addresses*
	between European Aeronautic Defence and Space Company EADS N.V. and its employees' representatives	BUSINESS PARTNERS Not defined.
Philip Morris (Kraft Jacobs)	Guidelines on information and consultation employment	Text not available
Unilever	Agreed joint statement UEWC and Unilever on protection of personal data	SUBSIDIARIES The Unilever policy has been written for all Unilever companies with the intention that a single global policy will ensure that the highest standards are maintained. The company has indicated that it will expect all its subsidiaries to comply fully with the policy. BUSINESS PARTNERS Not defined.
General Electric Plastics (Europe)	Agreement on Pre-employment screening ("background checks")	SUBSIDIARIES As this agreement is supposed to be used for all European sites of the company (…)". BUSINESS PARTNERS As doing backgroundchecks requires professional experience, network and time, GEP has chosen Kroll Background Europe (in the following referred to as "KBE") as preferred supplier and partner to do background checks. KBE will ensure that: It operates within the guidelines of European data privacy laws Their legal team works continuously to ensure that record handling and storage meets European and international legal requirements (…).

Company	*Title of the Agreement*	*Addresses*
Total	European agreement – social platform Total Group	SUBSIDIARIES This agreement applies to all the Total Group's legally autonomous entities mentioned in the 1st article of the agreement concerning the European Works Council (EWC) of Total dated 20 March 2001, provided that they have a personnel representation body. BUSINESS PARTNERS Not defined.
Deutsche Bank	Common Standpoint of the Deutsche Bank Group and the EWC	SUBSIDIARIES Not defined. BUSINESS PARTNERS Not defined.
Ford (Europe)	IOS restructuring: maintenance of jobs, investments, employability	Text not available
General Motors (Europe)	Restructuring Framework	SUBSIDIARIES This restructuring program will affect all brands, sites, plants and functions within GM Europe. BUSINESS PARTNERS Not defined.
General Electric Plastics (Europe)	Amendment to the GEPE EBR Agreement on the introduction of regulations (including methodology and practice) during negotiations between the GEPE Central Management ("CM") and the GEPE EWC ("EWC")	SUBSIDIARIES Not defined. BUSINESS PARTNERS Not defined.
Ford (Europe)	Ford of Europe and the Ford European Works Council (FEWC) Agreed upon Social Rights and Social Responsibility Principles	SUBSIDIARIES These Principles apply to Ford of Europe. BUSINESS PARTNERS Ford of Europe will encourage business partners throughout its value chain to adopt and enforce similar policies to those contained in these Principles, as the basis

Company	*Title of the Agreement*	*Addresses*
		for establishing mutual and durable business relationships. The Company will seek to identify and utilise business partners who aspire in the conduct of their business to standards that are consistent with this document.
General Electric Plastics (Europe)	GEPE Agreement on use of electronic communication systems	SUBSIDIARIES As this agreement is supposed to be used for all European sites of the company. BUSINESS PARTNERS Not defined.
General Motors (Europe)	General Motors Europe and the European Employee Forum agree on Principles of Social Responsibility	SUBSIDIARIES Not defined. BUSINESS PARTNERS We support and encourage the application of these principles by those with whom we do business. The principles will be shared with our business partners as a solid basis for a sustainable business relationship. They shall comply with all applicable laws and regulations that relate to wages, hours & conditions of employment, discrimination and occupational health & safety. Under contracts with GME, our suppliers represent and signify that they will not utilize forced or involuntary labor in the supply of goods or provision of services to GME.
Philip Morris (Kraft Jacobs)	Processing key HR data (part of EWC agreement)	Text not available
ENI	Agreement report	SUBSIDIARIES Not defined. BUSINESS PARTNERS Not defined.
Kraft Foods	Framework understanding concerning the protection and processing of employment related	Text not available

Company	*Title of the Agreement*	*Addresses*
	personal data of employees of Kraft Foods International in EU/EEA Countries	
Danone	Joint opinion on the applicable social standards for all the undertakings concerned by the restructuring program of the Biscuits Pole in Europe presented on 29 March 2001	SUBSIDIARIES No explicit reference but the EFA refers to the Danone Group. BUSINESS PARTNERS Not defined.
Bouygues	European Social Charter of the Bouygues Group	SUBSIDIARIES All employees will be made aware of this European Social Charter, which is applicable to all Bouygues Group activities. It is the Group's intention to extend this charter world-wide. BUSINESS PARTNERS Not defined.
Unilever	Responsible Restructuring	SUBSIDIARIES Not defined. BUSINESS PARTNERS Not defined.
General Motors (Europe)	European framework, dated 5 March 2001 at 20:30 ("The following framework agreement is in relation of GM's current restructuring initiatives")	SUBSIDIARIES Not defined. BUSINESS PARTNERS Not defined.
Philip Morris (Kraft Jacobs)	Agreement on the use of data recorded by sales forces	Text not available
Philip Morris (Kraft Jacobs)	Agreement by the EU Assembly for the workforce of Philip Morris tobacco companies in the european regions of Philip Morris on the protection of personal data processed by ITSC Europe S.A.R.L.	SUBSIDIARIES The parties agree to provide a copy of the agreement on data protection (see "annex") to all Philip Morris tobacco companies in the European area. BUSINESS PARTNERS Not defined.

Company	*Title of the Agreement*	*Addresses*
General Motors (Europe)	Framework "regarding "Project Olympia" initiatives"	SUBSIDIARIES Not defined. BUSINESS PARTNERS Not defined.
General Motors (Europe)	Framework	SUBSIDIARIES Not defined. BUSINESS PARTNERS Not defined.
Ford (Europe)	Joint Venture CFT: maintenance of Ford contracts, investments	Text not available
Ford	Agreement governing the separation of the Ford Visteon organisation	SUBSIDIARIES Not defined. BUSINESS PARTNERS Not defined.
Vivendi (Veolia Générale des Eaux)	Charter on the safety at the workplace in the Group	SUBSIDIARIES No explicit reference but the EFA speaks about Vivendi Group. BUSINESS PARTNERS Not defined.
Philip Morris (Kraft Jacobs)	Principles on the introduction of euro	Text not available
Philip Morris (Kraft Jacobs)	Code of conduct smoking at the workplace	Text not available
ENI	Agreement	SUBSIDIARIES No explicit reference but the text speaks about the ENI Group in Europe. BUSINESS PARTNERS Not defined.

Bibliography

BOOKS

Barnard, Catherine, *EU Employment Law* (Oxford University Press 2012).

Bercusson, Brian, *European Labour Law and the EU Charter of Fundamental Rights* (ETUI aisbl 2003).

Blanpain, Roger and Colucci, Michele, *The Globalization of Labour Standards: The Soft Law Track*, vol 52 Bulletin of Comparative Labour Relations (Kluwer Law International 2004).

Bronstein, Arturo, *International and Comparative Labour Law: Current Challenges* (Palgrave Macmillan 2009).

Friedman, Thomas, *The Lexus and The Olive Tree* (Anchor Books 2000).

Gore, Al, *The Future – Six Drivers of Global Change* (Random House 2013).

Servais, Jean-Michel, *International Labour Law* (2nd revised edn, Kluwer Law International 2009).

Senden, Linda, *Soft Law in European Community Law* (Hart Publishing 2004).

BOOK CONTRIBUTIONS

Blanpain, Roger, 'Multinational Enterprises and Codes of Conduct: The OECD Guidelines for MNEs in Perspective' in Blanpain, Roger (ed.), *Comparative Labour Law and Industrial Relations in Industrialized Market Economies* (Kluwer Law International 2010).

Bé, Dominique, 'A Report on the European Commission Initiative for a European Framework for Transnational Collective Bargaining' in Papadakis, Konstantinos (ed.), *Cross-Border Social Dialogue and Agreements: An Emerging Global Industrial Relations Framework?* (International Institute for Labour Studies 2008).

Boni, Guido, 'Introduction' in Schömann, Isabelle, et al., *Transnational Collective Bargaining at Company Level – A New Component of European Industrial Relations?* (ETUI aisbl 2012).

Clauwaert, Stefan, 'European Framework Agreements: "Nomina Nuda Tenemus" or What's in the Name? Experiences of the European Social Dialogue' in Schömann, Isabelle, et al., *Transnational Collective Bargaining at Company Level – A New Component of European Industrial Relations?* (ETUI aisbl 2012).

Da Costa, Isabel and Rehfeldt, Udo, 'Transnational Restructuring Agreements: General Overview and Specific Evidence from the European Automobile Sector' in Papadakis, Konstantinos (ed.), *Shaping Global Industrial Relations – The Impact of International Framework Agreements* (Palgrave Macmillan 2011).

Egels-Zandén, Niklas, 'Clean Clothes Campaign' in Hale, Thomas and Held, David (eds), *The Handbook of Transnational Governance: Institutions and Innovations* (Polity Pr 2011).

Fichter, Michael and Helfen, Markus and Schiederig, Katharina, 'Transnational Solidarity around Global Production Networks? Reflections on the Strategy of International Framework Agreements' in Fairbrother, Peter, Hennebert, Marc-Antonin and Lévesque, Christian (eds.), *Transnational Trade Unionism: Building Union Power* (Routledge 2013).

Gallin, Dan, 'International Framework Agreements: A Reassessment' in Papadakis, Konstantinos (ed.), *Cross-Border Social Dialogue and Agreements: An Emerging Global Industrial Relations Framework?* (International Institute for Labour Studies 2008).

Gumbrell-McCormick, Rebecca, 'The International Labour Movement: Structures and Dynamics' in Fairbrother, Peter, Hennebert, Marc-Antonin and Lévesque, Christian (eds.), *Transnational Trade Unionism: Building Union Power* (Routledge 2013).

Hammer, Nikolaus, 'International Framework Agreements in the Context of Global Production' in Papadakis, Konstantinos (ed.), *Cross-Border Social Dialogue and Agreements: An Emerging Global Industrial Relations Framework?* (International Institute for Labour Studies 2008).

Hayter Susan, 'The Social Dimension of Globalization: Striking the Balance' in Blanpain, Roger (ed.), *Confronting Globalization – The Quest for a Social Agenda*, vol 55 Bulletin of Comparative Labour Relations (Kluwer Law International 2005).

Howse, Rober and Langille, Brian A and Burda, Julien, 'The World Trade Organization and Labour Rights: Man Bites Dog' in Leary Virginia A and Warner Daniel (eds), *Social Issues, Globalisation and International Institutions: Labour Rights and the EU, ILO, OECD and WTO* (Martinus Nijhoff Publishers 2006).

Jagodzinski Romuald, 'Transnational Collective Bargaining: A Literature Review' in Schömann, Isabelle, et al., *Transnational Collective Bargaining at Company Level – A New Component of European Industrial Relations?* (ETUI aisbl, 2012).

Jagodzinski Romuald, 'European Works Councils and Transnational Company Agreements – Balancing on the Thin Line between Effective Consultation and Overstepping Competences' in Schömann, Isabelle, et al., *Transnational Collective Bargaining at Company Level – A New Component of European Industrial Relations?* (ETUI aisbl, 2012).

Jones, Karen, 'Corporate Codes, IFAs and Multi-National Corporate Social Responsibility 10 Years after the UN Global Compact' in Blanpain, Roger (ed.), *Labour*

Markets, Industrial Relations and Human Resources Management: From Recession to Recovery, vol 80 Bulletin of Comparative Labour Relations (Kluwer Law International 2012).

Kun, Attila and Hajdú, József, 'Conceptualization of Corporate Social Responsibility in the Context of Labor Law' in Blanpain, Roger (ed.), *Rethinking Corporate Governance: From Shareholder Value to Stakeholder Value*, vol 77 Bulletin of Comparative Labour Relations (Kluwer Law International 2011).

Miller, Doug, 'The ITGLWF's Policy on Cross-Border Dialogue in the Textiles, Clothing and Footwear Sector: Emerging Strategies in a Sector Ruled by Codes of Conduct and Resistant Companies' in Papadakis, Konstantinos (ed.), *Cross-Border Social Dialogue and Agreements: An Emerging Global Industrial Relations Framework?* (International Institue for Labour Studies 2008).

Papadakis, Konstantinos, 'Introduction' in Papadakis, Konstantinos (ed.), *Cross-Border Social Dialogue and Agreements: An Emerging Global Industrial Relations Framework?* (International Institute for Labour Studies 2008).

Papadakis, Konstantinos, Casale, Giuseppe and Tsotroudi, Katerina, 'International Framework Agreements as Elements of a Cross-Border Industrial Relations Framework' in Papadakis, Konstantinos (ed.), *Cross-Border Social Dialogue and Agreements: An Emerging Global Industrial Relations Framework?* (International Institute for Labour Studies 2008).

Papadakis, Konstantinos, 'Introduction and Overview' in Papadakis, Konstantinos (ed.), *Shaping Global Industrial Relations – The Impact of International Framework Agreements* (Palgrave Macmillan 2012).

Papadakis, Konstantinos, 'Adapting International Framework Agreements in the Russian Federation, South Africa and Japan: Management and Motivations' in Papadakis, Konstantinos, *Shaping Global Industrial Relations – The Impact of International Framework Agreements* (Palgrave Macmillan 2012).

Pulignano, Valeria, et al., 'Local Actors and Transnational Structures – Explaining Trends in Multinational Company-Level Negotiations in Europe' in Fairbrother, Peter, Hennebert, Marc-Antonin and Lévesque, Christian (eds), *Transnational Trade Unionism: Building Union Power* (Routledge 2013).

Schömann, Isabelle, 'The Impact of Transnational Company Agreements on Social Dialogue and Industrial Relations' in Papadakis, Konstantinos, *Shaping Global Industrial Relations – The Impact of International Framework Agreements* (Palgrave Macmillan 2012).

Schömann, Isabelle, 'Transnational Company Agreements: Towards an Internationalisation of Industrial Relations' in Schömann, Isabelle, et al., *Transnational Collective Bargaining at Company Level – A New Component of European Industrial Relations?* (ETUI aisbl 2012).

Schömann, Isabelle, 'Transnational Collective Bargaining: In Search of a Legal Framework' in Schömann, Isabelle, et al., *Transnational Collective Bargaining at Company Level – A New Component of European Industrial Relations?* (ETUI aisbl 2012).

Servais, Jean-Michel, 'International Labour Standards and Corporate Social Responsibility' in Blanpain, Roger (ed.), *Confronting Globalisation: The Quest for a*

Social Agenda, vol 55 Bulletin of Comparative Labour Relations (Kluwer Law International 2005).

Sobczak, André, 'Legal Dimensions of International Framework Agreements in the Field of Corporate Social Responsibility' in Papadakis, Konstantinos (ed.), *Cross-Border Social Dialogue and Agreements: An Emerging Global Industrial Relations Framework?* (International Institute for Labour Studies 2008).

Synder, Francis, 'Soft Law and Institutional Practice in the European Community' in Martin S (ed.), *The Construction of Europe: Essays in Honour of Emile Noël* (Kluwer Academic Publishers 1994).

Vos, Kees J, 'New Modes of Governance in Industrial Relations' in Blanpain, Roger (ed.), *Labour Markets, Industrial Relations and Human Resources Management: From Recession to Recovery*, vol 80 Bulletin of Comparative Labour Relations (Kluwer Law International 2012).

Welz, Christian, 'A Qualitative Analysis of International Framework Agreements: Implementation and Impact' in Papadakis, Konstantinos, *Shaping Global Industrial Relations – The Impact of International Framework Agreements* (Palgrave Macmillan 2012).

Windmuller John P, and Pursey Stephen K and Baker, Jim, 'The International Trade Union Movement' in Blanpain, Roger (ed.), *Comparative Labour Law and Industrial Relations in Industrialized Market Economies* (Kluwer Law International 2014).

ARTICLES

Ales, Edoardo, Dufresne, Anne, 'Transnational Collective Bargaining: Another (Problematic) Fragment of the European Multi-level Industrial Relations System' (2012) 18(2) European Journal of Industrial Relations 95.

Béthoux, Élodie and Didry, C Claude and Mias, A Arnaud, 'What Codes of Conduct Tell Us: Corporate Social Responsibility and the Nature of the Multinational Corporation' (2007) 15(1) Corporate Governance: An International Review 77.

Blanpain, Roger, 'European Works Councils: The European Directive 2009/38/EC of 6 May 2009' (2010) 1(1) European Labour Law Journal 107.

Crough, Colin, 'Modelling the Firm in its Market and Organizational Environment: Methodologies for Studying Corporate Social Responsibility' (2006) 27(10) Organization Studies 1533.

Drouin, Renee-Claude, 'Promoting Fundamental Labor Rights Through International Framework Agreements: Practical Outcomes and Present Challenges' (2010) 31 Comparative Labor Law and Policy Journal 591.

Hammer, Nikolaus, 'International Framework Agreements: Global Industrial Relations between Rights and Bargaining' (Winter 2005) 4(05) Transfer 511.

Herrnstadt, Owen E., 'Are International Framework Agreements a Path to Corporate Social Responsibility?' (2007) 10(1) The Journal of Business and Employment Law 187.

Jagodzinski, Romuald, 'Involving European Works Councils in Transnational Negotiations – A Positive Functional Advance in Their Operation or Trespassing?' (2007) 14(4) Industrielle Beziehungen 316.

Locke, Richard M., et al., 'Beyond Corporate Codes of Conduct: Work Organization and Labour Standards at Nike's Suppliers' (2007) (1-2) International Labour Review 21.

Lo Faro, Antonio, 'Bargaining in the Shadow of "Optional Frameworks"? The Rise of Transnational Collective Agreements and EU Law' (2012) 18(2) European Journal of Industrial Relations 153.

Müller, Torsten and Platzer, Hans-Wolfgang and Rüb, Stefan, 'European Collective Agreements at Company Level and the Relationship between EWCs and Trade Unions – Lessons from the Metal Sector' (2011) 17(1) Transfer: European Review of Labour and Research 217.

Pulignano, Valeria, 'European Integration and Transnational Employment Regulation: The Company-Level Experience of EFAs in the Metal Sector in Europe' (2010) 1(1) European Labour Law Journal 81.

Sobczak, André, 'Ensuring the Effective Implementation of Transnational Company Agreements' (2012) 18(2) European Journal of Industrial Relations 139.

Telljohann, Volker, et al., 'European and International Framework Agreements: New Tools of Transnational Industrial Relations' (2009) 3-4 Transfer 505.

Weiss, Manfred, 'The European Social Dialogue' (2011) 2(2) European Labour Law Journal 155.

Zimmer, Reingard, 'European Works Councils as Participants in Euro-Wide Collective Agreements: Analysis from a German Perspective' (2013) 4(4) European Labour Law Journal 313.

ONLINE ARTICLES

Hendrickx, Frank H R, 'The Development of Transnational Company Agreements in Europe' (2009) <https://pure.uvt.nl/portal/files/1305894/Hendrickx_Development_of_transnational_company_agreements_110209_postprint_embargo1y.pdf> accessed 11 August 2014.

Lim, Hoe, 'The Social Clause: Issues and Challenges' (International Labour Organizations – Bureau for Workers' Activities 2001) <www.actrav.itcilo.org/actrav-english/telearn/global/ilo/guide/hoelim.htm> accessed 24 August 2014.

Wilke, Peter and Schütze, Kim, 'Background Paper on International Framework Agreements for a Meeting of the Restructuring Forum devoted to Transnational Agreements at Company Level' (2008) <http://ec.europa.eu/social/BlobServlet?docId=4969&langId=en> accessed 17 May 2014.

ILO (ACTRAV), 'Labour and Business in the Global Market' <http://actrav.itcilo.org/actrav-english/telearn/global/ilo/guide/icftuart.htm> accessed 17 May 2014.

WORKING PAPERS

Béthoux, Élodie, 'Transnational agreements and texts negotiated or adopted at company level: European Development and Perspectives' (Background document) (2008) <http://ec.europa.eu/social/BlobServlet?docId=4968&langId=en> accessed 10 April 2014.

Edwards, Paul Tony, et al., 'Corporate Social Responsibility in Multinational Companies: Management Initiatives or Negotiated Agreements?' (2007) Discussion Paper No. 185, International Institute for Labour Studies <www.ilo.org/public/english/bureau/inst/publications/discussion/dp18507.pdf> accessed 1 April 2014.

Hopkins, Michael, 'Corporate Social Responsibility: an issues paper' (2004) International Labour Office Working Paper No. 27 <www.ilo.org/legacy/english/integration/download/publicat/4_3_285_wcsdg-wp-27.pdf> accessed 12 February 2014.

Papadakis, Konstantinos, 'Restructuring Enterprises through social dialogue and labour management agreements: Social responsibility practices in time of crisis' (International Labour Office 2010) <www.ilo.org/public/libdoc/jobcrisis/download/restructuring_enterprises.pdf> accessed 23 May 2014.

Rüb, Stefan, 'World works councils and other forms of global employee representation in transnational undertakings' Arbeitspapier No. 55 <http://www.boeckler.de/pdf/p_arbp_055.pdf> accessed 14 July 2014.

Senatori, Jacopo, 'Transnational Company Bargaining and the Discourse of the European Commission: A Critical Overview' (2013) Working Paper, <www.labourlawresearch.net/sites/default/files/papers/SENATORI.pdf> accessed 10 March 2014.

Stevis, Dimitris, 'International framework agreements and global social dialogue: Parameters and prospects' (2010) Employment Working Paper No. 47, <www.oit.org/wcmsp5/groups/public/@ed_emp/documents/publication/wcms_122176.pdf> accessed 14 April 2014.

REPORTS

Alaimo, Anna, 'Transnational Company Agreements and Sectoral Social Dialogue: Parallel Lines, No Convergence?' in Leonardi, Salvo, et al., *European Action on Transnational Company Agreements: A Stepping Stone towards a Real Internationalisation of Industrial Relations?* (IRES 2012).

Ales, Edoardo, et al., 'Transnational Collective Bargaining: Past, Present and Future' (Final Report 2006) available at <http://ec.europa.eu/social/BlobServlet?docId=4641&langId=en> accessed 14 March 2014.

Ales, Edoardo and Verrecchia, Giorgio, 'Transnational: The Emerging Multifaced Dimension of Industrial Relations' in Leonardi, Salvo, et al., *European Action on Transnational Company Agreements: A Stepping Stone towards a Real Internationalisation of Industrial Relations?* (IRES 2012).

Carley, Mark, 'Transnational Company Agreements. Dialogue, Rights, Anticipating Corporate Restructuring, Actors: A New Perspective' (Report of the French EU Presidency Conference, Lyon, 13-14 November 2008) <www.travail-emploi-sante.gouv.fr/IMG/pdf/ATNEactes.pdf> accessed 29 March 2014.

Cilento, Marco, 'Development of Transnational Negotiations with Multinational Companies in a Trade Union Perspective' in Leonardi, Salvo, et al. (eds), *European Action on Transnational Company Agreements: A Stepping Stone towards a Real Internationalisation of Industrial Relations?* (IRES 2012).

ITC-ILO, 'Key Issues for Management to Consider with regard to Transnational Company Agreements (TCAs)' (2010) <http://lempnet.itcilo.org/en/tcas/admin/final-pub> accessed 5 March 2014.

Van Hoek, Aukje and Hendrickx, Frank H R, 'International Private Law Aspects and Dispute Settlement Related to Transnational Company Agreements' (Final Report 2009 - VC/2009/0157) <http://ec.europa.eu/social/BlobServlet?docId=4815&langId=en> accessed 14 August 2014.

Leonardi, Salvo, 'Transnational Company Agreements: A Stepping Stone towards a Real Internationalization of Industrial Relations?' in Leonardi, Salvo, et al., *European Action on Transnational Company Agreements: A Stepping Stone towards a Real Internationalisation of Industrial Relations?* (IRES 2012).

Rocha, Fernando and Beneyto, Pere J., 'Trade Unions and Europeanisation of Industrial Relations: Challenges and Perspectives' in Leonardi, Salvo, et al., *European Action on Transnational Company Agreements: A Stepping Stone towards a Real Internationalisation of Industrial Relations?* (IRES 2012).

Rodríguez, Ricardo, et al., 'Study on the Characteristics and Legal Effects of Agreements between Companies and Workers' Representatives' (Final Report 2011) <http://ec.europa.eu/social/BlobServlet?docId=7631&langId=en> accessed 14 August 2014.

Schömann, Isabelle, et al., 'Codes of Conduct and International Framework Agreements: New Forms of Governance at Company Level' (Eurofound, Office for Official Publications of the European Communities 2008) <www.eurofound.europa.eu/pubdocs/2007/92/en/1/ef0792en.pdf> accessed 14 November 2013.

Schömann, Isabelle, et al., 'Codes of Conduct and International Framework Agreements: New Forms of Governance at Company Level, Case Study IKEA' (Eurofound, Office for Official Publications of the European Communities 2008) <www.eurofound.europa.eu/pubdocs/2007/927/en/1/ef07927en.pdf> accessed 14 May 2014.

Sobczak, André, et al., 'Codes of Conduct and International Framework Agreements: New Form of Governance at Company Level, Case Study: EDF' (Eurofound, Office for Official Publications of the European Communities 2008) <www.eurofound.europa.eu/pubdocs/2007/921/en/1/ef07921en.pdf> accessed 14 May 2014.

Telljohann, Volker, et al., 'European and International Framework Agreements: Practical Experiences and Strategic Approaches' (Eurofound, Office for Official

Publications of the European Communities 2009), <www.eurofound.europa.eu/pubdocs/2008/102/en/2/EF08102EN.pdf> accessed 14 March 2014.

Welz, Christian, 'IFAs and EFAs: – 'essai' of a Qualitative Analysis, Expert Group – Transnational Company Agreements' (2009) (Expert Group transnational company agreements) <http://ec.europa.eu/social/BlobServlet?docId=6369&langId=en> accessed 14 July 2014.

World Commission on the Social Dimension of Globalization, 'A Fair Globalization: Creating Opportunities for All' (2004) <www.ilo.org/public/english/wcsdg/docs/report.pdf> accessed 20 February 2014.

Zimmer, Reingard, 'Establish a Legal Frame for Transnational Collective Agreements in Europe: A Difficult Task' in Leonardi, Salvo, et al., *European Action on Transnational Company Agreements: A Stepping Stone towards a Real Internationalisation of Industrial Relations?* (IRES 2012).

OFFICIAL DOCUMENT

EU Documents and Legislation

Consolidated Version of the Treaty on the Functioning of the European Union [2012] OJ C 326/01.

Charter of Fundamental Rights of the European Union [2012] OJ C 326/02.

Explanations relating to the Charter of Fundamental Rights [2007] OJ C 303/17.

Council Directive 94/45/EC of 22 September 1994 on the establishment of a European Works Council or a procedure in Community-scale undertakings and Community-scale groups of undertakings for the purposes of informing and consulting employees [1994] OJ L 254.

Directive 2009/38/EC of 6 May 2009 on the establishment of a European Works Council or a procedure in Community-scale undertakings and Community-scale groups of undertakings for the purposes of informing and consulting employees [2009] OJ L 122.

Commission Decision 98/500/EC on the establishment of Sectoral Dialogue Committees promoting the Dialogue between the Social Partners at European level [1998] OJ l225/27.

Commission, 'Promoting a European Framework for Corporate Social Responsibility' (Green Paper), COM (2001) 366 final.

Commission, 'Communication concerning the application of the agreement on social policy presented by the Commission to the Council and the European Parliament' (Communication) COM (93) 600 final.

Commission, 'Communication from the Commission of 20 May 1998 adapting and promoting the social dialogue at Community level' (Communication) COM (98) 322 final.

Commission, 'Communication from the Commission on the Social Agenda' (Communication) COM (2005) 33 final.

Commission, 'The role of transnational company agreements in the contexts of increasing transnational integrations' (Staff Working Document), SEC (2008) 2155.

Commission, 'Transnational company agreements: realising the potential of social dialogue' (Staff Working Document), SWD (2012) 264 final.

Commission, 'The development of transnational agreements', First approach (March 2006) <http://ec.europa.eu/social/BlobServlet?docId=2895&langId=en> accessed on 14 July 2014.

Commission, 'Mapping of transnational texts negotiated at corporate level', EMPL F2 EP/bp 2008 (D) 14511.

Commission, 'Implementation and Dispute Settlement in Transnational Company Agreements' (Issues paper), EMPL F2 EP.

Commission, 'Second Meeting of the Expert Group on TCAs of 27 November 2009' (Minutes) EMPL F2 EP.

European Parliament, 'Resolution on cross-border collective bargaining and transnational social dialogue' (2012/2292(INI)).

International Labour Organization

ILO Recommendation R91: Collective Agreements Recommendation, (Recommendation concerning Collective Agreements) (34th Conference Session Geneva 29 June 1951).

International Labour Conference (86th Session) Declaration on Fundamental Principles and Rights at Work and its Follow-up (Geneva 18 June 1998).

Governing Body (204th Session) Tripartite Declaration of Principles concerning Multinational Enterprises and Social Policy (Geneva, November 1977 as amended at its 279th (November 2000) and 295th Session (March 2006)).

Governing Body (295th Session) InFocus Initiative on Corporate Social Responsibility (CSR) (Geneva March 2006).

Governing Body (301th Session) Proposal for evaluating the effect given to the Tripartite Declaration of Principles concerning Multinational Enterprises and Social Policy (Geneva, March 2008).

Governing Body (317th Session) Tripartite Declaration of Principles concerning Multinational Enterprises and Social Policy (MNE Declaration): Operational plan for promotional activities and proposal for the new survey (Geneva, 6–28 March 2013).

NAFTA

The North American Agreement on Labor Cooperation (adopted 14 September 1993, entered into force 1 January 1994) 32 I.L.M 1499 (NAALC).

OECD

OECD, OECD Guidelines for Multinational Enterprises (2011), OECD Publishing < http://www.oecd-ilibrary.org/governance/oecd-guidelines-for-multinational-enterprises_9789264115415-en > accessed 14 September 2014.

UN

Proposed Text of the Draft Code of Conduct on Transnational Corporations, U.N. E.C.O.S.O.C., 2d Sess., Annex, U.N. Doc. E/1990/94 (1990).

UNCHR (Sub-Commission), 'Norms on the responsibilities of transnational corporations and other business enterprises with regard to human rights' (2003) UN Document E/CN.4/Sub.2/2003/38/Rev.2 UNCHR Res 2005/69 (2005) UN Doc E/CN.4/RES/2005/69.

UNCHR, 'Report of the Special Representative of the Secretary-General John Ruggie on the issue of human rights and transnational corporations and other business enterprises' (2011) UN Doc A/HRC/17/31.

HRC, 'Human rights and transnational corporations and other business enterprises' (2011) UN Doc A/HRC/RES/17/4.

UNCTAD, 'World Investment Report 2013' (2013) UNCTAD/WIR/2013.

UNCTAD, 'World Investment Report 2009' (2009) UNCTAD/WIR/2009.

Others

WTO, Singapore Ministerial Declaration (13 December 1996) WT/MIN(96)/DEC.

WTO, 'World Trade Report 2013: Factors Shaping the Future of World Trade' (2013). < www.wto.org/english/res_e/booksp_e/world_trade_report13_e.pdf > accessed 20 September 2013.

World Bank Group, 'Legal Framework for the Treatment of Foreign Investment' Volume 2: Guidelines' (1992) Report No. 11415.

TRADE UNIONS' AND EMPLOYER REPRESENTATIVES' DOCUMENTS

BWI, 'BWI Targets Multinational Companies' (2013) < http://www.bwint.org/pdfs/EN_MNCbooklet.pdf accessed > 14 June 2014.

BWI, 'BWI, IndustriALL and Lafarge sign a new global framework agreement in presence of ILO Director-General' (Press Release 2013) < www.bwint.org/default.asp?Index = 4937&Language = EN > accessed 14 May 2014.

BWI, 'New BWI Model Framework Agreement' (Approved by BWI World Council on 3 December 2010) < www.bwint.org/default.asp?Index = 47&Language = EN > accessed 23 May 2014.

BWI, 'BWI Guidance on International Framework Agreements (IFAs)' (2007) < www.bwint.org/pdfs/FinalnoteIFAWCNov07.pdf > accessed 23 May 2014.

EMF, 'Internal EMF Procedure for negotiations at multinational company level' (2006) < www.emf-fem.org/Areas-of-work/Company-Policy/Adopted-documents-Position-papers-Publications/Position-papers2/Internal-EMF-Procedure-for-negotiations-at-multinational-company-level/2006-12-internal-proc.-nego.-mn.-cny-level-EN > accessed 15 August 2014.

ETUC (Executive Committee), 'More and Better European Company Framework Agreements: Enhancing Trade Unions in Transnational Negotiations with Transnational Companies' (Discussion Note 2012) EC198/EN/12 <http://collective.etuc.org/sites/default/files/12-EN-More-and-Better-European-Company-Framework-Agreements%20ADOPTED.pdf > accessed 15 August 2014.

See the ETUC, 'on the Resolution of the EU Parliament on Cross Border Collective Bargaining and Transnational Social Dialogue letter' (Letter 12 November 2013) < www.epsu.org/a/9917 > accessed 14 August 2014.

IFBWWW, 'IFBWWW experiences with Global Company Agreement' (2004) <http://www.newunionism.net/library/organizing/IFBWW%20-%20Experiences%20with%20Global%20Company%20Agreements%20-%202004.pdf > accessed 3 February2014.

IMF, 'Background to International Framework Agreements in the IMF' (Background paper prepared for the IFA World Conference Frankfurt am Main, Germany, 26-27 September 2006) <http://library.fes.de/pdf-files/gurn/00251.pdf> accessed 23 May 2014.

IMF, 'The Power of Framework Agreements' (2003) <http://library.fes.de/pdf-files/gurn/00257.pdf > accessed 10 April 2014.

IOE, 'Fact Sheet for Business: International Framework Agreements (IFAs)' (2013) < www.ioe-emp.org/fileadmin/ioe_documents/publications/Policy%20Areas/international_industrial_relations/EN/_2013-11-21__Fact_Sheet_for_Business_-_IFAs__final_.pdf > accessed 14 March 2014.

IOE, 'International Framework Agreements: An Employers' Guide' (2007) <http://apirnet.ilo.org/resources/ifas-an-employers-guide > accessed 24 May 2014.

IOE, 'Corporate Social Responsibility: An IOE Approach' (2003) < www.ioe-emp.org/fileadmin/ioe_documents/publications/Policy%20Areas/csr/EN/%282003-03-21%29%20Corporate%20Social%20Responsibility.pdf > accessed 1 April 2014.

Rackham L, 'An innovative social agreement' (Press Release 2010) < www.emf-fem.org/Press/Press-releases/An-innovative-social-agreement > accessed 14 April 2014.

UNI, 'Global Agreements' <http://mail.uniglobalunion.org/Apps/iportal.nsf/pages/20090226_ml9xEn > accessed 9 April 2014.

WEBSITES

Official website of BWI www.bwint.org/default.asp?Language = EN > accessed 14 May 2014.

Official website of EI <http://www.ei-ie.org/en/websections/content_detail/3247> accessed on 14 May 2014.

Official website of IAEA www.iaea-globalunion.org/> accessed 14 May 2014.

Official website of IndustriALL <www.industriall-union.org/about-us> accessed on 14 May 2014.

Official website of IFJ www.ifj.org/about-ifj/mission-statement/> accessed 14 May 2014.

Official website of ITF www.itfglobal.org/about-us/moreabout.cfm> accessed 14 May 2014.

Official website of IUF www.iuf.org/w/?q=node/149> accessed 14 May 2014.

Official website of PSI <www.world-psi.org/en/who-we-are> accessed on 14 May 2014.

Official website of SAI <www.sa-intl.org/index.cfm?fuseaction=Page.ViewPage&pageId=490> accessed 20 January 2014.

Official website of UNI Global Union <www.uniglobalunion.org/about-us> accessed on 14 May 2014.

Official website of the UN Global Compact: <www.unglobalcompact.org/AboutTheGC/index.html> accessed 23 February 2014.

Official website of the Office of the United States Trade Representative on the U.S. GSP <www.ustr.gov/trade-topics/trade-development/preference-programs/generalized-system-preference-gsp> accessed 15 November 2014.

Official website of the European Commission on the EU GSP <http://ec.europa.eu/trade/policy/countries-and-regions/development/generalised-scheme-of-preferences/index_en.htm> accessed 15 November 2013.

Eurofound, 'European industrial relations dictionary' <www.eurofound.europa.eu/areas/industrialrelations/dictionary/index.htm> accessed 14 July 2014.

European Commission, 'Social Dialogue' <http://ec.europa.eu/social/main.jsp?catId=329&langId=en> accessed 14 July 2014.

European Commission, 'Cross-industry social dialogue' <http://ec.europa.eu/social/main.jsp?catId=479&langId=en> accessed 14 July 2014.

European Commission, 'Sectoral Social Dialogue' <http://ec.europa.eu/social/main.jsp?catId=480&langId=en> accessed 14 March 2014.

European Commission, 'Social dialogue texts database' http://ec.europa.eu/social/main.jsp?catId=521&langId=en accessed 14 July 2014.

European Commission, 'List of European social partners' organisations consulted under Article 154 TFEU' <http://ec.europa.eu/social/BlobServlet?docId=2154&langId=en> accessed 14 July 2014.

ILO, 'Follow-up Surveys' <www.ilo.org/empent/Informationresources/WCMS_101251/lang--en/index.htm> accessed 12 January 2014.

ILO, 'Social Dialogue Sector' <www.ilo.org/public/english/dialogue/index.htm> accessed 14 July 2014.

ILO, 'Tripartite declaration of principles concerning multinational enterprises and social policy (MNE Declaration) – 4th Edition' <www.ilo.org/empent/Publications/WCMS_094386/lang--en/index.htm> accessed 14 November 2013.

ILO, NORMLEX (Information System on International Labour Standards' <www.ilo.org/dyn/normlex/en/f?p=NORMLEXPUB:1:0::NO:::> accessed 2 May 2014.

ISO, 'ISO 26000' <www.iso.org/obp/ui/#iso:std:iso:26000:ed-1:v1:en> accessed 20 January 2014.

OECD, 'National Contact Points' <http://mneguidelines.oecd.org/ncps/> accessed 1 May 2014.

OECD, 'Database of specific instances – Employment issues in Austria' <http://mneguidelines.oecd.org/database/instances/at0004.htm> accessed 1 May 2014.

OECD, 'Database of specific instances – Alleged violation of employee rights in Bangladesh' <http://mneguidelines.oecd.org/database/instances/br0021.htm> accessed 10 January 2014.

BCLR - BULLETIN OF COMPARATIVE LABOUR RELATIONS

Vol. Author/Title/Year/ISBN

1. Roger Blanpain, *Individual Employment Contracts: Collective Agreements*, 1970.
2. Roger Blanpain, *Social Planning*, 1971 (ISBN 90-312-0018-2).
3. Roger Blanpain, *Guaranteed Income Funds*, 1972 (ISBN 90-312-0019-0).
4. Roger Blanpain, *Employee Participation at the Level of the Enterprise*, 1973 (ISBN 90-312-0020-4).
5. Roger Blanpain, *Vastheid van Betrekking: Staking en Bezetting*, 1974.
6. Roger Blanpain, *Labour Law and Industrial Relations (International Bibliography)*, 1975 (ISBN 90-312-0023-9).
7. Roger Blanpain, *Multinational Enterprises*, 1976 (ISBN 90-312-0024-7).
8. Roger Blanpain, *Worker's Participation in the European Company*, 1977 (ISBN 90-312-0044-1).
9. Roger Blanpain, *Women and Labour*, 1978 (ISBN 90-312-0077-8).
10. Roger Blanpain, *European Conference on Labour Law and Industrial Relations: Multinational Enterprises*, 1979 (ISBN 90-312-0091-3).
11. Roger Blanpain, *Job Security and Industrial Relations*, 1980 (ISBN 90-312-0147-2).
12. Roger Blanpain, Greg Bamber & Russell Lansbury, *Technological Change and Industrial Relations: An International Symposium*, 1983 (ISBN 90-312-0205-3).
13. Roger Blanpain, James Janssen van Raay & A. Moulty, *Worker's Participation in the European Community: The Fifth Directive*, 1984 (ISBN 90-654-4187-5).
14. Roger Blanpain, *Equality and Prohibition of Discrimination in Employment*, 1985 (ISBN 90-654-4215-4).
15. Roger Blanpain, *Restructuring Labour in the Enterprise: Law and Practice in France, F.R. of Germany, Italy, Sweden and the United Kingdom*, 1986 (ISBN 90-654-4283-9).
16. Roger Blanpain & E. Kassalow, *Unions and Industrial Relations: Recent Trends and Prospect: A Comparative Treatment*, 1987 (ISBN 90-654-4294-4).
17. Roger Blanpain & Marco Biagi, *Trade Union Democracy and Industrial Relations*, 1988 (ISBN 90-654-4394-0).
18. Roger Blanpain & Jelle Visser, *In Search of Inclusive Unionism*, 1990 (ISBN 90-654-4439-4).
19. Roger Blanpain, *Flexibility and Wages: A Comparative Treatment*, 1990 (ISBN 90-654-4461-0).

20. Roger Blanpain, Stephen Frenkel & Oliver Clarke, *Economic Restructuring and Industrial Relations in Industrialised Countries,* 1990 (ISBN 90-654-4488-2).
21. Roger Blanpain & Friedrich Fürstenberg, *Structure and Strategy in Industrial Relations,* 1991 (ISBN 90-654-4559-5).
22. Roger Blanpain, Amira Galin & Ozer Carmi, *Flexible Work Patterns and Their Impact on Industrial Relations,* 1991 (ISBN 90-654-4572-2).
23. Roger Blanpain, *Workers' Participation: Influence on Management Decision-Making by Labour in the Private Sector,* 1992 (ISBN 90-654-4600-1).
24. Roger Blanpain, Brian Brooks & Chris Engels, *Employed or Self-Employed,* 1992 (ISBN 90-654-4613-3).
25. Roger Blanpain & Tiziano Treu, *Industrial Relations Developments in the Telecommunications Industry,* 1993 (ISBN 90-654-4642-7).
26. Roger Blanpain & Marco Biagi, *Industrial Relations in Small and Medium Sized Enterprises,* 1993 (ISBN 90-654-4696-6).
27. Roger Blanpain & Marco Biagi, *Participative Management and Industrial Relations in a Worldwide Perspective,* 1993 (ISBN 90-654-4769-5).
28. Roger Blanpain, Jacques Rojot & Hoyt N. Wheeler, *Employee Rights and Industrial Justice,* 1994 (ISBN 90-654-4804-7).
29. Roger Blanpain & Ruth Ben-Israel, *Strikes and Lock-Outs in Industrialized Market Economies,* 1994 (ISBN 90-654-4841-1).
30. Roger Blanpain, Kazuo Sugeno & Yasuo Suwa, *The Harmonization of Working Life and Family Life,* 1995 (ISBN 90-411-0064-4).
31. Roger Blanpain & Laszio Nagy, *Labour Law and Industrial Relations in Central and Eastern Europe,* 1996 (ISBN 90-411-0298-1).
32. Roger Blanpain, *Labour Law and Industrial Relations in the European Union,* 1997 (ISBN 90-411-0527-1).
33. Taco Van Peijpe, *Employment Protection under Strain,* 1998 (ISBN 90-411-0528-8).
34. Roger Blanpain, Takashi Araki & Ryuichi Yamakawa, *The Process of Industrialization and the Role of Labour Law in Asia,* 1999 (ISBN 9-041-1104-7-X).
35. Roger Blanpain & Marco Biagi, *Non-standard Work and Industrial Relations,* 1999 (ISBN 90-411-1117-4).
36. Roger Blanpain, *Private Employment Agencies: The Impact of ILO Convention 181 (1997) and the Judgment of the European Court of Justice of 11 December 1997,* 1999 (ISBN 90-411-1118-2).
37. Roger Blanpain, *Multinational Enterprises and the Social Challenges of the XXIst Century: The ILO Declaration on Fundamental* Principles *at Work, Public and Private Corporate Codes of Conduct,* 2000 (ISBN 90-411-1280-4).
38. Roger Blanpain, Ryuichi Yamakawa & Takashi Araki, *Deregulation and Labour Law: In Search of a Labour Concept for the 21st Century,* 2000 (ISBN 90-411-1370-3).
39. Roger Blanpain, *The Council of Europe and the Social Challenges of the XXIst Century,* 2001 (ISBN 90-411-1543-9).

40. Roger Blanpain, *On-Line Rights for Employees in the Information Society, Use & Monitoring of E-Mail & Internet at Work*, 2002 (ISBN 90-411-1626-5).
41. Roger Blanpain, *The Evolving Employment Relationship and the New Economy: The Role of Labour Law & Industrial Relations*, 2001 (ISBN 90-411-1691-5).
42. Roger Blanpain, *Involvement of Employees in the European Union, Works Councils, Company Statute, Information and Consultation Rights*, 2002 (ISBN 90-411-1760-1).
43. Michele Colucci, *The Impact of the Internet and New Technologies on the Workplace: A Legal Analysis from a Comparative Point of View*, 2002 (ISBN 90-411-1824-1).
44. Roger Blanpain, *White Paper on the Labour Market in Italy: The Quality of European Industrial Relations and Changing Industrial Relations*, 2002 (ISBN 90-411-1841-1).
45. Roger Blanpain, Russell D. Lansbury & Young-Bum Park, *Impact of Globalisation on Employment Relations: A Comparison of the Automobile and Banking Industries in Australia and Korea*, 2002 (ISBN 90-411-1850-0).
46. Roger Blanpain & Antoine Jacobs, *Employee Rights in Bankruptcy: A Comparative-Law Assessment*, 2002 (ISBN 90-411-1942-6).
47. Roger Blanpain, Takashi Araki & Shinya Ouchi, *Corporate Restructuring and the Role of Labour Law*, 2003 (ISBN 90-411-1949-3).
48. Roger Blanpain, *Collective Bargaining, Discrimination, Social Security and European Integration*, 2003 (ISBN 90-411-2010-6).
49. Roger Blanpain & Luis Aparicio-Valdez, *Labour Relations in the Asia- Pacific Countries*, 2004 (ISBN 90-411-2239-7).
50. Roger Blanpain & Ronnie Graham, *Temporary Agency Work and the Information Society*, 2004 (ISBN 90-411-2252-4).
51. Roger Blanpain, *The Actors of Collective Bargaining: A World Report*, 2004 (ISBN 90-411-2253-2).
52. Roger Blanpain & Michele Colucci, *The Globalisation of Labour Standards: The Soft Law Track*, 2004 (ISBN 90-411-2303-2).
53. Roger Blanpain, Takashi Araki & Shinya Ouchi, *Labour Law in Motion: Diversification of the Labour Force & Terms and Conditions of Employment*, 2005 (ISBN 90-411-2315-6).
54. Roger Blanpain, *Smoking and the Workplace*, 2005 (ISBN 90-411-2325-3).
55. Roger Blanpain, *Confronting Globalization: The Quest for a Social Agenda*, 2005 (ISBN 90-411-2381-4).
56. Roger Blanpain, Thomas Blanke & Edgar Rose, *Collective Bargaining Wages in Comparative Perspective: Germany, France, the Netherlands, Sweden and the United Kingdom*, 2005 (ISBN 90-411-2388-1).
57. Roger Blanpain & Anne Numhauser-Henning, *Women in Academia & Equality Law: Aiming High - Falling Short?*, 2006 (ISBN 978-90-411-2427-6).
58. Roger Blanpain, *Freedom of Services in the European Union: Labour and Social Security Law: The Bolkestein Initiative*, 2006 (ISBN 978-90-411-2453-5).
59. Roger Blanpain, Frans Pennings & Nurhan Sural, *Flexibilisation and Modernisation of the Turkish Labour Market*, 2006 (ISBN 978-90-411-2490-X).

60. Roger Blanpain & Boel Flodgren, *Corporate and Employment Perspectives in a Global Business Environment,* 2006 (ISBN 978-90-411-2537-X).
61. Roger Blanpain, Shinya Ouchi & Takashi Araki, *Decentralizing Industrial Relations and The Role of Labor Unions and Employee Representatives,* 2007 (ISBN 978-90-411-2583-3).
62. Roger Blanpain, *European Framework Agreements and Telework: Law and Practice: A European and Comparative Study,* 2007 (ISBN 978-90-411-2560-4).
63. Roger Blanpain, Jim Kitay, Leanne Cutcher & Nick Wailes, *Globalization and Employment Relations in Retail Banking,* 2007 (ISBN 978-90-411-2620-1).
64. Roger Blanpain, Russell Lansbury, Jim Kitay, Nick Wailes & Anja Kirsch, *Globalization and Employment Relations in the Auto Assembly Industry:* A *Study of Seven Countries,* 2008 (ISBN 978-90-411-2698-6).
65. Roger Blanpain & Michele Tiraboschi, *The Global Labour Market: From Globalization to Flexicurity,* 2008 (ISBN 978-90-411-2722-8).
66. Roger Blanpain, Michele Colucci & Frank Hendrickx, *The Future of Sport in the European Union: Beyond the EU Reform Treaty and the White Paper,* 2008 (ISBN 978-90-411-2761-7).
67. Roger Blanpain, Linda Dickens, *Challenges in European Employment Relations: Employment Regulation, Trade Union Organization, Equality, Flexicurity, Training and New Approaches to Pay,* 2008 (ISBN 978-90-411-2771-6).
68. Roger Blanpain, Hiroya Nakakubo & Takashi Araki, *New Developments in Employment Discrimination Law, 2008* (ISBN 978-90-411-2782-2).
69. Roger Blanpain, Andrzej Marian Świątkowski, *The Laval and Viking Cases: Freedom of Services and Establishment v. Industrial Conflict in the European Economic Area and Russia,* 2009 (ISBN 978-90-411-2850-8).
70. Roger Blanpain, William Bromwich, Olga Rymkevich, Silvia Spattini, *The Modernization of Labour Law and Industrial Relations in a Comparative Perspective,* 2009 (ISBN 978-90-411-2865-2).
71. Roger Blanpain, Juan Pablo Landa & Brian Langille, *Employment Policies and Multilevel Governance,* 2009 (ISBN 978-90-411-2866-9).
72. Roger Blanpain, European Works Councils; *The European Directive 2009/ 38/EC of 6 May 2009, 2009* (ISBN 978-90-411-3208-6).
73. Roger Blanpain, William Bromwich, Olga Rymkevich & Silvia Spattini, *Labour Productivity, Investment in Human Capital and Youth Employment: Comparative Developments and Global Responses,* 2010 (ISBN 978-90-411-3249-9).
74. Greg J. Bamber & Philippe Pochet, *Regulating Employment Relations, Work and Labour Laws: International Comparisons between Key Countries,* 2010 (ISBN 978-90-411-3199-7). General Editor: Roger Blanpain.
75. Roger Blanpain, Desislava Nikolaeva Dimitrova, *Seafarers' Rights in the Globalized Maritime Industry,* 2010 (ISBN 978-90-411-3349-6).
76. Roger Blanpain, Hiroya Nakakubo & Takashi Araki, *Regulation of Fixed- Term Employment Contracts,* 2010 (ISBN 978-90-411-3356-4).
77. Roger Blanpain, William Bromwich, Olga Rymkevich & Iacopo Senatori, *Rethinking Corporate Governance,* 2011 (ISBN 978-90-411-3450-9).

78. Roger Blanpain & Frank Hendrickx, *Labour Law between Change and Tradition: Liber Amicorum Antoine Jacobs*, 2011 (ISBN 978-90-411-3424-0).
79. Roger Blanpain, Thomas Klebe, Marlene Schmidt & Bernd Waas, *Trade Union Rights at the Workplace*, 2012 (ISBN 978-90-411-3460-8).
80. Roger Blanpain, William Bromwich, Olga Rymkevich & Iacopo Senatori, *Labour Markets, Industrial Relations and Human Resources Management: From Recession to Recovery*, 2012 (ISBN 978-90-411-4004-3).
81. Roger Blanpain, Hiroya Nakakubo & Takashi Araki, *Systems of Employee Representation at the Enterprise: A Comparative Study*, 2012 (ISBN 978-90-411-4080-7).
82. Roger Blanpain & Frank Hendrickx, *Temporary Agency Work in the European Union and the United States*, 2013 (ISBN 978-90-411-4769-1).
83. Roger Blanpain, Toker Dereli, Y. Pınar Soykut-Sarıca & Aslı en-Tabaı, *Emerging Patterns of Work and Turkish Labour Market Challenges under Globalization: Readings on Labour and Employment Relations*, 2014 (ISBN 978-90-411-4983-1).
84. Roger Blanpain, Pablo Arellano Ortiz, Marius Olivier & Gijsbert Vonk, *Social Security and Migrant Workers: Selected Studies of Cross-border Social Security Mechanisms*, 2014 (ISBN 978-90-411-4770-7).
85. Roger Blanpain & Nikita Lyutov, *Workers' Representation in Central and Eastern Europe: Challenges and Opportunities for the Works Councils' System*, 2014 (ISBN 978-90-411-4746-2).
86. Roger Blanpain, Ulla Liukkunen & Chen Yifeng, *China and ILO Fundamental Principles and Rights at Works*, 2014 (ISBN 978-90-411-4984-8).
87. Roger Blanpain, *The Use of Languages and Employment Relations*, 2014 (ISBN 978-90-411-5606-8).
88. Roger Blanpain, Hiroya Nakakubo & Takashi Araki, *Protection of Employees' Personal Information and Privacy*, 2014 (ISBN 978-90-411-5608-2).
89. Roger Blanpain, Jan Wouters, Glenn Rayp, Laura Beke & Axel Marx, *Protecting Labour Rights in a Multi-polar Supply Chain and Mobile Global Economy*, 2015 (ISBN 978-90-411-5662-4).
90. Roger Blanpain & Stefania Marassi, *Globalization and Transnational Collective Labour Relations: International and European Framework Agreements at Company Level*, 2015 (ISBN 978-90-411-4748-6).

www.ingramcontent.com/pod-product-compliance
Lightning Source LLC
LaVergne TN
LVHW011113300926
849160LV00008B/367
* 9 7 8 9 0 4 1 1 4 7 4 8 6 *